DESIGNING & IMPLEMENTING SUCCESSFUL DIVERSITY PROGRAMS

LAWRENCE M. BAYTOS

Co-published with the Society for Human Resource Management

PRENTICE HALL
Englewood Cliffs, New Jersey 07632

Prentice-Hall International (UK) Limited, *London*
Prentice-Hall of Australia Pty. Limited, *Sydney*
Prentice-Hall Canada, Inc., *Toronto*
Prentice-Hall Hispanoamericana, S.A., *Mexico*
Prentice-Hall of India Private Limited, *New Delhi*
Prentice-Hall of Japan, Inc., *Tokyo*
Simon & Schuster Asia Pte. Ltd., *Singapore*
Editora Prentice-Hall do Brasil, Ltda., *Rio de Janeiro*

10 9 8 7 6 5 4 3 2 1

Library of Congress Cataloging-in-Publication Data

Baytos, Lawrence M.
   Designing & implementing successful diversity programs / Lawrence
M. Baytos.
     p.   cm.
   Includes bibliographical references and index.
   ISBN 0-13-128034-1 :
   1. Minorities—Employment. 2. Multiculturalism. 3. Personnel
management. I. Title. II. Title: Designing and implementing
successful diversity prorams.
HF5549.5.M5B39 1995
658.3'041—dc20
                                    94-34051
                                       CIP

ISBN 0-13-128034-1

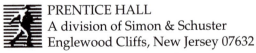
PRENTICE HALL
A division of Simon & Schuster
Englewood Cliffs, New Jersey 07632
Printed in the United States of America

DEDICATION

To my mentor in diversity, Dr. R. Roosevelt Thomas, Jr., and the dozens of other diversity pioneers who have blazed the trail in helping managers and their organizations recognize the issues, break the code of silence, create a vision for change and identify realistic avenues for progress.

CONTENTS

LIST OF EXERCISES AND EXHIBITS

ACKNOWLEDGMENTS

I am grateful for the support and advice provided by associates, fellow professionals and family that made it possible for me to conceive and write this book.

To C. Roland Stichweh, Vice President, Towers Perrin, and Mr. Robert L. Lattimer, Managing Director of Diversity Consultants Inc./Towers Perrin for their encouragement to share insights and experiences openly in hopes of advancing the state of the art.

To my colleagues at Diversity Consultants/Towers Perrin who served as chapter reviewers and whose practical experiences and subject matter expertise contributed greatly to the value of this book. That group of critics and colleagues includes the following: Barbara Adolf, Ken Boughrum, Bob Carey, Courtney Cosgrove, Ann Perkins-Delatte, Elaine Fuerst, Ilene Gochman, Judith Griffey, Mark Johnson, Dr. Toshi Ki, Bob Lattimer, Charles Lee, Belinda Morin, Tom Pawlak, Suzanne Peck, Margaret Regan, Cliff Rhodes, Lynn Sullivan, Carlos Vasquez.

To practitioners in industry who reviewed and helped shape several chapters: Mike Cohen, Vice President Management Development and Joan Green, Director of Diversity the Quaker Oats Company, Phyllis Hayes, Diversity/EEO Consultant Amoco Corporation, and Jim Kochanski, Director Human Resources Northern Telecom.

To individuals who shared their company experiences and granted permission to include those in the book: Bob Niles, Felice Cota-Robles, and Diane Falanga for sharing the Helene Curtis Industries work/family program information, Janice Fenn, Director of Human Resources, Sara Lee Corporation for the diversity strategy and communication information and Jim Kochanski, Director of Human Resources, Northern Telecom-U. S. for the diversity continuum vision.

To Linda Betzold of Towers Perrin who developed the illustrations used throughout the book, and Bob Cornet who helped me work through the publisher selection process.

To my clients and fellow practitioners who reaffirmed my view regarding the need for this book at this time.

To Karen Hansen and Sybil Grace of Prentice Hall Career & Personal Development for their skillful editorial guidance and patience in dealing with a strongly opinionated author.

To my friends and former colleagues at the American Institute for Managing Diversity in Atlanta for generously sharing their wisdom and enthusiasm over a period of years.

To the Diversity Group members who, by sharing with me some of their life experiences, helped me to better understand my own views and their limitations.

To my wife Carol for so patiently tolerating the countless hours I spent at the word processor, and to her and my daughters Laura and Lisa for their encouragement and unwavering support as I pursued this project.

ABOUT THE AUTHOR

Lawrence M. (Larry) Baytos is President of the Diversity Implementation Group, consultants focusing on the design and implementation of diversity strategies and programs. He previously was a senior consultant with Diversity Consultants Inc., a Towers Perrin Company and he was the first Chairman of Diversity Consultants under its previous ownership by the American Institute for Managing Diversity in Atlanta. He also served previously as Chairman of the Board of the Institute.

From 1977 to 1990 Larry was Senior Vice President for Human Resources for the Quaker Oats Company in Chicago. His job responsibilities took him to fifteen countries. During his career at Quaker Oats a number of leading edge diversity and work and family initiatives began, and the Company received from the Secretary of Labor an "EVE" award (Exemplary Voluntary Effort) for its innovative affirmative action programs. Prior to his 18 years at Quaker Oats he was an organization strategy and compensation consultant with Booz Allen & Hamilton, and Hewitt Associates. His business career started at the Procter & Gamble Company.

Mr. Baytos has pioneered in the application of diversity concepts in business, with a focus on strategy development and creating an organization environment and HR policies and programs that foster a diverse work force. He has shared his experiences through client assignments, speaking engagements with professional and corporate groups and through developing and teaching graduate level diversity seminars.

He has an MBA degree from the Harvard Graduate School of Business, and a B. S. in Business from Youngstown State University (Ohio).

Larry is the author of a dozen articles on human resources strategies, appearing in *Human Resource Planning, HR Magazine, Journal of Training and Development, Compensation and Benefit Review,* and *Personnel Journal.* He authored *Launching Successful Diversity Initiatives,* and was co-author of *Guidelines for Successful Diversity Training.*

Larry has served as President of the Human Resources Management Association of Chicago, and has been a Board member of a variety of Chicago area civic, charitable and health services organizations. He resides in Aurora, Illinois. He can be reached at (708) 717–2774.

HOW THIS BOOK WILL HELP YOU

The idea for the book came from my observations as a senior corporate human resources officer, and as a diversity consultant. In both these situations, I observed the following stages of diversity development in organizations:

1. *The Unaware.*   Some companies are not fully aware of the broad issues and diversity does not yet appear on their radar screen as a strategic opportunity or potential challenge.

2. *The Timid or Preoccupied.*   Many companies recognize that new approaches are needed to capitalize on work force diversity. However, they lack the confidence and understanding of how to move forward, or they see themselves operating in a survival mode that does not permit investment of funds and management time in long term issues.

3. *The Action Oriented.*   Some companies have moved into an action mode before determining a comprehensive strategy and understanding of the long term implications. Their efforts in a particular area [e. g., diversity training] have not had the broad impact they had expected. They are either discouraged and ready to give up the chase, or ready to circle back and develop the strategy that should have preceded the program.

4. *Companies Seeking a Leadership Position.*   There is a small group of leaders who have been working the issues hard for a number of years. While pleased with some aspects of their progress, they are always in search of useful new techniques and new ways of looking at old issues.

This book is intended to respond to the needs at each level of diversity development through the medium of an open sharing of the experiences of organizations that have been working at diversity. There is no single "right" answer that solves every company's issues, but you will see patterns of effective practices that may save you months of effort and frustration within your organization and will help you to get the maximum value from your external advisors as well.

WHO SHOULD READ THIS BOOK

The book will be a valuable source of practical guidance for individuals serving a wide range of roles in a diversity process. The gain may come from a number of different perspectives, such as the following:

- **Senior Executives:** Will help them make the link between managing diversity and the practical business benefits to the organization; and the leadership roles that senior executives should play to ensure diversity success and continuity of the efforts.

- **Diversity or Affirmative Action Managers:** Provides a practical guide to each phase of a diversity change process with specific action steps that can be applied to improve the programs of your organization.

- **Human Resource Generalists:** Provides a summary of the potential application of diversity issues to your area of expertise, whether it be communication, training, compensation, organization development or design.

- **Members of Diversity Task Forces:** Provides knowledge for enhancing personal awareness and skills on diversity issues, techniques for an effective change process, as well as adding to your understanding of the whole range of diversity activities that might be considered in your organization.

- **Diversity Trainers:** Summarizes the diversity training concepts and strategies, and provides a linkage of diversity education and training to other aspects of a diversity change process.

In short, anyone considering or actively involved in addressing issues of managing diversity will benefit from the material contained in this book.

HOW TO GET THE MOST BENEFITS—QUICKLY

If you want to understand each phase in a diversity change process, then you should simply move through the book on a sequential basis. If you are well along in a diversity process, you could jump in at the stage in the diversity change process that corresponds to the current stage of development—e. g., diversity research, communications, maintaining momentum and so forth.

If you are interested in considering the diversity aspects of a specific area of human resources management—affirmative action, compensation, career mobility systems, e.g.—simply go to the chapter bearing that title. However, some subjects touch many areas of planning and activity, such as communications, corporate culture, business rationale. Therefore, these subjects come up in a number of different places in the book and they can't be captured totally in a single chapter.

Those readers who have had limited exposure to diversity concepts should first build their knowledge foundation by reading Chapter 16, which provides more on the context for the strategies and tactics discussed in earlier chapters.

In some of the chapters an exercise or assessment instrument has been provided to give you the opportunity to test your knowledge and build skills for applying the information and techniques to the particular circumstances of your organization. These materials have been tested in various training situations, client assignments or graduate level seminars. You will find them very helpful in extending the value of the book to your organization and I encourage you to use them.

ABOUT THE EXAMPLES

Throughout the book examples of diversity research results are provided in the form of focus group comments, and scores from employee diversity research projects. Names of the companies from which the data was developed are withheld to protect the confidentiality. In fact, **none of the companies** represented in the data are mentioned anywhere within the book. The companies most often cited in the data range in size from 1500 to over 50,000 employees and include various services, high tech manufacturing and process industries that serve a variety of consumer and industrial markets.

Generally speaking, the scores for selected survey questions should be viewed as indicative rather than conclusive for the particular question. While survey information was statistically significant within the organization, the small number of companies does not warrant claims of a national norm. The scores should not be viewed as "best practices" norms, since results were garnered in organizations that were in the very early stages of a diversity process. On the other hand, since these are all financially successful companies, the results should also not be viewed as worst case scenarios.

Much of the information is taken from client situations or my own industry experience. However, to provide the broadest possible perspective, first hand experiences have been augmented by information provided by dozens of colleagues and acquaintances who are dealing with diversity issues on a daily basis. In any case, the examples used are not intended to be critical of any organization or individual. The purpose is to advance the state of the art in this important and still developing arena—tapping the full productivity potential of the diverse workforce.

Throughout the book data are broken out by various ethnic and gender groupings. The term "people of color" is used synonymously with the term "minority". In each case, individuals included under those broad umbrella EEOC categories terms include African Americans (Blacks), Asian Americans, Hispanic

(Latino), and Native Americans (American Indians). I recognize that these broad categories are somewhat artificial and do not capture the diversity of the members in the grouping. However, since the terms are generally well known, they must serve our purposes.

One of the limits of relying heavily on recent company experiences is that you end up talking about the issues on which those organizations are focusing their efforts or where it is relatively easy to identify the group members to obtain the input. Therefore, I regret that our data is limited regarding the perspectives of some important groups, such as people who are physically challenged, gays and lesbians, and Native Americans. Nevertheless, the principles and overriding vision quite clearly do respond to the issues and needs of such groups. The book is about all of us.

Note that this book is dedicated to my friend and diversity mentor Dr. R. Roosevelt Thomas, Jr. and his writings are referenced in several chapters. While I have built upon his broad concepts, the reader should not infer that Dr. Thomas's name in association with the book constitutes an endorsement of its contents, or of my ideas.

INTRODUCTION

This book is designed primarily to help you design and implement effective diversity strategies and programs. However, diversity still has many meanings, so it is important that the reader has an understanding of the basic conceptual starting point that I use for choosing and shaping the material in the book.

This introduction covers some of the basic background and concepts in a cursory fashion, including the following:

- Makes the case that diversity is a major issue for organizations and introduces the forces driving that concern.
- Defines what I mean by the term "diversity" in this book.
- Reviews a model for managing workforce diversity to present a vision for the future

Because this is a practitioner's book these items will be covered only very briefly here. Those who have not had exposure to the field or who may want to reinforce their understanding of the concepts should refer to Chapter 16 for a more detailed review.

DIVERSITY MANAGEMENT AS A STRATEGIC IMPERATIVE

During the past few years I have seen several surveys of human resources professionals which identify the broad area of diversity as one of the top priorities currently, and for the immediate future. Certainly the growth of consulting firms, seminars and publications is evidence of the interest. The staying power of diversity as a corporate priority has been demonstrated by the high level of interest that carried through the recession of the early '90s. In fact, as reported in a survey by Towers Perrin, 96% of the responding companies had either maintained or increased their support for diversity management during the recession. I know of instances where diversity efforts coincided with major downsizing efforts, both being viewed as essential activities.

The widespread corporate concern for diversity management is driven by the "3 Ds" that have affected virtually all organizations, whether you have 100 or 100,000 employees. The 3 Ds include:

1. **Demographics**   Females, minorities and foreign born are projected to produce 85% of the net growth in the U. S. work force between 1986 and the year 2000. White males will be a minority in the workforce by the year 2000. In 1960 nine out of ten consumers were white. In the year 2000, only six out of ten will be white. The changing demographics of the work place are also the changing demographics of the market place. Companies are looking for ways to align their organizations to the new realities of their customer base.

2. **Disappointment**   The traditional U. S. method for handling diversity was to bring women and people of color into the workforce under the banner of affirmative action. In so doing, it was often assumed that those individuals may harbor some deficiencies and perhaps would not have been hired were it not for affirmative action. It was also assumed that they should be willing to assimilate away their differences to better fit to the norms of the majority group [usually white males] and thereby enhance their opportunities for recognition and advancement.

   After more than two decades of affirmative action, it seems clear that the existing model has resulted in females and people of color being trapped in the lower levels of the corporate pyramid. Turnover, discontent and under-utilization of talent are the by-products of over two decades using the previous approaches.

3. **Demands**   The demands for new approaches to diversity come from employees who have become less willing than their predecessors to assimilate away their points of difference in hopes of gaining the elusive acceptance into the "club." Furthermore, the intense pressures of industry and global competition to "re-engineer" the corporation require that organizations tap the full potential of all their human assets.

DIVERSITY DEFINED FOR PURPOSES OF THIS BOOK

A general agreement seems to be evolving that there are two levels of diversity that organizations should recognize as they view issues and opportunities.

Primary Dimensions: The primary dimensions are the characteristics that are inborn and immutable.

- Gender
- Race
- Country of origin
- Age
- Physical challenge

These dimensions are critical because they generally are not subject to change and they determine our early associations in life. These characteristics usually determine our "in-groups" [others like us] and can dramatically affect our perceptions of those who are different from us.

[Author's note: There is a growing body of knowledge and opinion that suggests that sexual preference is also a primary dimension. The limits of this book do not permit an exploration of the scientific and sociological premises for this debate.]

Secondary Dimensions: The secondary dimensions are a virtually limitless array of individual characteristics. A few of the characteristics that are associated with life in our organizations include the following:

- Education
- Work Experience
- Marital/parental status
- Functional specialty
- Location
- Religion
- Problem solving approach
- Leadership style

Some important characteristics of the secondary dimensions are that they are usually subject to change by the individual; e. g., we can get married or unmarried, get additional schooling, change trades or professions, etc. Also these dimensions may have a widely varied impact on an individual. For example, one female employee giving birth may choose to drop out of the labor pool for a time, while another will pursue her career with a minimal delay.

DEFINING A VISION FOR DIVERSITY SUCCESS

If the affirmative action/assimilation model for utilizing diversity has not worked well for organizations, we need to develop a new model. For this book my model is the **Managing Diversity** vision spelled out by Dr. R. Roosevelt Thomas, Jr. of the American Institute for Managing Diversity in Atlanta:

Managing diversity is a comprehensive managerial process for developing an environment that works naturally for all employees. Managing Diversity seeks to tap the full potential of all employees, in pursuit of company objectives, where employ-

ees may progress without regard to [what should be] irrelevant considerations such as race, age, gender and other personal attributes.[1]

The power and clarity of the Managing Diversity [MD] model, aided by the popularity of Dr. Thomas's publications, have led many organizations in diversity change processes to adopt it as their diversity vision. Indeed, it is a powerful and compelling stage toward which companies can aim their efforts. However, managing diversity is a process requiring long term organizational commitment; it is not an event to be orchestrated. And if MD were an easy stage to arrive at, everyone would be there already. Unfortunately the road from affirmative action to managing diversity is littered with roadblocks and impediments to progress.

BREAKING THROUGH THE ROADBLOCKS TO DIVERSITY SUCCESS

This book will help you identify and work through the roadblocks or impediments to progress, which include the following:

- **Personal and Interpersonal Issues:** The biases and attitudes that we bring to the work place about people who are different from us can get in the way of productive working relationships and fair treatment.
- **Organization Culture:** The underlying assumptions about what is important to the organization and how its employees are valued may be very supportive of diversity, but often some adjustments to the culture are needed if diversity progress is to be sustainable.
- **Systems and Programs:** Human resources systems may be inadequate, or do not work equally well for all employees.

This book is about moving through the three different types of roadblocks described above, starting on a journey toward the managing diversity vision, or what I would like to call **Diversity Success.**

DEFINE THE CHARACTERISTICS OF DIVERSITY SUCCESS

Every organization should have a vision for diversity success that fits its needs. Some of the key characteristics I think of in relation to diversity success include the following:

[1]Reprinted with permission of the publisher from *Beyond Race and Gender: Unleashing the Power of Your Total Workforce by Managing Diversity,* © 1991, Dr. R. Roosevelt Thomas, Jr. Published by AMACOM, A Division of the American Management Association. All rights reserved.

- *Climate of Mutual Respect:* Employees at all levels treat their peers, subordinates and supervisors with the same respect, honesty and cooperation that they would seek in return.
- *Normalization:* Diversity is evident at all levels of the organization, and homogeneity is viewed as an exception rather than the norm.
- *Development:* The organization is committed to the long term recognition, development and advancement of all its employees. Efforts are continually made to adjust systems to work naturally for all employees.
- *Understanding and Valuing Differences:* Educational efforts, the corporate culture and values encourage the recognition of differences, leading to understanding and valuing both similarities and differences.
- *Strategic Imperative:* A strong business rationale drives the diversity activity, so that it will weather the periodic economic storms and management lapses of attention to the issues.
- *Contribution:* The business opinions of all employees are sought and none are discounted on the basis of the diversity dimensions of the contributor.
- *Collaboration:* In raising diversity issues for change, the emphasis is not on setting blame for past practices and patterns, but on developing collaborative relationships which move the company to a new performance plateau.
- *Universality:* Diversity is accepted as a natural part of doing business, and is woven into the fabric of the operations of the organization.
- *Accountability:* Everyone feels responsible for making progress on diversity, and for making the personal adjustments that create productive working relationships within a multicultural environment.

Skeptics may dismiss these diversity success characteristics as overly optimistic. I view such a challenge, however, as a necessary motivator to move to a new level of understanding and effectiveness. The question is not so much "Should we begin to worry about managing our diverse workforce?" Rather for me the question is, "Where do we start, how much resources can we allocate, and how fast can we move?" I hope you will find answers to those questions in this book that speak to the needs of your organization.

For those relatively new to diversity concepts, I again encourage you to deepen your understanding of some key diversity concepts in Chapter 16. For the more advanced readers, let's begin working our way through a diversity process with the book summary in Chapter 1.

Seven Key Actions for Designing and Implementing Successful Strategies and Programs

1

This chapter will provide you with seven guidelines for designing and implementing successful diversity strategies and programs. In addition, a timeline is provided that identifies the key activities and their sequence that should yield the most positive results.

Each organization has its own distinct character and its own diversity issues. Therefore, while each diversity study may have similarities with others, it also produces some share of surprises and unique insights. In looking at past personal experiences and information shared by other practitioners, there are some discernible activities, which if executed effectively, greatly increase the odds for success. There are seven key steps or guidelines that I have found helpful. These guidelines are described briefly below.

DEVELOP A STRATEGIC PERSPECTIVE TO GUIDE YOUR EFFORTS

To those contemplating action or who are early into a diversity change process, the range of activities and areas affected can be somewhat confusing or intimidating. For example, at various points in this book we will identify the following under way in various organizations:

- Approximately one hundred "diversity" activities
- Approximately seventy affirmative action activities that operate in conjunction with broader diversity efforts.
- About one hundred work and family activities sometimes included under the diversity umbrella.

In total, diversity activities can impact virtually every aspect of the employment relationship. With so many activities to choose from, targeting the needs of many different employee groups, where does one start? How can we view the process strategically?

In Exhibit 1.1 below, a model depicts the objective and forces involved in a diversity change process. The Kotter/Heskett [1] change model illustrated starts with the basic premise that if we are to manage diversity according to the vision described in the introduction, it will be necessary to change the behavior of the organization's employees—all employees.

Targeting Employee Behavior: There are a number of levers or forces that can be used to influence behavioral changes in the employees of the organization. Some are more important than others, but principally the levers include the following:

SYSTEMS/POLICIES/PLANS: One change lever is represented by the systems, plans, and policies that guide, reward and punish behavior. In the diversity context, these are generally processes, policies and practices developed and administered through the human resources department. (Those programs most closely relating to diversity are discussed in Chapters 7–12 and include career develop-

EXHIBIT 1.1 Model for Diversity Change Efforts

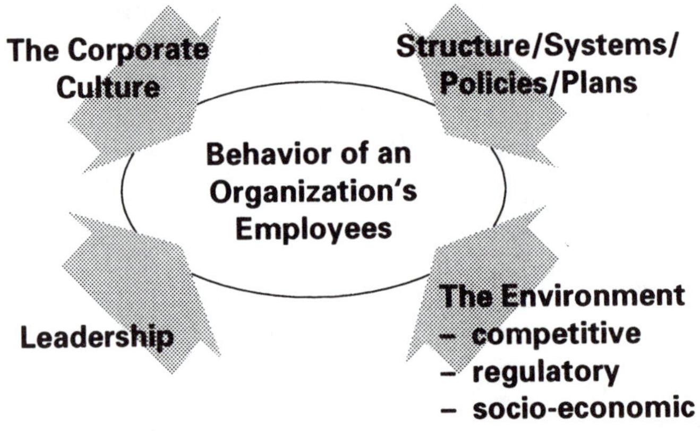

The Corporate Culture

Structure/Systems/ Policies/Plans

Behavior of an Organization's Employees

Leadership

The Environment
 – competitive
 – regulatory
 – socio-economic

ment systems, diversity education and training, affirmative action, work and family programs, compensation and communication.).

CORPORATE CULTURE: This is the vision, philosophy or underlying approach to "the way things are done around here." (Some of the issues in the corporate culture that most impact managing a diverse workforce are described in Chapter 13 along with suggestions for moving the culture in a slightly different direction.)

LEADERSHIP: The leadership referred to here is principally a senior management role to articulate a vision, build commitment, demonstrate desired behaviors, and enforce compliance. (Leadership activities are also described in a number of chapters, but particularly Chapter 3 on defining the business rationale, Chapter 13 on corporate culture and Chapter 14, relating to maintaining momentum on diversity.)

ENVIRONMENTAL INFLUENCES: These influences are external to the organization and could include regulatory requirements, socio-economic conditions, national issues of race relations, media reporting, and so forth. While one organization can rarely influence the existence and force of those environmental conditions, we can mitigate the adverse effects of those influences on our personal behavior and on the behavior of our employees. (See Chapters 2 and 8 for that discussion. The impact of external forces creating the interest in diversity is discussed in Chapter 16.)

As we move forward through the book, keep the overall change model in mind, or develop your own model. You will find it provides a conceptual framework for categorizing the long list of diversity activities in which you might be engaged, and is a constant reminder of your ultimate mission: to create conditions that motivate, facilitate, and reward behaviors that contribute to the effective management of your diverse workforce.

PREPARE YOURSELF FOR DIVERSITY LEADERSHIP

To be effective, credible and able to operate comfortably as a diversity change agent, it is critical that you come to grips with how you feel about people who are different than you. Biases may be inevitable, but if we let our biases influence our decisions we create an environment that will not work well for all employees. A better understanding of the nature, source, and severity of our own biases will also help us understand why others react in ways that we find surprising, hurtful, or dysfunctional.

SECURE COMMITMENT BASED ON A CLEAR BUSINESS RATIONALE

Diversity change processes require some application of your organization's financial resources and management commitment and involvement over an extended period of time. Any good business manager will want to make sure there is a good reason for applying the company resources toward this, rather than any number of other priorities crying for attention simultaneously.

Furthermore, you must cause people to change their attitudes, or at a minimum, to act in a different way than they have previously, while holding their attitudes in check. You must have clear and convincing reasons about how the behavior changes requested will help the organization if you want to secure their individual commitment. (See Chapter 3 for coverage of the business rationale.)

FOCUS THE ORGANIZATION FOR DIVERSITY SUCCESS

The traditional hierarchical methods for issue identification, action planning and implementation are not likely to be optimally effective for diversity planning and programming. You need different methods to make the process more inclusive, build commitment and create progress in a number of areas. (A variety of organizing activities and approaches are covered in Chapter 4, along with a description of some of the advantages and disadvantages of each.)

USE CREDIBLE DIVERSITY RESEARCH TO IDENTIFY ISSUES

Efficient allocation of resources requires the documentation of the perceptions of diverse employees regarding the culture, policies and programs of the organization. While some organizations already have such a diversity data base, many do not. The documentation of assessments will probably yield a few surprises to the organization and will help sort out the most pressing issues. The data can also be used as a yardstick to track future progress. (Employee research issues and planning for a research effort are covered in Chapter 5.)

MOVE QUICKLY FROM RESEARCH TO PRIORITIES TO ACTION PLANS

The organization should move forward quickly to address the issues identified through your diversity research. Your employee data may identify many practices or programs that should be addressed. Lack of consensus on priorities, or insufficient resources, can cause harmful delays in determining the direction of the efforts, or may result in the adoption of an overly ambitious scatter-shot approach to the subject.

(Some techniques for assessing diversity priorities are found in Chapter 6, along with examples of action plans used by two organizations. The subject-specific issues that generally surface are covered in Chapters 7–13.)

MEASURE DIVERSITY PROGRESS AND MAINTAIN MOMENTUM

Diversity changes of consequence will certainly take many months, and in some organizations could take several years. You can provide for revitalization of the activities and avoidance of loss of energy, or diversion to other company priorities by measuring progress and the tangible benefits to the organization, and reinforcing successes and dealing with failures. (Chapter 14 describes this area of ongoing concern.)

Much of this book describes the "what" and the "why" of the diversity change process. Frequently, in the early stages of a process, management will ask "How long will all this take?" Perhaps an underlying and unspoken question is, "When will we be finished with diversity so we can go on to other important issues?". In any case, one caution frequently repeated in the book is that a diversity intervention is not a "quick fix" for the problems of the organization. To provide for sustainable progress, a thorough and comprehensive approach requiring some months of extended effort is required. Some of the key steps in the process are outlined here. Some 40 steps covering five process stages are summarized in Exhibits 1.2 thru 1.6.

Note that the time line in Exhibit 1.2 assumes starting at "square one." Organizations who are farther along, might step into the process at some later point. For example, an organization may already be doing diversity training, which is listed in Exhibit 1.6, for implementation. However, for varying reasons, it may have launched the diversity training without first carefully researching the total needs and establishing priorities. In this case, it may find value in circling back and hooking into the process at the research stage as described in Exhibit 1.3.

Key Variables That Will Determine Your Rate of Progress: The time frame required for the guidelines shown in Exhibits 1.2–1.6 will vary according to numerous idiosyncratic organization characteristics, including the following:

- Priority that senior management assigns the activity. Is it a "must do" backed by the CEO, or a "nice to do"? Is it the highest priority on a five point scale or is it a three? Most organizations seldom get to their "three" priorities these days.

- Size and complexity of the organization which affects not only the range of

EXHIBIT 1.2 Timeline for a Diversity Change Process— Preparation Stage

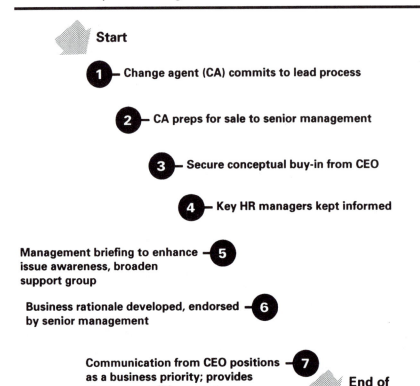

issues likely to surface, but the layers of organization that have to be motivated to change.

- Financial and staffing resources allocated to the effort. Will the activity be fully supported with a balance of internal and external resources?
- Other intervening priorities: restructuring, downsizing, delayering, corporate survival, etc. These divert attention from the diversity effort, even for organizations that are seriously committed to diversity progress.
- Capability and credibility of the human resources staff to support the task forces and initiatives going on at various levels and stages.
- The number and severity of the issues to be addressed.

As you go through the chapters in the book you will develop a better sense of where you are in the process and how long it might take to move to the next

EXHIBIT 1.3 Timeline for a Diversity Change Process—Organization Stage

Start of Second Quarter

1 — Diversity task force membership criteria developed, members identified

2 — Letter from CEO invites Diversity Task Force (DTF) to participate. Defines mission, authority

3 — HR determines support staffing and divisional involvement

DTF trained in diversity concepts and company issues — **4**

DTF makes preliminary — **5** assessment of needs
- data on issues
- staffing and budget
- timetable for deliverables

Preliminary identification for — **6** targeted activity areas

End of Second Quarter

plateau. Whether your diversity programming is still in the planning stage, or if it is well under way, these guidelines will have relevance to your eventual success.

IMPORTANT POINTS TO REMEMBER

Base your planning on the seven guidelines for moving toward diversity success:

1. Guide your efforts with a strategic perspective on what diversity is, and how each of the diversity initiatives will impact the organization.
2. Start the change process with a careful assessment of your own biases that could interfere with your effectiveness in a diversity leadership role.
3. Secure commitment from senior management and the entire organization by developing a clear and convincing business rationale for the organization's diversity commitment.

EXHIBIT 1.4 Timeline for a Diversity Change Process—
Research Stage

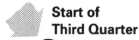 **Start of
Third Quarter**

1 — **Interviews with key influencers:**
  - **identify preliminary issues**
  - **understand culture**
  - **identify related prioirities (TQM, etc.)**

2 — **Research project designed on basis
of interviews. Proposal received detailing
methodologies, timing, responsibilities**

Proposal reviewed, modified —3

**DTF and consultants finalize —4
key research issues:**
  - **sample size**
  - **specifiic questions**
  - **format for reporting**
  - **key target dates**

Company identifies target participants —5

 **End of
Third Quarter**

**Start of
Fourth Quarter**

6 — **Questionnaires mailed. Focus groups scheduled;
letters sent to participants**

7 — **Questionnaires returned. Focus groups
conducted and summarized**

8 — **Analysis of data. Development of
findings and recommendations**

9 — **Presentation to DTF**

**End of
Fourth Quarter**

EXHIBIT 1.5 Timeline for a Diversity Change Process—Establishing Priorities and Action Plans

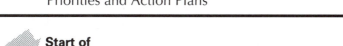

Start of Fifth Quarter

1 – DTF divides in sub-teams to work with data and issues more closely, (e.g., work and family, recruitment)

2 – Priorities set in each area with:
  – action plans
  – budgets
  – timetables

3 – Availability of resources assessed (e.g., trainers for diversity awareness)

4 – DTF prepares and presents overall plan to senior management for approval

Final action plan reflecting senior management input, resources allocated – **5**

Communication materials prepared – **6**

Key managers briefed on: – **7**
  – survey results
  – action plans
  – communication plans
  – Q&A preparation

Written communication/department – **8** meetings to discuss findings and action plans, manage expectations

Detailed policies and programs – **9** developed for DTF review

End of Fifth Quarter

EXHIBIT 1.6 Timeline for a Diversity Change Process—Implementing
Programs and Monitoring Progress

4. Focus the organization for diversity success by using nontraditional organization approaches to addressing issues.
5. Conduct solid diversity research to identify issues and serve as a base from which to measure progress.
6. Move quickly from research results to program implementation.
7. Measure progress and impact of diversity efforts, and use the results to reinforce the commitment of the organization.

Each of the above guidelines will be elaborated on in the chapters which follow.

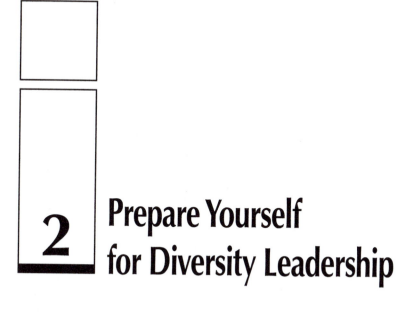

2 Prepare Yourself for Diversity Leadership

Whether we like it or not, it is difficult to escape the reality that prejudices or biases, and the "ism's" (racism, sexism, ageism, etc.) are very much at the heart of corporate diversity issues. Speaking from personal experience, it is difficult to serve effectively in a diversity leadership role unless you have come to grips with the attitudes that you bring to the task. Therefore, if you expect to serve on a diversity task force, participate in an affinity/advocacy group or serve in the role of diversity trainer, program developer or implementer, consultant, role model, human resources manager, affirmative action manager, or executive who approves programs, this chapter will help you.

This chapter will do the following:

- Explain that we all have prejudices, and why it is important for us to understand the impact of those prejudices on our own behavior and that of others.
- Provide a working definition of prejudices, and describe some of the methods by which we acquire them.
- Describe some of the ways that prejudice exhibits itself in the job setting.
- Explore a variety of approaches that individuals may use to heighten their awareness and understanding of prejudices, and to extend that understanding to on-the-job behaviors.

The examples used throughout the chapter are not intended to lay blame for past patterns of discrimination in business, or to further reinforce biases and stereotypes by raising them for discussion. The purpose is simply to lay the foundation for progress by addressing these issues up front.

UNDERSTANDING THE PERCEPTION GULF: WHOSE REALITY IS IT ANYWAY?

One of the characteristics of diversity research results (described in Chapter 5) is the strikingly different way in which individuals of differing race and gender react to the culture, programs, and opportunities they find in the company in which they are employed. A straightforward question used in some research projects to assess the general environment within a company reads as follows:

"The manner in which employees of Anonymous Company are treated is not affected by gender/age/race or physical ability." In Exhibit 2.1, the results are graphed for a salaried workforce of about 5,000 employees. You can see what wide variations there are among the various groups, with approval ratings ranging from 65% for white male respondents all the way down to 8% for African American female respondents.

EXHIBIT 2.1 Perceptual Differences: By Race

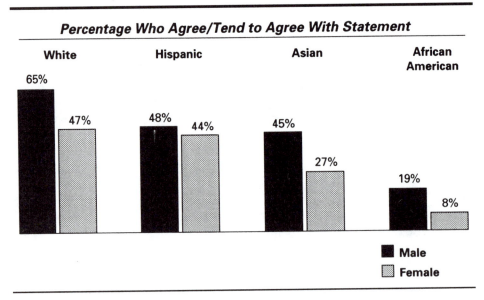

The pattern of widely disparate *perceptions* shown above for one organization is by no means unusual. Wide differences in perception levels along racial and gender lines have been noted in national surveys. For example, a survey conducted every two years asks the question whether blacks are discriminated against in their search for management jobs. (1) Over the years about 60–70% of the black respondents typically respond yes, versus only 20–30% of the white respondents who perceived such discrimination against blacks. This gap has remained relatively constant over the 10 years that the survey has been conducted.

When examining the widely varying perceptions of different employee groups you should consider the following:

- Our perceptions vary based on experiences and influences *before* we even enter the workplace.

- Each of us has different *actual* experiences within an organization; some get a sponsor or mentor; some do not. Some are invited into key informal communication networks; some are not.

- The *interpretation* of our workplace experiences is likely to be affected by our previous experiences. If two individuals lose out in the competition for a key promotion, one may see it as an unfortunate but fair result; another may view the decision as driven by the outright bias of the decision maker.

Each of us walking through our employer's door each morning brings with us a strong set of beliefs about our own "ingroup" as well as opinions about members of various "outgroups." Those attitudes may be reinforced in our minds by experiences in the work place. No group is without its strong biases and we will examine the source of some of those attitudes. Whatever the source of the bias, progress in managing diversity requires some individual understanding and self awareness about those beliefs. That understanding and awareness may motivate an individual to change his or her thinking, and to practice behaviors that are supportive of diversity. Even if we can't or are unwilling to change our basic attitudes, we can learn to become better at recognizing those attitudes and separating the attitudes from our behavior in the work setting.

WE MUST UNDERSTAND PREJUDICE BEFORE WE CAN DEAL WITH IT

One of the problems in discussing this subject is that the words have different meaning to different people, and they are often laden with emotional or moral overtones. The tonality gets in the way of reasoned and measured debate. So let's begin with a definition of bias/prejudice and contrast it with its malignant cousin—racism/discrimination/sexism. These distinctions are important.

Let's begin with the key definitions. In reviewing a number of different definitions of prejudice and discrimination, I found a definition provided by Loden/Rosener (1) to be especially helpful to our perspective, the workplace.

Prejudice/Bias Defined: Prejudices are judgments made that reinforce a superiority/inferiority belief system. Typically a prejudice will exaggerate the value of one's own group, while it diminishes the value of other groups of which we are not members.

Discrimination: When we combine a biased belief system with institutional power to impose our beliefs and to disadvantage others, then we are engaging in the *"ism's"*: racism, sexism, ageism, etc. Examples of institutional power in this context are the authority to hire, fire, reward employees in our organization.

The distinctions between the terms prejudice and discrimination are critical to understanding both the impact of our own behavior and the dynamics of prejudice in the work place. Furthermore, there are two key elements of the definition:

- The notion of organizational power as a prerequisite to discrimination; for example, the African American secretary who works for me may dislike me intensely (for any number of real or imagined reasons). She is biased against me, but she probably doesn't have the organization power to discriminate against me in a way that puts me at a disadvantage.
- The notion of a continuum of attitudes, moving from the acceptable to the unacceptable.

With regard to this latter point, you can construct a conceptual measuring device for judging where you are in the attitudinal continuum. Exhibit 2.2 is an illustration of a gauge that shows the range of bias/discrimination. After looking at the scale, review the description of the severity index below the illustration.

You may have your own terms for describing the principles described above. For example, in *The Rage Of A Privileged Class*, Ellis Cose lists the "dozen demons" that adversely affect African Americans and other racial minorities within organizations. Most of these "demons" fall on the right side of the scale in Exhibit 2.2, including exclusion from the club, low expectations, presumption of failure, and assigning guilt by association. (4)

Some might take comfort in the notion that our prejudices in many cases are harmless to others. However, the scale provides a misleadingly easy approach to keep our behavior under control. In the real world, we are too often unaware when we have passed from one intensity level to another. By the time you read this chapter and do the exercises, you will be in a better position to evaluate where you are on the scale and to change your position.

EXHIBIT 2.2 Workplace Bias and Discrimination: A Severity Scale*

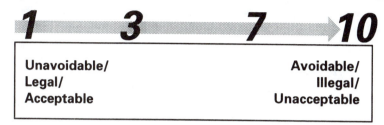

| Unavoidable/
Legal/
Acceptable | Avoidable/
Illegal/
Unacceptable |

The severity of workplace bias/discrimination corresponding to the scale* above are as follows:

1. **Privately held bias:** Held consciously or unconsciously, but is neither spoken of or acted upon.

3. **Anti-locution:** Expressing a prejudice, often to a like-minded friend or trusted social group.

7. **Avoidance:** Withdraw to avoid contact with disliked or distrusted group, surround self with those with whom you are comfortable.

10. **Discrimination:** Intentional or unintentional application of the prejudice to disadvantage others in the work setting, social situations, housing, etc.

YES, I HAVE PREJUDICES: THE NORMALITY OF PREJUDGMENT

How many times have you heard people say in various ways, "I'm not prejudiced" or words to that effect. It can be especially difficult for well-educated individuals who basically see themselves as having lofty ideals and good intentions, to readily accept that they have strong prejudices against other groups.

In Allport's classic on the subject, *The Nature of Prejudice,* he concludes prejudice is an ancient and universal condition. (3) There are two essential elements of prejudice: *denigration* and gross *over-generalization* concerning the faults or limitations of the target group of the prejudice. Many times the attitude is based on partial or faulty information.

Anthropologists and social psychologists support the notion of universal prejudice with historical perspectives which demonstrate that always (and in every society) we find separateness of groups. It requires less effort to deal with people who have similar presuppositions, so we bond together for comfort, strength and common cause.

Process of Categorization: Allport's research described how we think with the aid of categories, or generalizations. In fact we can scarcely avoid the generalization process, for our orderly living depends upon it. Characteristics of categorization used in forming judgments include:

- Forms large clusters for guiding our daily judgments, i.e., deciding what we think about a person based on his or her group identification. Open mindedness, strictly speaking, cannot occur. New experiences must be fit in with old categories. When making placement decisions, for example, it may be difficult for the prejudiced person to deal with people as individuals, to separate the person from the category. (For example, *"She is Hispanic, so she will probably have difficulty communicating with our Anglo customers."*)

- The mind tends to categorize environmental events in the "grossest" manner compatible with the need for action. This takes less effort, but in the work setting often has the effect of foreclosing opportunities. (e.g., *"Women are not rising as fast as they want here. But I see a lack of initiative, which is characteristic of women. It makes them less promotable."*)

- Categories have an immediate tie with what we see, how we judge, and what we do. They facilitate perception and conduct, making life smoother and more consistent. How much easier for us to make judgments about people without the drudgery of actually digging below the surface characteristic that we associate with the label!

- Categories can be more or less rational, that is, have a kernel of truth, e.g., (*"About one third of our female employees don't return to full time employment after they give birth. So I guess it may be a waste to spend too much development time on them early in their careers."*)

Perhaps one of the strangest features of prejudice is holding on to prejudgments in the face of evidence disproving the validity of the attitude (*"Chang seems to be doing well in his new management role, but he is an exception to the typical Asian American."*)

Formation of In-groups: An in-group can be roughly defined as a group that uses the term *WE* with the same social significance. Some memberships come with birth and are ascribed according to the primary dimensions of diversity. (e.g., female—American born—Vietnamese). Other memberships are achieved or selected (For example, Registered Nurse, Riverdale Country Club).

One reason that we have a hard time recognizing our biases and dealing with them is that the attitudes about other groups are formed so early in life. Developmental psychologists have verified that as early as age five, a child is capable of understanding that he or she is a member of various in-groups sharing characteristics and interests. By age nine or ten, the child will understand some of the differences between groups, but fierce in-group loyalties are developed before that. Friendliness with members of different ethnic groups usually disappears by the fifth grade for example. Boys lose (temporarily for most) their interest in friendship with females at about age eight.

Our attitudes have been influenced from an early age and continue to be shaped by a variety of forces, such as the following.

Experiential Shapers of Attitudes
- Personally encountered
- Personally observed
- Report from a witness
- Third hand report

Familial/Association Influences
- Parents/grandparents
- Siblings
- Friends
- School/work associates
- Clubs/churches, etc.

Environmental Influences
- Movies, TV, dramas
- Newspapers, magazines
- Books and studies
- Political campaigns

What we see and how we react to the information is heavily determined by the primary and secondary diversity dimensions of our families. Unfortunately, it is also true in virtually every society that the child is regarded as a member of his or her parents' groups. The child is expected to acquire the parents' loyalties and prejudices. And, sadly, if the parent is a victim of prejudice, the child is also automatically victimized.

How Prejudice Leads to Stereotyping in the Workplace: The tendency to categorize often leads to *stereotyping*. One definition of a stereotype is when an exaggerated belief (favorable or unfavorable) is associated with a category. The function of a stereotype is to rationalize our conduct in relation to that category.

Some stereotypes are totally unsupported by facts; others develop from a sharpening and over-generalization of facts. For example, here is a comment taken from a focus group of white males: *"If you're a manager and get a Black or Hispanic, you are likely to have a communication problem. You can't understand them. That's a fact, but it should not be confused with racism."* Once formed, stereotyped assessments such as these cause their possessor to view future evidence in terms of the available categories.

A stereotype is not identical with a category. It is a fixed idea that accompanies the category. For example, the category Black can be held in mind simply as a neutral, factual, non-evaluative concept, pertaining merely to a racial group. Stereotyping occurs when the initial category is contaminated with "pictures in our head" so that judgments made about individuals help us to fit the member of that group into the mental filing cabinet that we have reserved for that group. For example, one of my consulting associates happens to be a tall black male. One of the ice breakers he encounters in meetings with corporate executives are questions about whether he played basketball in college. While he was, in fact, a modestly successful college athlete, he finds it disappointing that the executives fall into the stereotype of associating Black males with athletic prowess. Unfortunately no one asks him questions which could lead to a discussion of his academic achievements (top 10% in his MBA class). My associate is stuck with what I describe as a *"positive-limiting stereotype."* In this form of categorizing, the other party perceives it as a compliment. However, the target of the positive-limiting stereotype sees it as limiting the ways in which he will be viewed by others (e.g., tall black male equals basketball player).

Individuals who are *not* members of the dominant group can become quite frustrated when they are viewed by members of the dominant group primarily in terms of their diversity characteristics, even if those characteristics are of marginal importance to the individual holding them. They must adhere to the customs, values, manners, and laws of the dominant group. However, if they attempt to develop a relationship on equal terms, they are rejected on the basis of the marginal characteristic (female, Hispanic, Asian, physically challenged) which they feel should be irrelevant. Below are some focus group comments from individuals who have been the target of workplace stereotyping and how they reacted to those experiences:

African American Male:
"If a white employee shows up late, management assumes it was probably for a valid reason. Those kinds of courtesies are never extended to us."

Asian American Male:
"I think we're often seen as good technicians, but incapable of making decisions. So we get more autonomy than we should on technical tasks and no autonomy on problem solving and decision making."

African American Male:
"I had one manager, when I first came here, tell me that he didn't know that black people could write as well as whites! At least he was honest about it."

Hispanic Female:
"When I complained of a racial slur my manager actually told me, 'There you go, being hot-blooded again. It was just a harmless joke.'"

White Female:
"I had an older woman supervisor who resented that I was trying to have both a career and a family. She said you had to be 'married to the job'. She felt males made better employees because they didn't have divided loyalties, the way women did."

In some later exercises we will explore how you can identify some of your stereotypes that underlay the assumptions about various groups in your organization, and how they affect their treatment and advancement opportunities.

Our discussion has tended to focus on issues of racism and sexism and other "protected classes" under various civil rights legislation. However, there are other forms of bias that may be stronger than those mentioned. For example, individuals who are severely obese are likely to be victims of blatant bias and the target of openly hostile remarks, (5) and the same applies to those who may be openly gay or lesbian. As one focus group participant said, *"The gays and lesbians are the only ones we can still beat up on and get away with it. As a result there are many jokes about them."*

USING EXERCISES TO DEAL WITH PREJUDICES AT THE WORKPLACE

Let's assume that the experts are right—that no matter who we are, and what groups we are members of, we will have strong biases about other groups that could get in the way of effectively working with others. Such impediments could be especially important for those leading or participating in the diversity efforts of your organization. To help you understand and address your issues, it will be useful to go through the exercises listed below.

- Tracing our cultural *roots* exercise to identify the nature and sources of our attitudes,

- Raising *awareness* of our attitudes toward others through reading, training exercises and case studies.

- Building *relationships* based on the achievement of mutually beneficial objectives.

- Creating *fail-safe* options that can be used in new situations as we build our understanding and skills.

If you have already had extensive diversity awareness training (and it worked), you may want to move directly to the next chapter.

Tracing Our Roots: As we noted earlier, attitudes regarding others different from ourselves are placed in our heads at very early ages, because in every society on earth the child is expected to acquire parents' loyalties and prejudices. Furthermore, the family characteristics will often determine where the child is raised, and the kinds of persons he or she will interact with during the formative years. One exercise I have used is to ask participants to revisit their upbringing and reflect upon the associations and experiences that have influenced their attitudes toward their own group and other groups.

EXERCISE 2.1 Tracing the Roots of Our Attitudes Toward Others

The objective of this exercise is to identify some of the sources or influences on attitudes that we have developed about our own ethnic/gender group and members of other groups. Think back to your childhood and later years, and answer the following:

1. Were you raised in the country, city or suburbs?
2. Was your neighborhood ethnically or racially diverse or somewhat like your own family?
3. How many children are there in your family? Are they older or younger than you? What gender?
4. Did your mother work outside the home?
5. Was your school ethnically or racially or economically diverse, or were students somewhat like yourself? How about your close friends?
6. Think back to a time when you became aware of having particular feelings (positive or negative) about someone who was not like you:
   a. How did that person (or members of that group) differ from you?
   b. How did you develop your opinion about them:
      - A personal encounter or experience with the person/group?
      - From comments made by a member of the family, friend or acquaintance?
      - From something you read or saw in a movie or television program?
      - Some other means?
7. Referring to the responses in 6, did your feelings about the other persons affect your behavior toward them? Did you avoid or seek them out, praise or criticize them, ignore them or seek to learn more about them?
8. In recent years, has there been any change in your thinking about the other person/group?
   - Do you have a better opinion now, or worse?
   - How did the change in opinion come about? Personal experience, learned more about them?
9. If you had it to do over, what would you change in the way you felt and behaved toward individuals or members of the other group?

Three Exercise Scenarios: Exercise 2.1 is good for warming people up to the subject of diversity and enabling them to make some connections between where their attitudes are now and the environment in which they were shaped. Let's look at just a few samples to illustrate a variety of situations rather than a pattern.

FARMER JONES: THE WOMAN'S PLACE IS IN THE HOME: A white male grew up in a Midwestern farm community. It was a closely knit family with an older brother and a younger sister. The women in the family had all the work they could handle helping out on the farm. Young Mr. Jones grew up thinking that women were the key to an efficient and positive family experience, and it was important to have them around the house. After-dinner gossip sometimes touched on some of the few wives in the community who attempted to work outside the home. Often this conversation was in the context of strains that the arrangement put on the family.

DANCES WITH BIGOTS: IMPACT OF SHARED PAIN: A female of Cherokee/Anglo parents was raised in a large Midwestern city. Her family lived on the "wrong side of the tracks" along with other low income families, including a number who were black. A strong grandmother impressed upon her the importance of getting along with everyone. She went to schools that had diverse student bodies and most of her childhood friends were persons of color. Although her superficial features were Caucasian, the slights and insults she endured in school relating to her Native American ancestry caused her to identify with the concerns of people of color and to be wary of people from the "right side of the tracks."

BIG CITY BLUES: BUILDING A BASE FOR RESENTMENT: An inner-city African American youth was raised in a primarily black neighborhood. Members of his extended family suffered through periodic unemployment, and conversations often revolved around how to get to "the man" for a job interview. In his current relationships, he tended to view whites with a mixture of resentment and exaggerated awe. He recognized that his underlying anger was related to difficult family circumstances and perceived injustices that contributed to his reluctance to build working relationships with his white supervisors.

These are just a sampling of the infinite variety of personal histories that could come from the roots exercise. People who have applied themselves seriously to the exercise found that introspection helped them develop a better understanding of the nature and source of some of their attitudes; a step forward in self understanding.

Building Awareness Of Your Blindspots: There are at least three basic approaches to building awareness of ourselves and of other cultures.

INTELLECTUALLY BASED ACTIVITIES: The first avenue to understanding includes activities such as reading, watching movies and television programs covering the topics. For example, there is a wealth of reading material available. A partial list can be found in the bibliography at the end of this book. Reading and other activities are a low risk way to broaden your understanding, but they require a conscious desire to objectively weigh the validity of new information.

INTERACTION WITH OTHERS: A second approach involving slightly more risk would be to seek out opportunities for personal contact to become better acquainted with individuals who are different. Such a relationship can enhance your cultural understanding and provide other important benefits as well. Some examples of multi-benefit programs include the following:

- Establish an informal mentoring or information-sharing arrangement with someone of a different gender, race or ethnic group.
- Establish a volunteer tutor program where employees develop a one-to-one relationship with inner city high school youths.
- Do volunteer work with an organization whose clientele is somewhat different from groups with which you normally associate.

Personal associations help to reinforce your efforts to begin relating to your peers, subordinates, and bosses based on individual characteristics, rather than basing your attitudes on untested stereotypes associated with members of a given group.

A third approach to enhancing your awareness would be through participation in education and training program exercises (such as those discussed in Chapter 8). Let's look at one of those exercises that specifically addresses the issue of personal biases and stereotyping in the work environment. One example of an awareness building exercise is the Johari Window adaptation described in Exercise 2.2. The Johari Window concept has been used with good results for many years in various training programs. In this example, I have given the basic concept a "diversity twist" to tie the overall concept directly to the topic at hand.

EXERCISE 2.2 The Johari Window Exercise

Purposes of the Johari Window Exercise:
> To create an understanding that

- We are not always aware of our behavior toward others (much less the effect the behavior has on the recipient).
- We are not always aware of the influences which drive that behavior.

> The exercise also provides an opportunity to admit to biases without guilt, since the individual may legitimately claim a lack of awareness of the attitude and/or behavior.

The Exercise Set Up:
> The Johari window is divided into four panes. Each pane represents the degree to which the individual is aware of his attitudes and behavior.

EXHIBIT 2.3 The Johari Window—The Panes of Prejudice

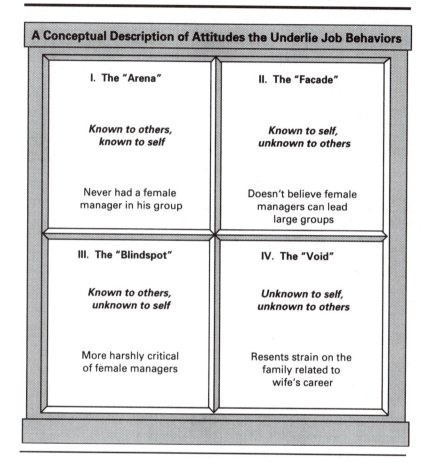

A Conceptual Description of Attitudes the Underlie Job Behaviors

I. The "Arena"

Known to others, known to self

Never had a female manager in his group

II. The "Facade"

Known to self, unknown to others

Doesn't believe female managers can lead large groups

III. The "Blindspot"

Known to others, unknown to self

More harshly critical of female managers

IV. The "Void"

Unknown to self, unknown to others

Resents strain on the family related to wife's career

Using the basic description in each pane, you can apply a type of diversity related behavior to the conceptual model. For example, let's take the male manager who is observed as having a history of being unsupportive of the employment and advancement of female managers in his area of responsibility. This lack of women in his group is in the *"Arena"* pane, readily observed by all, and is within his own sphere of recognition. The arena pane is the easiest to deal with, because you can focus on the facts of the situation.

The manager also knows he has a negative attitude toward female managers and that his feelings on the subject are not consistent with company policy. Therefore, he puts on a *"Facade,"* meeting minimal compliance requirements while keeping his true feelings to himself. In any diversity effort a significant number of managers don't really accept the program. However, they know that resistance is futile, and even perhaps career threatening. In such cases, they simply go through the motions of support and compliance. Unfortunately, you won't find out who is providing lip service until the program is well under way, and the behavior can be documented.

At the *"Blindspot"* awareness level, the person's co-workers may observe that the manager is caustically critical of female managers he observes. The manager is not aware of his overt behavior until someone points it out to him. The observations of others may be sufficient to stimulate a behavior change if the individual is motivated.

The *"Void"* pane is truly an unknown, and would require some expert digging, perhaps involving psychoanalysis. The void pane is not susceptible to the typical diversity training techniques and lies beyond the scope of the book.

Building Relationships Across Cultural Lines: The reality of workforce diversity requires that we develop effective working relationships with people who are not like us, and perhaps have no desire to be like us. The "Great Expectations Exercise" was created for this purpose.

EXERCISE 2.3 The "Great Expectations" Exercise

Objectives:

1. Identify our feelings and preconceptions about individuals who are different from ourselves.
2. Learn to deal directly with those feelings in a realistic business setting.
3. Provide participants an opportunity to discuss stereotyping and its potential effects on a working relationship (when used in a group setting).

GREAT EXPECTATIONS: STEREOTYPES AT WORK

This situation takes place at Monolith Financial Services Company which is based in a suburb of New York City. Two Monolith managers, Bill Bresinski and Louella Jones, have just been informed about some changes in reporting relationships.

Bill Bresinski: Bill Bresinski is a 55-year-old accounting manager in the corporate controller's department. He has worked in various internal financial departments of the company for nearly 25 years.

Bill is a second generation American. All of Bill's grandparents had emigrated from Eastern Europe to the U.S. in the early 1900's. His father had worked as a longshoreman in the New York shipyards.

Bill received his bachelor degree in accounting from the local branch of the state university. Much of his course work was taken at night so he could work to pay for his college and support his young family. Bill was the first member of his immediate family to obtain a college degree. He had joined Monolith as an accounting trainee, and his progress through the accounting department had been unspectacular, but steady. He was regarded by his supervisors as an extremely dependable and honest employee. He was frequently critical of some of the company's computer activities, which he viewed as too expensive for what they achieved. He was a hard worker but valued his involvement with his family and community activities. His children were now on their own, but he was guardian for his ailing mother who lived nearby.

Bill had just learned that a 32-year-old, African American woman had just been named Assistant Controller, and that he would be reporting to her. Bill had been passed over several times previously for the position of Assistant Controller. Most of Monolith's middle and senior managers were white males, and Bill had never reported to a female or minority in any of his positions.

Louella Jones: Louella Jones received her undergraduate degree at the main campus of the state university. She worked for two years and then quit to obtain an MBA in finance from Wharton. While a student in the MBA program, she helped start a support group for black students.

Louella was the first of her immediate family to move into a professional capacity in the business world. She had been recruited to Monolith several years ago from one of its competitors. She was on the company "fast track" program for career development.

Louella's initial assignments were in the treasury and planning areas. She did well and enjoyed the work, which included developing some interesting new computer applications. She was not deeply interested in the accounting side of the finance division. However, she had been encouraged to take the Assistant Controller position to broaden herself and to get some experience supervising others.

Louella is not married, but has a steady boyfriend. She likes to travel and is active in the local NAACP chapter. Her parents work in professional positions in the Boston public school system.

Today's Meeting: Louella and Bill were separately planning for their first meeting with each other on Tuesday morning. Each one was reviewing expectations of what the other would be like, and what kind of working relationship might evolve.

Working the Exercise: Bill's and Louella's expectations of one another may be influenced by preconceptions or stereotypes that they bring to the meeting.

1. What primary and secondary dimensions of diversity may each of their stereotypes touch upon?

	Bill Bresinski	Louella Jones
Primary Dimensions [e.g., age]	_____	_____
	_____	_____
	_____	_____
	_____	_____
Secondary Dimensions [e.g., education]	_____	_____
	_____	_____
	_____	_____
	_____	_____
	_____	_____

2. Within each of the diversity dimensions identified in 1, list one or more stereotypes [a word or phrase] that you have heard applied to persons in that group. The list does not necessarily represent a feeling that you hold, but simply acknowledges that such attitudes may exist among certain members of our society, e.g.,

Diversity Dimension	*Stereotype Word/Phrase*
A. Example: Bill's Age	Resistant to change
	Coasting into retirement
	Can't learn new skills
	Difficult to fire

You should be able to come up with several stereotypes for each of the diversity dimensions identified in step 1.

3. How might the relationship between Bill and Louella develop if either individual fails to recognize the preconceptions and attitudes each brings to the situation? For example, consider the effects on communications, comfort, performance expectations.

4. What kinds of activities might they employ, or what personal perspectives can help them create an effective working relationship?

The Great Expectations exercise can be quite revealing and discomforting to participants especially when done in a group setting. Phyllis Hayes, Diversity Consultant at Amoco Corporation, has led similar exercises a number of times as an internal and external consultant. Phyllis indicates that the kinds of stereotyping labels that come up through this and similar exercises have been very consistent over a period of years. The issues are not new ones, but breaking the "code of silence" provides participants the opportunity to address sensitive issues openly.

Providing Fail-Safe Mechanisms: Let's assume that you have done your homework. You have worked hard at identifying the nature of your biases and their sources. And yet you are still unsure whether your decisions and interactions with people different from you are not affected by your biases. Some of the activities that you might wish to consider are as follows:

ASK FOR A SECOND OPINION: For example, when doing a performance evaluation for a subordinate, seek out the perspectives of others with whom the individual has contact. The incorporation may be part of a formal system (such as the 360 degree appraisal process described in Chapter 7). The additional inputs may also be solicited on an informal basis. If you are the individual being evaluated, initiate the request for a multi-view evaluation, which can be useful for your development, if for no other reason.

TEST FOR MUTUAL UNDERSTANDING: Communications can be a problem between any boss and subordinate, and communicating across cultures may require new skills and experiences. There are materials that can increase your skills. For example, the American Society for Training and Development has a monograph on *The Basics of Intercultural Communication* (4) in which are described some of the key dimensions to be considered:

LANGUAGE: including accents, linguistics, gross translation errors and nuance errors.

PLACE: including personal space and technology.

THOUGHT PROCESSING: including social organization, contexting, authority, and concept of time.

NONVERBAL BEHAVIOR: including appearance, body language and touching.

The cultural context can be critical to understanding differences and communicating. For example, in some Asian cultures, averting the eyes during conversation is a sign of respect or deference to authority, but in Western cultures it may be taken as evidence of low self-confidence or evasiveness. Touching the other person while conversing may be interpreted as a sign of support and intimacy in one culture, but will be seen as an attempt to dominate in another.

The exercises described in this chapter are but two examples of the type that might be used to help each of us and our co-workers begin to recognize and come to grips with the biases that we bring to the work place. (Some others are described in Chapter 8, diversity education and training.) The objective is not to rid everyone of all their biases. While bias eradication may be a laudable goal, it won't happen. However, what may happen with hard work, is that we will be much more aware of our own attitudes, how those attitudes affect our behavior, and the reactions which those behaviors engender in others.

Diversity progress in an organization is like building a brick house—it happens one brick at a time. You can better help that progress through enhanced self awareness and behavior modeling.

IMPORTANT POINTS TO REMEMBER

1. We must first understand prejudice and discrimination before we can begin to deal with its presence and effects in the workplace. Prejudice is an attitude. Discrimination combines attitude with power to put someone at a disadvantage.

2. It is "normal" to make prejudgments about people who are different from our own group based on assigning them to a category. However, the biases we have can result in evaluating individuals according to stereotypes that get in the way of judging people on their own merits.

3. There are a variety of techniques and exercises that can be useful in enhancing our self awareness of our attitudes toward people who are different from us:

   • Tracing our roots to determine the preconceptions that were implanted in us by others.

- Building a greater awareness of our blind spots with regard to both our attitudes and our behavior.
- Working on attitudes and biases to develop effective working relationships.
- Utilizing a fail-safe device in the event the preceding activities are not entirely successful.

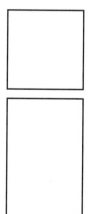

How to Develop the Business Rationale to Drive Diversity Commitment

3

This chapter explains the strategic and tactical importance of identifying and communicating the business rationale that drives your sustained commitment to diversity progress. The chapter also describes some of the typical rationale used by a variety of organizations, and provides an assessment guide to apply both for a general understanding of the principles and to use for your own organization. Some guidelines are provided for developing a written statement for your organization, and some examples to demonstrate how the rationale can be communicated.

A SOUND BUSINESS RATIONALE IS CRITICAL TO DIVERSITY SUCCESS

Perhaps in the "good old days" a vague reference to "improved morale" could be sufficient justification for the introduction of a new human resource program or activity. However, the profit pressures of corporate America seldom permit such luxuries any more. Furthermore, in the case of diversity initiatives, the need for the business justification is especially critical, for the reasons explained below.

Sustained Diversity Progress Requires Culture Change: Some changes in organizational culture and programs are often needed to foster an environment that values and capitalizes on workforce diversity. Corporate cultures can be extraordinarily resistant to change. Resistance will be especially keen if a company has been successful for 20, 50 or 100 years. You will need strong weapons to overcome the guardians of the corporation's cultural roots, who will defend their territory from change of any kind.

Diversity Progress Requires New Personal Perspectives: As noted in Chapter 2, attitudes toward people who are different from ourselves are implanted early in our lives and reinforced frequently through the media, our acquaintances, and personal experiences. We bring a strong mindset to the work place. Why should we trouble ourselves to tinker with this comfortable state of mind unless there is a satisfactory answer to "What's in it for me?"

Short Corporate Attention Spans Can Cause Loss Of Focus Before Diversity Gains Are Secured: U.S. corporations are well noted for their short attention spans. In many cases, the short term focus is driven by intense profit pressures and shifting competitive challenges. When short term thinking reigns supreme, a senior leader may flit from one management fad to the next, creating a "program du jour" approach to priorities, with little sense of commitment to the philosophical premise or strategic purpose for the intervention. (1)

In one organization, the CEO had quickly moved from Total Quality to Empowerment and now he was trying to get his team fired up about diversity. One key manager said that the others at his level would simply "fake it" for a period of time regarding diversity. While they did not question the sincerity of his interest in diversity, they assumed the CEO would soon go on to another pet project or cause. They saw no point in their really getting personally committed to the diversity program.

Other Corporate Priorities Compete For Management Attention: Setting aside for the moment comments about jumping from one management fad to another, the commitments for diversity programs must compete with other important and wholly justified priorities. As one angry manager said in a focus group, "*I want to become a better manager of diversity. Anyone can see the growing importance. However, if the first thing I think of every morning is 'Will they eliminate my job today?', then I will have a hard time focusing on the subject.*"

In a survey of 785 companies, respondents were asked to rate diversity against other priorities that the organization was facing. (2) Respondents ranked issues of profitability, market share, capital investment, total quality management, restructuring, workforce downsizing and going global ahead of diversity in importance. Given the intense competitive pressures that organizations face, the business rationale helps diversity compete for its place on the crowded corporate priority list.

Diversity Issues May Create Discomfort Among Employees: In many organizations there will be a significant number of employees suggesting that the company "leave well enough alone," rather than stir things up by raising touchy issues. As in any change process, for diversity "no pain = no gain". In our society we frequently find it difficult to discuss diversity issues on a one-to-one basis. If we are going to put the issues on the table, you first want to determine that the potential business benefits justify the risks that attend open discussion of issues.

Many Managers Retain Unfavorable Attitudes on Diversity: While there has been much progress in raising awareness about diversity issues and approaches, there is still a significant educational job to be done, right up through senior management. For example, a 1993 survey (2), revealed the following examples of unfavorable attitudes toward diversity among managers:

- 47% of managers felt that greater diversity in the workforce will make their job more difficult.
- 27% feel that diversity is just a politically correct term for affirmative action.
- 29% believe that special treatment for various groups reinforces negative stereotypes.
- 34% believe that diversity programs are motivated primarily by a desire to meet regulations and avoid lawsuits.
- One quarter of respondents predicted that greater diversity would increase the cost of doing business.

Senior management in many companies is quite well informed about diversity. However, the survey data indicates that negative perceptions are common and can present stumbling blocks to garnering commitment. In these days of "politically correct" speech, most employees will be reluctant to express their reservations openly, but you know that the negative attitudes are common and must be addressed in your planning.

UNDERSTAND THE SEVEN BUSINESS DRIVERS OF DIVERSITY COMMITMENTS

Let's assume you accept one or more of the arguments for establishing a business rationale, as described above. Now you are left with the task of defining that rationale with sufficient clarity that it serves as a stimulus to action and basis for commitment on the part of your organization. The issues are broad, and can include present conditions and future trends, as well as external influences and internal considerations. Therefore the impact on the organization of the various factors requires careful analysis. The paragraphs following describe the key business issues that drive diversity commitments.

1. Changing Market and Workforce Demographics: Many of today's senior managers started their careers in the 1960s when nine out of ten consumers were white. However, by the year 2000, four out of ten consumers will be non-white. Ethnic minorities purchased $600 billion in consumer products in 1992. Most organizations have not yet made the mental and strategic adjustments necessary to accommodate to market changes. The CEO of a major consumer goods company confided his concerns: *"I can't seem to get my marketing team to understand that the changing demographics of the workforce that we talk about every day will be the changing demographics of our market place. We sell to people like us! But "us" now, isn't the same "us" that it used to be. Our traditional markets are not growing and we have to develop the right mindset to anticipate and capitalize on the opportunities that are emerging."*

The changing demographics of the workforce represent the changing demographics of the market place for many companies, but not all companies. Markets are becoming more segmented, and companies are trying to find niches where they have some competitive edge. To some organizations the market issues lead them to want to have an employee group that reflects the market place to a reasonable degree. The payoff desired is the ability of the organization to better understand and respond to customer needs, and relate to the new consumer or buyer on a personal basis.

The principle of targeting diverse markets and market segments is well established. Let's look at how three organizations are incorporating diversity considerations into their strategic planning.

RETAIL EXAMPLE: A large chain of retail stores had most of its outlets in major metropolitan areas comprised of racially and ethnically diverse populations. The company was receiving questions from customers in some stores about the fact that they did not see too many people like themselves among the store staff. The company was already in the process of doing a demographic survey of the clientele of each store for marketing and product selection purposes. It used the market data to develop staffing goals that would gradually lead to the store staffs more closely reflecting the diversity of the store clientele. The change is being gradually implemented over a period of several years to permit an orderly adjustment of succession planning efforts.

AUTOMOBILE MARKETING EXAMPLE: The Cadillac division of General Motors suffered a decline in its 40% share of the black buyers market for luxury autos in 1989 to 21% in 1994. To attract black consumers they initiated a program of donating $50 for each test drive to a minority-oriented charity. They also established a program of racial sensitivity seminars so that auto dealer personnel would not lightly dismiss black prospects in the showroom simply because they dressed or acted differently than white prospects. (3)

CONSUMER GOODS EXAMPLE: A specialty foods manufacturer came to recognize that its product had a very low utilization rate among blacks and Hispanics. The predominantly white marketing group had not developed the interest or expertise to address those markets. To bring an appropriate focus on the subject, it formed an internal (diverse) task force to identify opportunities and prepare to tap the new markets. The group also drew upon the services of outside market-ing consultants who had special expertise in (what for this company were) non-traditional markets. As test markets have proven successful, the company is now struggling with the organization issue of keeping the diverse marketing effort separate, or "mainstreaming" it into existing organization groups.

The market rationale will be particularly important for companies that sell directly to consumers (e.g., steam irons rather than steam turbines). The fact re-mains that females and minorities tend to be concentrated at the lower levels of the corporate pyramid, rather than at the middle and upper management levels. However, decision makers in nearly all kinds of organizations are becoming more diverse. If you can reflect, at least in some general way, the increasing di-versity of the individuals making buying decisions on your products and ser-vices, you might improve your chances for making the sale. Let's look at an ex-ample of the diversity impact for business-to-business products and services.

TECHNICAL PRODUCTS AND SERVICES EXAMPLE: A company providing high technology communication services had a management team that was predomi-nantly white male. However, the disparity between the makeup of the customer group and the management team was becoming increasingly apparent. For ex-ample, at a users conference, about half the audience was female, but the com-pany presenters were almost entirely white males. An instance of a difficult client relationship was cited where the customer team consisted of two females and a minority male, and the sales/account management team were all white males. They began to accept that matching up more closely with the customer would not solve all their problems, but it could provide advantages in some instances.

2. Present or Projected Recruitment Needs Require Effective Management of Di-versity: Companies may wish to position themselves to be employers of choice for a talent pool that in the 1990s and beyond will be characterized as follows:

- Growing at a slower rate than in previous decades
- Increasing proportion of new entrants are females, minorities and foreign born.
- New entrants may have significant educational/skills gaps
- New entrants have different values on the importance of work and what they are willing to do to succeed.

The recruitment rationale may not be important in the short term for the many companies in the process of retrenchment or who have little hiring planned in the near term. However, even for these, the issue may have long term impor-tance when the business strengthens, and hiring must be resumed. Even for those operating currently at a "steady state" or needing to add new skills, replacement recruiting is usually necessary.

There have been several instances where companies began their diversity initiatives during the same calendar quarter in which they announced significant headcount reductions. Admittedly this is not an ideal environment in which to begin introducing notions of diversity. However, the juxtaposition does illustrate that the organizations were able to separate the short term tactical issue (reducing headcount) from the long term strategic need to remain an employer of choice for the diverse labor pool.

3. *Talent Retention Requires that Diversity Issues Be Addressed:* To provide high quality service, effectively utilize training investments and provide for future continuity, companies will attempt to value and retain diverse employees. Companies often report turnover rates for female and minority employees that are 10% to 50% higher than for white males. The pattern of female/minority clustering below the glass ceiling will never be improved if excessive numbers are opting out of the organization before the advancement and development systems have a chance to work.

Planning for improved retention may be an especially important rationale for organizations such as the following:

- The organization already experiences high turnover (such as restaurants and retail stores) and quality and customer service will be affected by a worsening of the high turnover.
- If the work requires significant upfront training for the new employee to be productive (e.g., technical sales, operators of complicated processes and machinery), turnover may be very expensive. You don't want to lose your training investment to a competitor that can portray itself as more accommodating to the needs of diverse employees.
- Employee retention is critical where product or user safety is a critical element of the product or service (e.g., air traffic controllers, medical products and services).
- "Personal" customer service links are critical to customer loyalty (e.g., personal banker representatives) and may be threatened by excessive turnover.

4. *Productivity is an Inherent Driver of Diversity Efforts:* As companies face increasingly stiff global competition, managers feel the need to utilize the full abilities that reside in all members of the workforce. The pressures for performance have a way of sweeping aside some of the irrelevant personal considerations. The words of one manager captures the spirit: *"I don't care if they come from Mars, as long as they can get the work done."* This productivity factor may be especially important in organizations where people costs are a significant portion of total expenses.

Sara Lee Corporation has an extensive diversity program throughout its many U.S. facilities. Janice Fenn, Director of Human Resources, states that the programs are tied to the company's strategic goal of being the low cost producer in its various market segments. The basic focal points are developed on a company wide basis, with considerable autonomy exercised at the local level to bring the concepts to reality. The credibility of the performance linkage is underscored by providing reports two or three times per year to the Board of Directors.

5. *Improved Diversity Management Can Enhance Teamwork:* Many companies are working through change processes such as *total quality management, total customer service, high performing organization,* etc. in which the team concept is fundamental to the operating philosophy. In the team environment, the contributions of all individuals are valued in order to maximize their commitment and productivity. Robert Lattimer of Diversity Consultants finds a growing body of research and client experience which suggests that heterogeneous work groups can outperform homogeneous work groups, especially in decision making and problem solving contexts.

The notion that diverse work teams may outperform homogeneous work teams, unfortunately, is counter-intuitive for U.S. managers. U.S. managers often are impressed by the Japanese management theory that it is more difficult to manage diverse work teams. Perhaps managers are reacting to an observation in some diversity research projects where employees (not in the mainstream) saw the teams as being more like exclusive clubs, where individuals from their department/function/gender, and so on, were not valued as contributors. In these situations the perception of the team was that it simply was an official recognition of the desire of managers to work together with people like themselves.

The Ortho Pharmaceutical Division of Johnson & Johnson is one organization that has used the teamwork rationale to drive its efforts. The division president determined that prejudices were getting in the way of the intense collaboration and flexible performance required of their teams. The diversity focus became a means to address those issues. (4)

6. *Going Global Requires Adaptation to Many Cultures:* The growth and profits of U.S. based companies are becoming increasingly dependent upon generating sales and profits outside their North American market base. Some well known names such as Colgate, Coca-Cola® and Procter and Gamble have brands that are borderless and already generate half or more of their income from sources outside the U.S.

In the global company, managers will need to have the ability to effectively interact with the company's employees from dozens of countries. Understanding and accepting different cultures, managerial styles and value systems will be necessary for global success, rather than trying to enforce assimilation to the traditional North America mode of doing business.

7. *Legal/Compliance Pressures Will Not Go Away:* Affirmative action programs historically have been driven by legal mandates and fear of the loss of reputation or financial penalties. While occasional multi-million dollar discrimination settlements have been made, they are not frequent. However, when it does happen, the adverse publicity, large financial settlements and loss of business which have befallen some organizations suggest that these can be both expensive and humbling experiences. Even in the more typical, more limited EEO charges and trials, settlements can be an expensive and disruptive experience for an organization, motivating it to "clean up its act".

Companies seeking federal or other governmental contracts have for decades been required to meet certain EEO/Affirmative Action requirements in order to qualify as bidders. It may not be noble or high-minded, but meeting the local, state or federal contract compliance requirements can be a real and important motivator. One response is for the organization to commit to establishing and utilizing diversity. Unfortunately, a second and more common response is simply to get the numbers to look good enough to meet minimum standards.

Caution: Balance the Business Focus with the Human Side: The emphasis on business rationale notwithstanding, your diverse employees will want to see a balance in the company's interest. You need to consider the way non-traditional employees will view senior management's message. Marty Marquez, of Denver-based Paragon Management Group, cautions that people of color want to be valued for who they are, to have their humanity and dignity respected along with their talents. This won't happen if they believe the organization regards them as just another revenue stream, benefitting the shareholders, but not them. Diverse people will be wary of being used anew, without the organization committing to dismantle unfair practices that have kept these individuals from rising to the proper level in the first place.

Along a similar vein, Norbert Hill, Jr. (Oneida), Executive Director of the American Indian Science and Engineering Society, uses the phrase "to work in two canoes," which captures the need to balance the focus of your efforts. Norbert says with Native Americans, for example, it is "R before I"—relationships before issues. You won't be heard on temporal issues until you have satisfied the spiritual side.

Unfortunately modern organizations are saddled with the country's history of economic exploitation of people of color. The shocking treatment of American Indians was based upon economic grounds—we wanted their lands. Slavery was basically an economic proposition for the Southern plantation owners. (5) While modern corporations can't be blamed for our history, it would be myopic to ignore the cynicism that some groups will bring to efforts that deal one-sidedly with economic issues.

Application to Other Entities: In discussing the seven types of rationale that drive corporate diversity efforts, note that the issues of business rationale can just as easily apply to non-profit institutions, governmental bodies and the like. A museum, for example, must be able to relate to its "market" if it is to draw attendance and generate funds. Medical centers need to consider how culture-based concerns for privacy may affect their planning of examination facilities and rooms. (6) Governmental agencies at every level can be more effective if the group is able to attract and retain a workforce that is indicative of the population that it serves.

HOW TO EVALUATE THE BUSINESS CRITERIA IMPORTANT TO YOUR ORGANIZATION

Having described what we have found to be the primary business drivers of diversity issues, we have now reached the point where you should be ready to apply the concepts. Exercise 3.1, at the end of this chapter, is a rating instrument for evaluating the business drivers for your organization. Let's look at how the instrument might be applied to one business, and then you can use it for your own organization. We will use the mythical Trans-National Bottlers Co. (TNB) as the example.

Trans-National Bottlers is a producer and marketer of a broad range of beers, soft drinks and bottled water. TNB headquarters are located in a major metropolitan center in the Northeastern U.S. Most of its sales are in the Midwest and Northeast, but they are seeking to broaden their market foothold in the Southwestern and Southeastern parts of the country.

Through acquisitions and internal growth it has developed its international business (primarily the Common Market) to the point where it now represents 10% of the total company sales. The international market has been profitable and they would like to expand further in the current countries as well as consider entry into Latin American and Far Eastern markets.

In the U.S. their consumer targets are middle class, age 30+ wage earners. TNB share of the ethnic markets is only 2/3 of the share they have maintained for traditional markets. Males are the most frequent decision makers for beer products, whereas women make up over 50% of the market for the soft drinks and bottled waters.

TNB has had limited success in developing and advancing women and minorities into middle and upper management ranks. Advancement has usually required a series of moves through various sales and marketing positions requiring geographic relocation. The culture of the company has been heavily influenced by the "macho" image often associated with beer drinking, even though beer was now only 2/3 of the company sales.

Using the limited TNB information provided above and your imagination, turn to Exercise 3.1. Along the left side of the form is a brief description of characteristics that might apply to TNB. For each factor you need to circle the appropriate number that relates to the importance of the priority. After you have gone through the exercise for TNB you can use the same principles to evaluate the business rationale that are applicable for your own organization. You will find that this approach will help you work toward a specific and sound rationale.

HOW TO WRITE THE DIVERSITY BUSINESS RATIONALE FOR YOUR COMPANY

The wording and communication media appropriate to your organization will depend upon the nature of the products or services being provided, the culture of the organization, the types of jobs and educational level of the workforce and related factors. Thus some variations in emphasis will be needed to cover all your internal and external audiences.

Some guidelines that you may wish to keep in mind as you prepare and communicate your business rationale include the following:

- While your full statement may be lengthy for senior management purposes, use a condensed version for communicating to target audiences.
- Don't include too many factors or the explanation may lose clarity and power.
- Use many examples that are relevant to your own organization.
- Minimize jargon and technical terms to be understood both on the shop floor and in the executive suite.
- Relate the conditions and issues the organization now faces to those previously encountered. Identify the cost of not addressing the issues.
- Don't obfuscate. If one of the main reasons you are "doing diversity" is to keep your government contracts, admit it.

Now let's look at Exhibit 3.1, the sample business rationale developed for Trans-National Bottlers. Refer to Exercise 3.1, the evaluation worksheet that you did to determine if the most important factors have been included in the writeup. How does it stack up against the criteria described above?

EXHIBIT 3.1 Sample Business Rationale for Trans-National Bottlers, Inc.

The Management Committee of the Trans-National Bottling Company has completed a preliminary review of issues that should be addressed with regard to meeting the needs and fully utilizing the abilities of our diverse workforce. We have concluded that our *Succeeding Through Diversity* effort will be a principal priority for the company for the reasons described below:

Marketing and Sales Opportunities

The strong base of consumers of TNB products has historically been white males in our core Midwestern markets. However, future growth will come from outside this historical base, and must recognize these realities:

EXHIBIT 3.1 Continued

- We will be entering markets in the south and southwest that have heavy concentrations of Hispanic consumers. We have little experience in targeting such markets.
- Our market share among black consumers is only 4% versus our 6% share of white consumers.
- Females currently make the purchasing decision for 18% of total alcohol beverage sales and 65% of other sales. However, our marketing approach has not been effective with female consumers.
- The buyers in store chains that make decisions about whether or not to stock our products are becoming increasingly diverse. We no longer look like our customers, and there may be some effect on results if we don't address the issue.

The continued growth and profitability of the company is dependent upon maintaining our positions in core geographic and demographic segments, while improving our success in the areas listed above. To achieve that success we must have a workforce and management team who reflects the changing market place and who can understand and respond to the needs of the changing consumer. We must also reassess our community relations programs, corporate contribution programs, purchasing from minority and women-owned enterprises so that we target the total resources of the company toward the pursuit of this goal.

Recruitment and Retention

As stated in our corporate objectives, we intend to be a world class employer, utilizing to the fullest the skills and talents of our entire workforce. However, we are aware that the culture, the systems or the programs have not been equally effective for all employees. For example:

- Overall voluntary separations increased from 8% to 12% during the past two years. We have lost a lot of good talent.
- The turnover rate for minority employees increased from 10% to 16% during that same time period.
- Turnover for female employees is at 16%. About 40% of our female employees do not return to work after delivering their first child.
- Our extensive affirmative action efforts have succeeded in recruiting a diverse workforce. However, we have been relatively unsuccessful in promoting females and minorities to the director or officer level.

The issues described above have a tremendous bottom line impact in recruitment, training and productivity costs. We cannot consider ourselves a world class employer and our continued growth and success cannot be sustained unless we create an environment that values and fully utilizes all employees.

The Trans-National Bottlers business rationale above is but an example of how you might develop and communicate one for your company's diversity efforts. A review of Exercise 3.1 will help you make the important diversity-business connection that makes sense for your company.

EXERCISE 3.1 Identification of Business Rationale for Diversity Initiatives

Exercise Instructions: The resources that organizations choose to devote to diversity initiatives should be determined by how effectively those initiatives contribute to achievement of strategic and operational objectives and reinforce the core values of the company. Referring to the scale and information below, rate the importance of the various issues by circling the number that best describes the situation:

1. Not a priority issue at this time, or uncertain.
2. Issue has some importance, but not critical to growth/profits
4. Issue seen as having significant strategic and/or operational importance.

ASSESSMENT STATEMENTS	Trans-National Bottlers			Your Company		
A. Marketing/Sales & Customer Service	Low Priority	Not Critical	Critical & Strategic	Low Priority	Not Critical	Critical & Strategic
1. Customer base is now diverse, or becoming more so.	1	2	4	1	2	4
2. There are particular ethnic groups for which the company is not getting its "fair share" or would like to more strongly penetrate.	1	2	4	1	2	4
3. Positioning in target markets may be stronger by capturing the input of diverse employees at all levels of the company.	1	2	4	1	2	4
4. Buying decisions are made primarily by one gender and your position may be strengthened by expanding the gender base.	1	2	4	1	2	4
5. The company has a strong image in the markets it is trying to serve or penetrate.	1	2	4	1	2	4
TOTAL MARKETING & SALES POINTS						

B. Recruitment

	Low Priority	Not Critical	Critical & Strategic	Low Priority	Not Critical	Critical & Strategic
1. The company will be in a recruiting mode on a regular basis in the coming years.	1	2	4	1	2	4
2. There is a significant demographic group that the company seems unable to attract through its recruiting efforts.	1	2	4	1	2	4

EXERCISE 3.1 Continued

ASSESSMENT STATEMENTS	Trans-National Bottlers			Your Company		
B. Recruitment (cont.)	Low Priority	Not Critical	Critical & Strategic	Low Priority	Not Critical	Critical & Strategic
3. There are particular skills or formal training required in applicants which is now, or may become, in short supply.	1	2	4	1	2	4
4. Perceptions of the industry or the types of jobs you offer meet resistance among some target groups.	1	2	4	1	2	4
TOTAL RECRUITMENT POINTS						

C. Retention of Talent

	Low Priority	Not Critical	Critical & Strategic	Low Priority	Not Critical	Critical & Strategic
1. Turnover rates for females and minorities are somewhat higher than for white males.	1	2	4	1	2	4
2. Turnover has an identifiable cost or effect on business efficiency, quality, or customer service.	1	2	4	1	2	4
3. Turnover may disrupt management succession plans.	1	2	4	1	2	4
4. Excessive female and minority turnover may create a negative recruiting and/or marketing image.	1	2	4	1	2	4
TOTAL RETENTION POINTS						

D. Enhanced Productivity

	Low Priority	Not Critical	Critical & Strategic	Low Priority	Not Critical	Critical & Strategic
1. Improved idea generation and decision making possible through better utilization of diverse input.	1	2	4	1	2	4
2. Headcount pressures require fullest possible utilization of all human resources.	1	2	4	1	2	4
TOTAL PRODUCTIVITY POINTS						

(continued)

EXERCISE 3.1 Continued

ASSESSMENT STATEMENTS	Trans-National Bottlers			Your Company		
E. Team Management	Low Priority	Not Critical	Critical & Strategic	Low Priority	Not Critical	Critical & Strategic
1. The company is committed to TQM, HPO or other concepts which place emphasis on team-work and empowerment.	1	2	4	1	2	4
2. Communication difficulties or tensions between various employee groups hamper the effectiveness of teams.	1	2	4	1	2	4
3. Primary or secondary diversity dimensions of an individual have a significant impact on how well the team accepts them.	1	2	4	1	2	4
TOTAL TEAMWORK POINTS						

F. Globalization

	Low Priority	Not Critical	Critical & Strategic	Low Priority	Not Critical	Critical & Strategic
1. A significant share of sales and earnings comes from outside the U.S.						
a. An understanding of local consumer needs and marketing approaches is needed.	1	2	4	1	2	4
b. Skills needed to manage a multinational, multi-cultural workforce.	1	2	4	1	2	4
2. Employees from outside the U.S. must be effectively utilized in U.S. assignments.	1	2	4	1	2	4
3. The Company's effectiveness in managing diversity is carefully watched by employees in other countries.	1	2	4	1	2	4
TOTAL GLOBALIZATION POINTS						

G. Legal/Compliance

	Low Priority	Not Critical	Critical & Strategic	Low Priority	Not Critical	Critical & Strategic
1. The company has been the subject of expensive and time consuming charges and law-suits on EEO/Affirmative Action issues.	1	2	4	1	2	4

EXERCISE 3.1   Continued

ASSESSMENT STATEMENTS	Trans-National Bottlers			Your Company		
G. Legal/Compliance (cont.)	**Low Priority**	**Not Critical**	**Critical & Strategic**	**Low Priority**	**Not Critical**	**Critical & Strategic**
2. The company may lose its status as an approved government contractor if it does not demonstrate a proactive stance.	1	2	4	1	2	4
3. Company sales may be adversely affected by publicity relating to EEO issues.	1	2	4	1	2	4
TOTAL LEGAL/COMPLIANCE POINTS						

H. Moral/Social & Other Unique Factors

1. A social responsibility commitment is supportive of company values/credos.	1	2	4	1	2	4
2. Other factors specific to the organization not mentioned in categories A through H [above].	1	2	4	1	2	4
TOTAL FACTOR POINTS						

SUMMARY OF BUSINESS RATIONALE EVALUATION

	Evaluation Points	
Category	TNB	Your Company
A. Marketing & Sales	_____	_____
B. Recruitment	_____	_____
C. Retention	_____	_____
D. Productivity	_____	_____
E. Teamwork	_____	_____
F. Globalization	_____	_____
G. Legal	_____	_____
H. Moral/Societal & Other	_____	_____
Total Points	_____	

(continued)

EXERCISE 3.1 Continued

SCALE FOR EVALUATION OF BUSINESS RATIONALE

Evaluation
Point Total >suggests:> Diversity Management *as a Business Priority*

25–40   **Low priority.** Commit beyond legal requirements only selectively.

40–55   **Moderately important.** Implement priority initiatives in addition to fulfillment of legal requirements.

55 +   **Vital and strategic priority.** Represents an opportunity for business competitive advantage. Major financial/management commitment justified.

Caution: The scale above is intended simply to provide a frame of reference. The importance of a single factor (e.g., loss of key accounts or market segments, potential class action suits) could be important enough, in itself, for some companies to rate diversity as a high priority for the organization.

IMPORTANT POINTS TO REMEMBER

1. A sound business rationale is essential for successful diversity change efforts for the following reasons:

   - To justify changes in the corporate culture
   - To motivate individuals to modify personal views
   - To counteract the effects of short corporate attention spans
   - To allow diversity to fairly compete against other priorities that cry out for management attention
   - To make it worthwhile for employees to endure the possible discomforts raised in diversity processes
   - To provide objective information offsetting unfavorable attitudes toward workforce diversity that are held by many employees

2. There are seven business drivers of commitments to diversity programs.

   - To position the organization to respond to and take advantage of changing market demographics
   - To position the organization as an employer of choice
   - To retain and develop the best employees of all backgrounds
   - To improve total productivity
   - To improve the performance of diverse work teams

- To enable the organization to adapt to the diversity associated with a global business strategy
- To comply with regulatory and legal requirements and to maintain the organization's reputation as a good employer

3. The focus on the business rationale should be balanced with a demonstrated concern for the human dimensions of your workforce.

4

How to Organize
for Diversity Success

Broad diversity programs pose potential management challenges, and special efforts should be taken to structure the organization for the tasks that lie ahead. This chapter describes the principal task forces, diversity councils, advocacy groups and team alternatives you might choose as a means to mobilize the resources of the organization. The action steps that will lead to success are examined. Also, the basic options are demonstrated for positioning diversity support within the human resources function.

WHY YOU SHOULD INCLUDE NEW ORGANIZATION APPROACHES TO SUPPORT DIVERSITY INITIATIVES

When companies prepare to develop a diversity strategy, investigate their diversity issues, or launch a comprehensive program of diversity initiatives, they will frequently utilize a highly specialized organization unit or combination of units. There are a variety of reasons why most companies decide to involve special organization adaptations for guidance, decision making and general leadership of the diversity initiatives:

- To ease senior management discomfort associated with emotion-laden issues that may be raised.

- To spread the work load required to push forward simultaneously on five to twenty priorities that are generated through issues/needs analysis.

- To enhance the quality of input by reaching out to those not normally consulted in policy and program introductions.

- To serve as senior management's "sales force" to promote credibility for the company's efforts and enhance the likelihood of employee support for the strategies and actions which emerge during a change process.

- To send a signal to employees that the diversity issues will be taken seriously and will not be dealt with on a business-as-usual basis.

- To expand "ownership" of the issues beyond the traditional supporters or interested parties.

Four distinctly different approaches for organizing for diversity initiatives which can be seen operating singly or in combination include: *Diversity Task Force, Employee Diversity Council, Employee Advocacy/Affinity Groups,* and a *Diversity Quality Team.* Each of these approaches is described in the following pages in the context of their typical *membership* and *mission,* an *example* illustrating the model, and a listing of some of the *action steps* which will significantly affect the potential for the success or failure of each approach.

HOW TO DEVELOP A STRONG DIVERSITY TASK FORCE

The most frequently encountered approach is the executive level steering committee, referred to here as the Diversity Task Force.

Membership of a Diversity Task Force: The Diversity Task Force (DTF for short) is typically a small (8 to 15) group with half or more of the members composed of line and staff officers of the company. The group may include one or more members of the operating/executive committee, and in some cases the CEO himself may choose to participate. Non-executive employees are also invited to participate so that adequate numbers of female and minority participants will be included, both to improve the quality of the input and to provide credibility for the outcomes of the group.

Mission of the Diversity Task Force: A DTF is often charged with developing a vision and strategy for the diversity initiatives, and it may also develop the business case for the efforts. The group can provide guidance on the assessment and resolution of diversity issues which the organization may face by sponsoring appropriate interventions and programs. The tonality of such a group is *"Let's get the facts, and get it done,"* and *"This is a business issue, not just a human resources department issue."*

Example of a Diversity Task Force Mission Statement: *"The purpose of the Anonymous Company Diversity Steering Committee is to recommend policies and programs which will help create an environment that utilizes the full potential of all members of our diverse work force for strategic advantage.*

Key responsibilities of the Diversity Steering Committee include the following:

- *Identify the primary strategic diversity issues which Anonymous Company faces now, and will face over the next ten years.*
- *Recommend priorities for addressing issues identified, and recommend the policies, plans and programs which will address those priorities.*
- *Support and guide the Human Resources department in the effective implementation and operation of the programs recommended by the Diversity Steering Committee and approved by the Anonymous Company Executive Committee.*
- *Serve as diversity program champions and models of effective behavior.*
- *Provide ongoing feedback to the Executive Committee on the results and progress of initiatives approved, and on newly emerging diversity issues facing Anonymous Company and competitive trends that may affect our efforts.*

Specific Action Steps for a Successful Diversity Task Force: The senior line officer of the organization should personally take responsibility for the following activities or delegate the responsibility to knowledgeable parties.

- Select participants for the DTF who have the personal interest, and who commit to make the time available to contribute in a meaningful way to the work of the DTF. They should also have broad organizational credibility as being objective and results oriented.
- Provide the DTF with a clear mission and accountabilities along with a timetable for the achievement of key action steps.
- Encourage the DTF to seek broad employee input into the nature and severity of the issues perceived by employees. This increases the quality of the input and enhances the credibility and chances of acceptance of resulting initiatives.
- Compress activities into a tight time frame to meet the participants' need to see "results" and to help manage employees' expectations for results.
- If executives selected for participation become too busy to meet with sufficient frequency to move projects toward completion on a timely basis, replace them on the DTF.

- When selecting females and minorities and other non-traditional employees to participate on a DTF, don't base the choices on the degree of comfort that the white male officers have with an individual, or on how successfully those individuals have assimilated into the "mainstream" of the company.

The Diversity Task Force is the form most like traditional hierarchical decision processes, which may account in part for its popularity.

THE EMPLOYEE DIVERSITY COUNCIL ORGANIZATION OPTION

Companies who are trying to embrace the broad diversity visions will utilize an organization approach embracing all key diversity dimensions of the organization. The tonality of the group is that *"differences are welcome and to be understood"* and that *"all inputs have value."* Issues should be addressed through a deliberate consensual process, rather than through the usual top-down processes.

Group Membership in an Employee Diversity Council: The Employee Diversity Council (EDC) is a deliberately inclusive approach, and might involve 20 to 30 employees. The membership is intended to be representative of the diverse employee population. Therefore, care is taken to include individuals representing a wide range of primary and secondary diversity dimensions, such as those listed below:

INDIVIDUALS WHO MAY BE INCLUDED IN THE DIVERSITY COUNCIL

Primary Dimensions	*Secondary Dimensions*
- Race	- Service with company
- Ethnicity	- Department, function
- Gender	- Location (plant, office R & D, sales, etc.)
- Age	- Single/married
- Differently abled	- Working parent/non-parent
- Sexual orientation	- Management/non-management

Assigned Mission of Employee Diversity Council: The EDC may be asked to identify policies, programs and practices which are in need of revision to meet the needs of a diverse work force. The business case probably has already been developed and provided to the Council. Members would draw upon personal experiences, as well as input from their like counterparts in the organization.

Example of an EDC Mission Statement: *"The mission of the Employee Diversity Council is to identify strategies and tactics that the Anonymous Company can implement to create:*

- *Individual and cultural diversity that are accepted and valued*
- *Open lines of communication among all levels of management and employees*
- *Opportunities that exist for all employees to achieve their career potential*
- *Systems, structure, culture and leadership that exist to foster management of diversity*

All of which are directed toward leveraging Anonymous Company resources to achieve a competitive advantage in the market place.

Action Steps for a Successful Employee Diversity Council

- Council members should be appointed by the CEO or the local organization equivalent.
- A clear and realistic mission should be given to the council, along with adequate support and resources, with a timetable for achievement of key milestones.
- Training should be provided to council members at an early stage regarding diversity definitions, typical diversity issues and approaches and current company programs.
- Subcommittees are formed within the council to focus on specific areas, to ease scheduling conflicts, speed progress on developing consensus and limit the time required for the members' participation.
- Participants are cautioned at the outset about the long term nature of the effort, and the need for both commitment and patience.
- White males are included in the Committee and processes and are viewed as on an equal footing with all other participants.
- Procedures are established to replace participants who get tired of the process before momentum has been established, or who may have lacked a strong commitment from the outset.
- Team building activities should be used to help the EDC work through the possible wide variation in perceptions of the issues that could slow down decision making.
- Supervisors of the EDC members should be advised in advance of the appointments and instructed to provide encouragement, flexibility and support for their employees' participation.
- A formal linkage is made between the EDC and the relevant human resources staff. Significant logistical support, technical guidance and implementation assistance should be established to recognize the time and technical limitations of the EDC participants.

CAPTURING THE ENERGY OF EMPLOYEE ADVOCACY/AFFINITY GROUPS

The Diversity Task Force and Employee Diversity Council are approaches conceived at the upper levels of the organization and implemented as a top-down initiative. The third approach, employee advocacy groups, is more of a bottom-up phenomenon. (Advocacy groups may also be known as networking, support or affinity groups.)

Advocacy/Affinity Group Membership: Membership in advocacy/affinity groups is usually limited to individuals of like race or gender grouping, sometimes including a functional/level twist such as:

- Black employees
- Hispanic employees
- Minority Engineers
- Career Moms
- Female employees
- Asian employees
- Women in Management
- Gay & Lesbian Alliance

Groups might be organized upon employee initiative, and may operate for a period of time before management becomes aware of their existence. In other cases, management might subtly or openly encourage the formation of such groups. White males usually do not have a group of their own.

Mission of Advocacy/Affinity Groups: The group members are likely to focus on the issues most relevant to its own membership, e.g., glass ceiling issues for females, perceived disparities in application of programs to members of the individuals' racial/ethnic group. The tonality is *"we must band together to provide mutual support, draw attention to our issues and get fair treatment."*

Example of an Advocacy Group Mission Statement: *"The Women's Career Network is an advisory task force to Senior Management and the Human Resources department. It is comprised of employees from all Anonymous Company Divisions and reflects a mix of functional areas, levels of experience and length of Anonymous Company service.*
The Women's Career Network will focus on the following issues:

- *Identifying areas of the company where the climate is not supportive of female employees*
- *Advancing the achievement of corporate wide Affirmative Action efforts specifically related to women*
- *Ensuring that there is equal access and opportunity for women to reach their full potential across all functional areas and management levels."*

Action Steps for Successful Advocacy Groups

- Senior management should support the existence of the group, or at least tacitly recognize the validity of employees' interests in forming such groups.

- A close linkage should be established with the Human Resources department so that the employee input is captured, realistic expectations can be established and competing priorities of various groups can be balanced and sequenced. If HR staff happen to participate in the group, they do so as individuals, not as representatives of the HR department.

- Senior line managers should meet directly with groups on occasion to demonstrate their interest in their direct feedback, to provide assurance that the input of the group to the process is valued and that legitimate issues will be addressed.

- Give advocacy groups a specific role in important aspects of the diversity change process such as helping to surface issues, consultant/vendor selection, testing of training or program ideas, etc.

- Balance attention and resources so that no single ethnic/gender group is seen as receiving a disproportionate share of benefits or having excessive clout.

- Provide a forum to develop white male input (who are typically excluded from such groups). Effort should be made to avoid the structure looking like affirmative action, and generating resentment in the process.

- Senior management should not view groups as complainers or troublemakers, but as a legitimate conduit for input that is not being captured by the traditional processes of the company. Resolve the issues, and the need for the groups will disappear.

- Provide groups with education and training to help them develop a broad perspective that goes beyond the needs of their particular group.

USE DIVERSITY QUALITY TEAMS AS A NATURAL EXTENSION OF TOTAL QUALITY MANAGEMENT

For companies that are in a total quality management program (TQM), total customer focus, or some other version of team management, it is very natural to use the team approach to address diversity issues.

Membership of the Diversity Quality Team: A diversity quality team may limit the scope of its activities to the particular facility at which it is based. Consistent with the TQM philosophy, the team is likely to be multi-functional and from different employee levels, such as those listed in the Table 4.1.

TABLE 4.1 Membership in Southern Division Manufacturing Diversity Team

Departments	Positions	Employee Diversity
Receiving	Shift superintendent	Under age 25 to over age 55
Forging and Stamping	Department managers	Under one year's service to over 30 years service
Sub-assembly	Shift supervisors	
Finish assembly	Human Resources supervisor	All major race/ethnic groups
Painting	Hourly team members from each department. [see left]	Females/Males
Shipping		Married/Single
	Office supervisor	

Example of a Diversity Quality Team Mission Statement: *The Southern Manufacturing Diversity Team will identify issues regarding workforce diversity which may have an impact on the quality or productivity of the facility, or impact its cost of operation or morale of its employees. Using TQM group productivity techniques, they will focus on issues within the control of each local facility to change, and develop quick and practical solutions to the issues. The Team may recommend appropriate actions to the Plant Management Committee for approval and implementation. They will serve as liaison with the diversity teams at the Western and Northeastern production facilities.*

Actions to Establish a Successful Quality Team

- Use a diversity quality team where TQM (or Total Customer Focus, or the company equivalent) is a firmly established management technique, is used comfortably by employees at all levels of the facility, and has broad credibility for its effectiveness in achieving specific results.
- Train the TQM teams in group processes and analytical and problem solving techniques.
- Provide for diversity in the team appointments, and consider candidates' interest and support for diversity as a criterion for membership.
- Keep the team focus on limited scope problems which lend themselves to correction through local level interventions.
- Don't allow the pressures of day-to-day operational issues to get in the way of an extended focus on the more intangible diversity issues.
- Avoid selecting participants who are "teamed out" due to numerous existing overlapping committees competing for their attention.

A brief summary of the features and advantages and disadvantages of each organization approach is found in Table 4.2.

TABLE 4.2 Comparative Summary of Diversity Organization Approaches

Feature	Task Force	Employee Council	Advocacy Group	Quality Team
Mission	Set vision, budgets. Build commitment	Define issues and provide diverse input	Support and network with like persons	Identify, work issues of that facility
Number in Group	8 to 15	20 to 30	Dozens to hundreds	10 to 20
Levels in Group	Mostly key managers	Officer to clerical	All levels, more at entry and first line manager	Hourly thru local key managers
How Selected	Appointed by the CEO	Invited by CEO	Self select partici- pation	Appointed by local top manager; union picks own member
Key Strength	Link to Senior de- cision makers	-Inclusive -Diverse input	-Unity of purpose -Voluntary	Builds on accepted model for dealing with issues
Key Limitation	Limited diversity of input	Slow moving	-Narrow focus -Those not included may be suspicious	Members may lack clout to tackle is- sues
Diversity Model	Traditional, hierarchical	Managing Diversity	Affirmative Action	Total Quality Man- agement

HOW TO ANTICIPATE AND DEAL WITH SPECIAL ISSUES IN DIVERSITY STRUCTURES

While structures of the type described can be an invaluable aid to progress, they are not without their drawbacks and complications. Five potential issues that may require advance planning are described below, along with some suggested techniques for dealing with each issue.

Clearly Define Mission Authority: On occasion diversity groups of the type de- scribed earlier in the chapter are appointed because the senior management doesn't have a clue as to what they want to do or how they wish to go about it. They will start the process but leave the mission too open ended. It will come as no big surprise that a lack of mission clarity will often lead to lack of results. Time will be wasted trying to figure out just what is expected of them. Both the committee members and the employee population at large will become disenchanted and skeptical if months pass by without anything of consequence coming from the committee's efforts.

Senior management ambiguity may also be reflected in a failure to provide a clear picture of the group's authority to take action during the diversity process. Two examples illustrate the authority confusion problem.

SITUATION A: The diversity steering committee for a large organization was informed that it was "empowered" to take whatever steps necessary to address and correct the issues. However, the group soon found that it could not even send out a meeting announcement without the memo going through three levels of approval. The group quickly learned that the empowerment was illusory.

SITUATION B: A diversity task force had been evaluating diversity consultants who might be used for an employee research project. It selected a consultant and negotiated the terms of an assignment. However, at this point senior management indicated the group had not been given authority to approve a study. Therefore, it had to put the study on hold, and circle back to get approvals, causing a delay of several months.

The chairperson of the committee should not accept the responsibility unless there is a clear charter for the group. If the charter does not exist the first month, one should be developed and signed off by the Executive Board before the committee wastes its time and energy.

Establish Credible Senior Management Involvement: In some organizations, senior management is seen as remote and uninvolved in the diversity process. On the other extreme, there have been instances where the company CEO decided to personally chair the diversity task force to demonstrate commitment to identifying and resolving issues. While this senior level commitment may be admirable in intent, it is not always practical. Consider the following situations:

- The chairman discovers that he cannot find the time in his schedule to meet with the committee, or some emergency causes a last minute withdrawal from the scheduled meeting, or causes him to disrupt the meeting flow by popping in and out of the meeting room. Some members of the task force may incorrectly conclude that the CEO's behavior is evidence that he is not that interested after all.

- The presence of the CEO may intimidate participants who occupy somewhat lower positions in the organization from being candid on the nature and extent of the diversity issues the company is facing. This risk is particularly high where upward feedback from the ranks historically has not been valued.

- The corporate culture may be unfavorable for diversity. Since the CEO is typically a major shaper of the culture, employees may feel that the CEO will view their critique as a direct or indirect criticism of his or her leadership. His or her presence in itself simply precludes an open discussion of the subject.

Rather than have the CEO as chairperson, consider the selection of a respected senior officer at the next level to shepherd the efforts. Thus, the committee will have the credibility that goes with senior involvement, without the constraints of the CEO dominating the meetings.

Plan for Local Diversity Involvement in Large Organizations: In a typical large national or multi-national organization, the nature and extent of diversity issues may vary significantly from one location to another. The frictions that develop on the factory floor will differ from headquarters and the research lab both in subject matter and severity, requiring different approaches. Thus, if the organization has a headquarters-dominated diversity group, the output of that group may be dismissed by field personnel as *"more fog emanating from the ivory tower."*

To capture broader input and build commitment for results, it is important to incorporate the involvement of major locations and widely dispersed employees. This can be done within the framework of a broad outline put forward by the committee. For example, employee diversity research may be provided as a requirement for all locations, but the timing and nature (for example, questionnaires, focus groups, etc.) could be adapted to the local needs and executed within an overall time framework that is acceptable to all.

If the initiatives are to cover many parts of the company, you might consider having local committees. One representative from the local committee could participate in the corporate group. That person serves as an information source to the corporate group, and a link back to the activities being researched and addressed at the local level.

Involve the Hourly Workforce: A number of organizations have chosen not to involve hourly employees in the early stages of a diversity change process. Reasons given for a delay in addressing the issues of hourly employees may include the following:

- Desire to "get it right" in our own shop (with salaried employees) before applying the principles more broadly.
- Issues may have a different shading for hourly employees. For example, performance feedback and job posting approaches may be totally different from those of salaried employees. Instances of racism, sexism are sometimes more blatant and outspoken among the hourly workforce. As one hourly worker said, *"It can get pretty rough out there (in the plant). It's 'bitch this, bitch*

that'. We resort to racial name calling just to fight boredom. Some take it the wrong way."

- The work load could simply be too great if the organization attempts to address issues with all groups simultaneously. The potential for overload will become clear as we move through some of the later chapters.

- Some, or all of the hourly employees may be represented by a union. Some of the issues raised may be subject to collective bargaining and may not be proper to handle outside the scope of the labor agreement. For example, in one case younger hourly employees expressed strong dissatisfaction with advancement opportunities. However, the promotion process (primarily on the basis of seniority) is spelled out in five pages of small print in the contract, and was considered inviolate by longer service union members.

When unionized employees are to be involved, an understanding with the union is needed prior to the involvement as to the type of issues that might be raised and assurances given that the company is not trying to subvert the bargaining process. Where a reasonable degree of trust between labor and management exists, the issues should be manageable and could strengthen the relationships.

Avoid Human Resources Domination of the Group: One issue that frequently arises is the extent to which the human resources department should be represented on, be seen as providing leadership for, the diversity task force or other group. There is a natural tendency for HR people to overtly or covertly attempt to take ownership of the diversity issue:

- Because HR feels they have the subject matter expertise

- Because HR will want to keep the process from getting out of control

- Because the CEO told them to "fix the problem"

- Because almost anything done in the diversity area will overlap with their existing responsibility for recruitment, affirmative action, performance management, and so on.

Having personally gone through the process in a large organization, and observed the difficulties and successes that other organizations have had, my advice is simple. HR should maintain a low profile, support role, rather than a high profile dominant leadership role. There are several reasons for this advice.

HR is frequently seen as part of the problem. Write in comments or focus group discussion will on occasion single out HR, along the following lines:

EXAMPLE A: *"I've always questioned why in my years with this company I have never seen a black person in a key job in the human resources department."*

EXAMPLE B: *"I went to HR on a confidential basis, because I wasn't sure how hard I wanted to push my complaint. By the time I got back to my office my boss was waiting for me. So much for confidentiality."*

EXAMPLE C: *In a diversity survey, about 60% of the respondents said they would be reluctant to go to the HR department with a complaint about fair treatment or discrimination.*

Sometimes the criticism may not be entirely fair, since HR may simply be enforcing management dictates or be forced to defend aspects of a corporate culture that they themselves do not agree with, but are unable to change. In the circumstances just described, HR is simply the lightning rod that draws the thunder bolts from employees.

In other cases HR simply has not performed in a way that engenders the trust of all employees. As one employee said, *"I know that they are management's representatives. But just once, I would like to see them operate like they represented the interests of all employees as well."* In any event, an HR-dominated activity will be viewed with suspicion by individuals who have not been well served by its presence in the past.

HR domination of diversity activities will enable line managers to dismiss the activity as "just another HR giveaway program." Diversity will not attract the line support necessary to become a lasting way of life in the organization. There is one organization that put together a diversity steering committee that was comprised of the head of human resources and three direct reports (three of four were white males). The Vice President of Human Resources somehow could not grasp the limitations he was building into the process with this kind of HR-centric approach.

Some degree of distancing may enable HR to objectively view the developing process. If HR can limit the necessity to defend their past activities and programs, they can be true facilitators of the process and not viewed as roadblocks or management toadies. At the other extreme, HR cannot appear to be disinterested or uncommitted to the diversity process. As in many areas, they provide leadership by motivating others to take ownership.

Aside from the way in which HR is involved with the steering committee, there is the need to figure out how to set up the relevant groups within the department. Some options for organizing within HR are described later in this chapter.

Prepare the Diversity Leadership Group for Their Roles: Regardless of the structure utilized to support the diversity efforts, i.e., task force, advocacy groups, or teams, the group will need preparation and education to be effective in its role. The preparation falls under four general categories.

- Clear mission and roles: What is to be done and what is expected of each participant.
- Conceptual clarity: What is diversity, what should it look like in that organization.
- Company issues: What is the current situation? What has been done to date, with what results?

- Team Effectiveness: What skills and insights are needed for the group to work together effectively, given the mix of organization levels, cultures, and so on.

Some of the information can be provided by sources internal to the organization, e.g., sharing data on mobility, recruitment, etc. In other instances, external sources such as consultants, training seminars, and reading materials may advance understanding. If the members are not accustomed to working in a diverse work group, team building activities with a cross-cultural focus will be helpful to develop comfort and productive work patterns. Gardenswartz and Rowe (1) describe cross cultural team building as incorporating the following steps:

1. Acknowledge the obvious and subtle differences represented in the group.
2. Find a common ground that all can embrace, that unites the differences discussed in 1.
3. Identify individual interests, strengths and preferences so that the talents and interests of the entire group can be best met.
4. Clarify expectations about the need to be flexible in assigning priorities and developing action plans.
5. Shape the group culture to facilitate having all the experiences of the members utilized and recognized.
6. Create a feedback loop on how well the organization is functioning, and how the performance will be measured.

POSITION THE DIVERSITY STAFF TO SUPPORT THE PROCESS

The positioning of the day-to-day leadership of the human resources diversity activities may impact on the chances for success. In companies that have made progress, HR has played a key role in helping senior management build commitment, and in removing roadblocks and supporting the work of diversity committees and councils. Let's look at two basic approaches commonly used to position functional leadership of diversity activities.

Challenge the "Traditional" HR Organization Option: The first approach, referred to as the "Traditional Division of Labor", is described in Exhibit 4.1. It seeks to spread diversity responsibility around among the existing functional HR structure. Advantages of this approach are that it does not disturb the role comfort associated with the status quo, and therefore may make the specialists feel more at ease. However, it may also lead to uncoordinated efforts and lack of a central point for coordination with the diversity task force.

The Diversity **Umbrella** *Approach Within HR:* The *Diversity Umbrella Approach* assumes that a diversity change process requires a new way of looking at old pro-

EXHIBIT 4.1 Organizing HR for Diversity Initiatives: Traditional Division of Labor

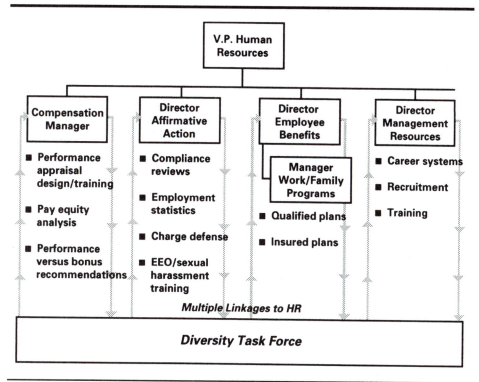

grams and practices. All related programs are brought under one person, The Director of Diversity and Work Life programs. The Director of Diversity and Work/Life serves as the link and chief support to the diversity task force or other diversity organization unit. The Director draws upon the functional experts of the HR department for technical expertise, and keeps them informed of issues and action plans that might influence their own position. The formation of the position also sends a message to the organization that the company recognizes that past approaches have not been entirely successful in dealing with diversity issues, so new organization options are required. See Exhibit 4.2 for a schematic view of the HR diversity umbrella organization.

The **High Profile Positioning** *of HR Diversity Support:* While it is most common to see the technical support positioned within the HR departments, some organizations feel that diversity activities are too important to be left to HR. Baxter Healthcare Corporation and Kraft/General Foods, for example, have elected to establish a diversity leadership group reporting directly to the CEO or the organization equivalent. The rationale for such a high profile positioning might include the following:

EXHIBIT 4.2 Organizing HR for Diversity Initiatives: The "Diversity Umbrella" Organization Plan

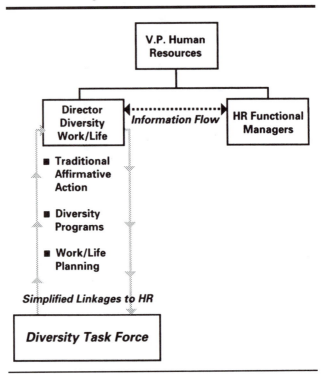

- Sends a clear message to the organization that the subject is important to the CEO.
- The CEO linkage may help ease resistance to the program among line managers.
- Permits budgeting, resource allocation and performance measurement separately from the HR department.
- Provides diversity activity leader with an entry to meetings and visibility not otherwise possible.
- Allows diversity activity leader to tie initiatives to other strategic directions of the company.
- May permit the recruitment (internal or external) of a stronger manager for the position than would otherwise be possible.

There are also downsides to the high profile approach. For some organizations it will appear artificial, or inconsistent with the norms for jobs reporting directly to the CEO. If the CEO changes the reporting relationship at a later date, or if the budget for the group is cut, people in the organization will be left to speculate whether diversity is *really* that important to the leadership? Also the diversity function could lose touch with HR and be put in a position of competing for resources. As a practical matter, only a relatively small number of large organizations will be comfortable with the high profile approach.

The complexity, sensitivity and far-reaching nature of diversity interventions suggests the opportunity for special organizational adaptations. The "right" answer for any given company or institution will vary according to its size, geographic dispersion, and past success experiences with alternative forms. The approaches suggested illustrate some typical approaches and consideration of this information can save you time and frustration.

IMPORTANT POINTS TO REMEMBER

1. Use special organization approaches to support the unique challenges of a diversity change process.
   - Diversity Task Force
   - Employee Diversity Council
   - Employee Advocacy Groups
   - Diversity Quality Teams
2. Anticipate the typical challenges faced by special diversity organization units and take action to provide optimal productivity.
   - Clearly define the mission and authority of the group.
   - Establish credible senior management involvement.
   - Plan for local involvement in large organizations.
   - Involve the hourly workforce—at the appropriate time.
   - Avoid human resources department domination of the diversity steering group.
   - Train the diversity steering group for leadership roles.
3. Gather all diversity support activities under an "umbrella" within human resources to effectively support the steering group.

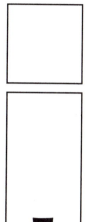

5

Diversity Research Strategies: What to Look for and How To Get It

A strategic approach to diversity management requires a reliable data base. This chapter provides a review of key elements of diversity research in organizations. It includes the following specific items:

- A review of the objectives of diversity research within organizations and why it is important
- Suggested criteria for evaluating the usefulness of data that you may already have available
- Guidelines and a checklist for structuring a research project
- Comparison of the various research methods and the pros and cons of each
- Examples of diversity research output and some of the key themes that tend to appear

DETERMINE WHAT EMPLOYEE DIVERSITY RESEARCH CAN DO FOR YOU

It is a relatively straightforward task to describe what diversity research should be helping you to accomplish:

- Determine the perceptions and behaviors as differentiated by race, gender, function, level, or other situation-specific dimensions.
- Evaluate the effects of organizational culture on organizational behavior affecting the climate for diversity.
- Evaluate the perceived effectiveness of systems and programs.
- Aid in the assignment of priorities to issues and to develop specific action plans.

In addition to the utilitarian rationale for employee diversity research, there are other tactical and pragmatic reasons to consider employee research. Those key reasons for a credible diversity data base are described in the paragraphs which follow:

Anticipate the Denial Syndrome: It is quite common for the senior management of organizations to be caught off guard by the degree of negativity expressed in employee opinions and perceptions in a confidential diversity research process. All too often, executives equate the degree of satisfaction of their minority and female employees to the number of EEO complaints. Unfortunately, formal complaints are only the **tip of the tip of the iceberg**.

Filing a charge or lodging a formal complaint is viewed by many employees as a last resort, possibly damaging to their career prospects. Even if the complaining employee "wins" on that issue, he or she may still lose in the long run. The reaction of the employee's supervisor may be subtle resentment rather than obvious retaliation, but the employee loses nonetheless. Thus, the perceived slights and inequities are usually borne quietly, with feelings shared candidly with acquaintances of like race and gender, but rarely expressed openly to people in the power structure. Of course the company loses as well if employees react to issues by "tuning out" or performing below their capabilities.

Thus, when the feelings of employees of all races and gender (which to date were carefully guarded) are set forth with clarity and certainty, executives find it difficult to accept. Company management may attempt to dismiss the survey instrument as invalid, the focus group leader as an agitator, or the negative write-in comments as the feelings of an isolated group of malcontents. A credible data base including quantitative and qualitative dimensions is needed to get buy-in for the necessary corrective actions.

Deal with Multiple Agendas: It is not uncommon for a given group to feel that they are the ones receiving the worst treatment. The black employees may feel their problems are the most severe, female managers feel they have serious issues, white males feel left out, and so on. To rise above the competing agendas which arise naturally from in-group biases and self interest, a strong data base can provide objective assessments for balanced decision making on priorities.

Treat It as a Business Issue: To be taken seriously, you must support statements about the scope and severity of diversity issues with analytical data. Few large organizations of any kind will decide to allocate large amounts of funds and management time to an issue that has not been systematically established to be of some importance to the organization. Gut feel is great, but it is unlikely to carry the day when time comes to allocate budgets to competing priorities. Organizations that describe themselves as having a "numbers driven" culture are especially insistent on specificity.

Deal with the Broad Scope of Issues: As you will read in later chapters, nearly every aspect of corporate life may have diversity implications. Even if the review is limited to human resources programs, climate for diversity, etc. the range of issues can be broad and, at times, intimidating. Application of sound data will help bring the issues into perspective, and sort out the interrelationships among a number of issues.

Create a Base Line for Measuring Future Progress: One of the most frequently asked questions is "How will you know if your diversity initiatives are working?" It is a fair question, and there are some measures that will be readily available, such as reduced turnover of females and minorities and their advancement to higher levels. However, you will also want to measure progress on the "soft" issues of employee attitudes and perceptions. The repetition of a diversity survey at two to three year intervals can provide important ongoing feedback and justification of continuing efforts and a basis for amending strategies and programs.

Counter Backlash: Generally speaking, the aspects of the corporate culture that impede diversity progress are not as quickly recognized by the dominant group in the organization (usually white males). Since those in the dominant group have not personally experienced the problem, they may believe others feel the same way. In the absence of knowledge of the issues, they may resist the solutions later prescribed. A sound data base doesn't make backlash go away, but is important to ameliorate its presence.

LOOK FOR OPPORTUNITIES TO USE DATA ALREADY AVAILABLE

Many organizations routinely carry out employee climate surveys, and use those surveys to determine priorities for action on a wide range of issues. If a data base documenting perceptions of programs, practices and the organization culture already exists and is current, you have a good head start. However, before you conclude that you have all the data you need, ask some of these questions:

Are the Responses Broken Out by the Race and Gender of Employees? Overall scores can be rather comforting, but if some groups of the population are totally disenchanted, the overall score report can be quite misleading. For example, the two statements in Table 5.1 were among those used in an employee survey.

The wide variances in perceptions among the different groups in the two statements reproduced in Table 5.1 provide ample justification for analysis of data on the basis of diversity variables. But there is always the exception. In one organization the human resources officer noted that the approval ratings given by females and people of color were really not much worse than ratings provided by white male employees. The senior HR person explained the minimal differences by the fact that *"Everyone dislikes it here. There just isn't a good reason for women and minorities to hate it worse than others do."*

Is There a High Level of Survey Participation Among Women and People of Color? Some companies find that women and minority employees are less likely than white males to participate in routine internal company attitude questionnaires. One organization used focus groups to gain an understanding for the basis of the differences in participation rates. The critique of the survey included the following:

- The detailed demographic information requested of respondents could reveal their identity, and reprisals might result. "Confidentiality is the number one issue" as one participant put it.

- Participants saw two extremes of how the data might be utilized. Some felt disappointed with the results of previous surveys. *"I haven't seen any results on the attitude survey or the family issues survey. You can only get your hopes up*

TABLE 5.1 Variations in Employee Responses:

Statement:	Percentage Who Agree With Statement				
	Overall	Black	Asian	Hispanic	White
Business opinions of women are	55%	26%	50%	50%	62%
respected as well as those of	Male	57%	67%	80%	75%
men.	Female	18%*	36%	38%	45%
The manner in which employees are	47%	6%	35%	47%	57%
treated is **not** affected by gender,	Male	17%*	44%	20%*	66%
ethnicity, age, etc.	Female	4%*	27%	62%	46%

Boxed scores indicate highest scores
*Lowest scores

so many times!" On the other extreme, some individuals had seen an overreaction, with supervisors being terminated shortly after results were available. Being candid could endanger someone's career.

- Individuals referred to the fact that the questions failed to address issues that they felt were important: racism, sexism, etc. They couldn't describe how they "feel" about issues due to lack of open-ended opportunities for responses.

- The manner in which feedback of survey results was handled had a big impact on their willingness to participate in anything again. In some cases there was no feedback on results to the participants, and in other cases the feedback was viewed as "sugar coated" and not truly indicative of the actual results. Some felt that when feedback was given it covered such a large piece of the organization that participants did not have a sense that it related to the particular circumstances in their department.

All of these issues provide direction for the design of a diversity research program suitable to the needs of your organization.

Does Your Survey Ask the Tough Questions? Many routine employee surveys consciously stay away from questions that could be considered controversial, or where the company does not want to really know the answer. Thus, there is more than adequate information on how employees feel about the cafeteria and company newspaper. However, there may not be sufficient questions dealing with employees' feelings about the respect they are shown, their perceptions about the fairness in the administration of company policies and programs, the relationships between white employees and people of color. What you ask is what you get. If you feel that data currently available does not fully reveal the diversity issues of the organization, you need to consider a specific diversity research probe.

HOW TO STRUCTURE A DIVERSITY RESEARCH PROJECT

When one considers the various diversity dimensions, and the range of issues on which opinions may be sought, one quickly concludes that the potential list of data groupings can be staggering. The key combinations that have proven most popular are itemized in Table 5.2.

I would like to clarify that no one should attempt to capture this complete list. The trend is for organizations to ask for too much information, so they end up with more data than could be analyzed in depth or utilized in the strategy and planning process.

TABLE 5.2 Potential Research Data Cuts: The Long List

Primary Diversity Dimensions	Secondary Dimensions
White Male	Exempt/Nonexempt
White Female	
African American Male	Division/Department
African American Female	
Hispanic Male	Hourly/Salaried
Hispanic Female	
Asian American Male	Service < 10 yrs., 10–19, etc.
Asian American Female	Plant/Headquarters/Sales
Age	Marital/parental status
Physical Ability	Age of children
	Day care needs

Partial List of Subject Variables

Culture/environment—Fairness—Respect
Performance management—Working Relationships
Communication—Teamwork—Development and Training
Career advancement—Compensation—Work and family program—
   Perceptions of Racism/Sexism, Ageism—Business opinions of f/m valued

HOW TO PLAN FOR EFFECTIVE AND AFFORDABLE RESEARCH

What are some criteria that may be utilized in determining how to structure your research process to be comprehensive yet affordable? A sampling of key issues is summarized below.

- **Numbers of employees to be included should be sufficient to warrant the effort and provide a reliable picture.** For example, surveys often reveal some gender-based differences in scores in various groups, so separate reporting can be useful. However, one company had very few black male exempt employees, so the black males were grouped with black female exempts for research purposes.

   As stated earlier, data denial is a common occurrence in diversity research. If the information is not specific enough on an organization cut basis, it becomes too easy for someone to say that "I'm sure my employees feel differently. Those low ratings must have come from _____ Department." On the other hand, attempts at micro-identification could be counter-productive, as groups become too small to provide statistical validity.

- **Anonymity of Respondents should be protected.** This is a function of numbers to be included and how detailed the demographic breakdown will be. One company felt that the information by location was very important. However, the detailed race/gender/position/department information request caused respondents to be reluctant to participate for fear that their input would be recognizable. Many either did not respond at all, or did not fill out the demographic detail. Thus, the specificity objective was not achieved.

- **Viewpoints may vary significantly by groups.** As shown in Table 5.1, there may be wide differences in perceptions. To lump all minorities into one cohort could mask some important variations between groups. In one situation a differentiation was revealed on an organization level basis. Analysis of exempt versus nonexempt scores revealed that employees perceived the company as having a "class system." However, in other situations this may not be an issue.

- **The cost of collecting, reporting and analyzing the various data cuts must be considered.** With computer-scored questionnaires, the processing costs of another data breakout may be insignificant. However, in more labor intensive activities such as focus groups and data analysis, the added complexity may drive up the cost out of proportion to the value of the data derived.

- **Make sure that employees feel their voice has been heard; their special needs have been recognized.** In one plant situation, there were very few female exempt employees, so there was no data breakout to capture their input. Some one-on-one interviews were needed to create the sense of inclusion in the process. Gay/lesbian and physically challenged employees could represent other instances where special data gathering efforts are required. In one instance, employees of Philippine extraction objected to being included with other Asian nationalities in a focus group for Asian American employees. However, the cost of breaking the research into many small segments (Japanese, Taiwanese, etc.) caused the company to deny the request for a special Filipino focus group.

- **Do not include too many areas of inquiry**. If you have 80 questions covering 10 subject areas, broken out by 16 demographic cuts, you may have a problem of data overload.

    Use interviews and discussion groups early in the process to determine what areas are of most concern and concentrate the research efforts on those areas of perceived concern. Discussions with advocacy groups, review of EEO complaints and examination of exit interview information may also help you narrow the focus.

- **Have a representative sampling of employees participate in the process.** For example, older/longer service employees in many cases will express more positive opinions about the company than younger, short service employees. If you over-sample, or under-weight your research with one group versus another, you could get aggregate results that are misleading. Put another way, if you put together a focus group of your most content employees, your results will be as misleading as if you stacked the list only with the discontented employees.

There is no magic formula for structuring a diversity research effort that can be applied across a whole range of companies. Even within a single company, the approach used at a factory may have to differ significantly from headquarters, depending on the issues, the demographics of the work force, etc. However, we hope the criteria listed are of value in assessing your own needs.

USE A BALANCE OF DIVERSITY RESEARCH METHODOLOGIES

There is a wide range of techniques used in conducting diversity research. A description of the six most commonly used techniques and the advantages and disadvantages of each follows.

Written Questionnaire—usually targeted at all, or a statistically valid sampling of employees. These yield specific data that sheds "light" on differing perceptions. Questionnaires may be sent to the home, or distributed at work. Completed questionnaires should be routed through a "safe" channel to reassure concerns on confidentiality.

Advantages	Disadvantages
• Can include large numbers at a low cost per participant	• Difficult to ascertain the "why" behind the answers
• Preserves anonymity	• May look too much like other previous company surveys, leading to low response rates
• Provides "hard numbers" for those who place high value on quantitative analysis	• May require active follow-up to obtain an adequate number of completed questionnaires.

Focus Groups—usually conducted in groupings of 8 to 15, selecting employees on the basis of the same gender, ethnicity and position level. The group moderator preferably is of the same ethnicity and gender. Structured 2- to 3- hour sessions can ferret out the passion that surrounds some issues, and the "why" behind a numerical answer on the survey. The sessions may also be used to involve employees in structuring solutions to issues they have identified.

Advantages	*Disadvantages*
▪ Captures "heat" as well as light on issues	▪ Can be expensive on a per-participant basis
▪ Sends powerful message about the company's interest in that group's input	▪ Must be wary of potential bias of focus group moderators
▪ Involvement of employees in problem solving generates useful input and helps manage expectations	▪ Can degenerate into gripe session if not properly planned and facilitated
	▪ Requires strong client logistical support to assure you have the right participants, at the right place, at the right time and matched with the right focus group leader.

Individual Interviews—conducted with senior management, or key influencers such as union officials, affinity group leaders, or where numbers are insufficient to develop a separate data breakout (e.g., physically challenged). Interviews may be helpful to define issues to address in the research effort, develop a sense of the commitment to diversity in the organization, and start a "buy-in" process.

Advantages	*Disadvantages*
▪ Privacy provides opportunity to surface potential resistance	▪ Can be expensive on a per-participant basis
▪ Can dwell on "soft" areas such as corporate culture that are not readily captured by a written instrument	▪ Interview structure must minimize opportunity for interviewer bias to affect outcome
	▪ Respondents may use interview for posturing, or give politically correct responses regardless of their real feelings

Diversity Scan—Intensive review of issues, using quality control diagnostic techniques with groups of 10 to 20 employees. The process may take 10 or more hours of meeting time, spread over several days. Output includes identification of root causes and issues, setting of priorities and recommendations of an action plan to management. Electronic feedback systems may be used to provide confidential and instantaneous feedback to the group as they work through the issues.

Advantages	*Disadvantages*
• Fits well in a culture in which TQM is well established and well regarded • Intensive time commitment permits development of detailed action plans	• Requires significant time commitment from participants • Cost and time constraints limit numbers who can participate • Group leader skills critical to the success of the effort

Program and Policy Review—to determine which programs, communications and practices currently exist which may have a bearing on diversity issues (e.g., affirmative action programs, career mobility systems, communications on diversity).

Advantages	*Disadvantages*
• Provides understanding of context for employee comments on the programs • Permits best practices comparison	• May waste time if done too early in the process • The paper trail may be misleading since bias more frequently shows in the administration of programs rather than in the design

External Benchmarking—to determine the types of practices and programs which have proven effective in "leading edge" companies, or companies in your industry or geographic proximity.

Advantages	*Disadvantages*
• Gain from the investment and experience of others • May help avoid common pitfalls	• Can be time consuming and costly to gather data • For many companies it is too early to tell if the activity is working well • May create tendency to follow the leaders, even if not appropriate to your organization

The mix of techniques is determined by the range of issues, numbers of employees and breakouts, geographical dispersion, costs, company culture and recent experience with like techniques. For example, one large company recognized that questionnaires would be the most economical way to reach employees throughout the U.S. However, they felt that employees had been "surveyed to death" in other activities. They didn't want to confuse employees with yet another instrument, so they opted for a series of focus groups.

To aid you in planning your research effort, I have prepared a diversity research planning tool, which is found in Exercise 5.1.

EXERCISE 5.1 Diversity Research Planning Guide

1. Identify the areas which you believe would be of greatest concern to employees and the company.

	Top 5 Priority [Y/N]
General Area for Concern	
a. Corporate culture that fosters diversity	_____
b. Fairness in the design and application of HR policies and programs	_____
c. Timely, useful and fair performance appraisals	_____
d. Cooperative and respectful working relationships between different ethnic and gender groups.	_____
e. Upward, downward, lateral communications	_____
f. Teamwork, effectiveness of diverse teams	_____
g. Training and development	
▪ For current positions	_____
▪ For future opportunities	_____
h. Career development and advancement	_____
i. Work and family programs	_____
j. Compensation and reward systems	_____
k. Recruitment of a diverse workforce	_____
l. Perceptions of racism, sexism, ageism and other "isms" in the work setting	_____
m. Encouraging and valuing diverse input into business issues	_____
n. Other areas of importance	

_____

_____

2. What is the size of the groups from which the research data will be drawn? [use work sheet below]

CENSUS GROUP SUMMARY

	NUMBERS IN EACH GROUP/LOCATION =			Total
GROUPS	*Location A*	*Location B*	*Location C*	*In Group*
Exempt Employees				
White Female				
Black Female				
Hispanic Female				
Asian Female				
White Male				
Black Male				
Hispanic Male				
Asian Male				
Other Groupings:				
e.g., Native American,				
Gay & Lesbian,				
Differently Abled				

(continued)

EXERCISE 5.1 Continued

GROUPS	NUMBERS IN EACH GROUP/LOCATION =			Total
	Location A	Location B	Location C	In Group
Nonexempt Employees				
White Female				
Black Female				
Hispanic Female				
Asian Female				
White Male				
Black Male				
Hispanic Male				
Asian Male				
Other Groups:				
TOTALS				

3. In the last two years, which of the above groups participated in some form of employee input:
   a. Written questionnaire
   b. Focus groups
   c. Individual interviews
   d. Team discussions

4. What is the budget for the research phase of the diversity process? _____

5. What is the time frame for completion?   Target Date

   ▪ Selection of methodologies   _____

   ▪ Selection of sample groups   _____

   ▪ Development of questionnaires   _____

   ▪ Scheduling of mailings and/or meetings   _____

   ▪ Employee communication   _____

   ▪ Administration of surveys and focus groups   _____

   ▪ Preliminary report of findings   _____

   ▪ Final report of findings and recommendations   _____

6. What other activities might be competing for attention at the same time as the research is being conducted?

   ▪ Vacation or holiday period

   ▪ Layoffs, downsizing, reorganization

   ▪ Budgeting or performance review cycle

   ▪ Other

7. Is the organization preference highly quantitative, somewhat qualitative, or somewhere in between?_____

8. What group's buy-in is essential for credibility and commitment? _____
   _____

9. Who will analyze the data and develop recommendations?_____
   _____

EXERCISE 5.1 Continued

10. Who will present findings and recommendations:
    - To the diversity task force
    - To senior management
    - To other groups, e.g. _____
11. Who will prepare the communications for providing feedback to the general employee population? _____

WHAT DOES THE RESEARCH OUTPUT LOOK LIKE?

The most frequently used approaches for reaching the employee groups will be the questionnaires and focus groups. Within each technique there is a range of detail that might be presented, depending on the wishes of the client and the budget for the project.

Survey Results Example—Raw Data: The computer output on one survey question is shown in Table 5.3 for the "Top 2 Boxes" (those who agree or tend to agree with statement) and "Bottom 2 Boxes" (those who disagree or tend to disagree with the statement).

The demographic breakouts will reflect the distribution of individuals in

TABLE 5.3 Survey Data Compilation
Anonymous Corporation—Gotham City Division

Question: Agree/Disagree: Anonymous senior management values different views and opinions in the decision making process.

	Total Respondents	Blacks		Asian		Hispanic		White	
		Fem	MI	Fem	MI	Fem	MI	Fem	MI
Total Employees Answering	2980	280	70	110	90	210	100	870	1110
% Favorable	38%	33%	50%	36%	33%	52%	60%	33%	49%
% Unfavorable	32%	46%	34%	27%	22%	33%	30%	33%	28%
Not sure	30%								

each work force. Using data from a series of related questions, conclusions are then drawn about an area of activity, such as communications, advancement and development, fair and equitable working relationships, etc. Summaries can be developed so that the data is in an understandable and user friendly format.

Focus Group Examples: The form in which focus group information is fed back will vary widely depending on the needs of the client, the budget for the collection and reproduction of commentary, the need to protect the anonymity of the focus group participants. There are several different approaches to providing feedback from focus groups:

Summary: In this approach the client is merely interested in the key issues which developed among the various groups. This information can be used as a cross check against the written survey information gathered separately. The summary may require subsets of priorities identified that are separated by focus group. An example of an overall summary can be found in the data appendix in the Panoply Products Case (Chapter 15).

Specific Commentary: Where there are some specific issues which the researchers wish to bring to management's attention, they may provide a sampling of specific quotes from the focus groups which illustrate the different groups' attitudes toward the particular issue. Throughout this book specific comments have been used to highlight attitudes toward career mobility systems, white backlash, stereotyping, etc. Commentary on one issue, performance appraisal, is shown below. In this particular case, a broad range of employees were critical of the effectiveness of the current program, indicating that it should be a priority for improvement.

EXAMPLE OF FOCUS GROUP CRITIQUE ON A SPECIFIC SUBJECT: PERFORMANCE APPRAISAL

White Male:
"Performance appraisals here are a joke. If they give you a low rating they will hear about it from personnel. If the rating is high, their boss will question them. So they play it safe and put you in the middle."

"We get very little feedback. Our supervisors don't seem to have the time or energy to devote to the truly managerial functions like performance appraisal or even informal feedback."

"I know that performance reviews are universally late. I am out there trying, but without feedback, I don't know if I am doing the right things."

African American Male:
"Everyone feels that the performance appraisal process is a travesty. It just affects African-Americans more, because the appraisals are the only tangible means for advancement in money and position, whereas white employees have other avenues."

"Sometime we are given exceptional ratings for doing something that would be considered mediocre in a white male. They just don't expect a black person to be up to that standard, and so their shock gets registered on the form."

White Female:
"It is a formality one goes through, but it isn't taken seriously unless they want to advance or terminate you. Otherwise, you sit down, you read, you sign, you walk out."

Hispanic Male:
"I rarely get informal feedback and I am not comfortable asking for it. If you ask, they seem to think you are pushy or negative. You get a reputation."

Asian Female:
"Since many Asians are taught not to complain, our tendency is to sign the form, whether or not we agree with what it says about us. Managers don't understand the need to draw us out, so that both points of view will be represented."

ANTICIPATING WHAT THE DATA WILL SAY

Quite frequently before companies embark on a research process, they will ask "What will the results be?". The concern is understandable, because the act of merely asking questions is part of a change process, and it sends signals to employees. On the other hand, every organization truly is different in terms of its employee mix, company culture, human resources programs, etc. In every company there will be some findings which come as a surprise to the client and the consultant. However, I have seen some general patterns of response emerge which I call the **nexus** of diversity issues (1). The nexus issues are listed in Exhibit 5.1. Those issues include the following:

Issues of Minorities/People of Color

UPWARD MOBILITY: the opportunity to push through the glass ceiling after proving themselves at the entry level. Concerns may show themselves in the form of observations about the limited number of persons of color in key management jobs.

FAIRNESS: is sought in terms of policies and programs that are neutral for all races both in content and administration (for example, performance appraisal, job posting, tuition reimbursement).

RESPECT: granted by bosses, peers and subordinates when it has been earned. Includes having their business-related opinions taken seriously.

EXHIBIT 5.1 Nexus of Diversity Issues

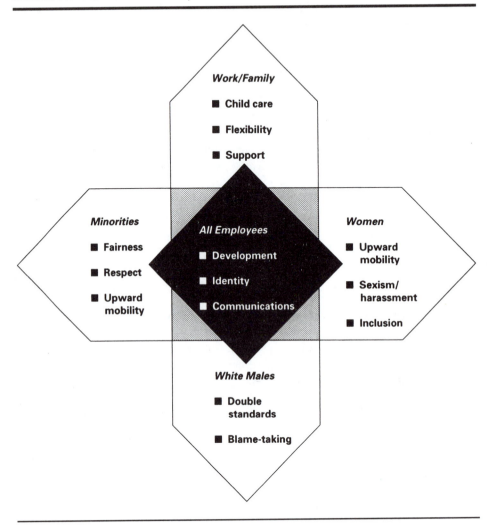

Work and Family Issues

CHILD CARE: concerns focus on the availability, quality and cost of child care for working parents.

FLEXIBILITY: is sought in areas that help employees to responsibly balance and fulfill their roles as both employees and parents (for example, parental leave policies, flexible hours, job sharing).

CLIMATE: that recognizes the validity of dependent care issues and supports employees in their utilizing the flexibility and programs that are available.

Women's Issues

UPWARD MOBILITY: is an issue just as it is for minorities. Here the concern may be about being shunted into "women's jobs" where there may be little opportunity for escape.

SEXUAL HARASSMENT: does not come up frequently, but when it does, the intensity of the concern is great. They want an environment that does not condone it, and if it occurs as an aberration, their complaint will be taken seriously and handled with utmost sensitivity.

INCLUSION: usually shows up as a negative reaction to "the old boys' club" approach to business and informal relationships. They may not want to go on the fishing trip with the guys, but they might like some other opportunity to informally associate with their boss and male peers without being at a disadvantage in the setting.

White Males: Let's not forget that white male employees still form an important part of our diversity fabric. They may worry about the denial of opportunities due to what they may view as the *Double Standard* of affirmative action. They also do not wish to be saddled with the *blame* for all the failures of our society or the organization which led to the current conditions.

All Employees: There is usually widespread concern across all employee groups about the **Development** opportunities that are available, whether or not employees expect to progress. They also wish to retain aspects of their personal uniqueness that are critical to their **Identity** and sense of self worth. **Communication** [up, down, across] is often deemed insufficient in the fast changing environment.

HOW TO USE YOUR DATA FOR MAXIMUM IMPACT

When the time comes to begin dealing with the data generated through your research effort, there are some patterns and issues for which you should be prepared. Some useful guidelines for the weeks following completion of the research include the following.

Anticipate the Data Denial Syndrome: Occasionally an organization is caught completely off guard by the intensity of the negative employee input. Sometimes the surprise is followed by attempts to challenge the methodology used, the sample group, or some other aspect of the mechanics. This issue was covered at the outset of the chapter, and the chances of it occurring can be minimized through realistic preparation of the management team for the results.

Diversity Is Everywhere: Sometimes participants in a diversity survey or focus group will express surprise that there were not more "diversity related" questions involved. This perception is caused by a mindset that managing diversity is equivalent to affirmative action; thus they are looking for more detail on hiring practices and discrimination complaints.

If you accept that diversity issues relate to corporate culture, systems, programs, and the like you can see that any question may have diversity implications. For example, let's say that 70% of the employees report that they receive a fair and accurate performance appraisal. On further review, you note that the 70% figure obscures the fact that white employees have responded positively 80% of the time. However, only 40% of the minority employees agree with the statement. In the situation described, there are some important diversity dimensions to a seemingly innocuous question.

Not Everything Can Be Explained: Occasionally there will be bits of data that you will find puzzling and you will need to dig deeper. For example, in one company the female Hispanic employees rated the company higher on a number of issues than did any other ethnic/gender group in the survey. Upon further review, it was learned that many of the females were in one department that was headed by an effective and supportive manager. The overall satisfaction with the working relationship led individuals to answer almost any question positively.

In other cases the differences on a given question simply may not be readily explained, or you will not have the time or resources to satisfy your curiosity. Having a range of questions relating to a given issue provides multiple opportunities to understand the underlying issues driving the responses.

The Same Question Can Have Different Meaning to Different Groups of Employees: If you are researching both hourly and salaried employees, you may need a different set of questions. For example, if you ask a question about satisfaction with advancement opportunities, hourly employees may respond more negatively than salaried employees. The more negative response of hourly employees may be a result of union agreements containing language that promotions are based primarily on seniority. In a seniority-driven promotion system, younger and shorter service employees may feel frustrated that their advancement is not related to their performance. With salaried promotion criteria usually being more open, there is the potential (but not the guarantee) for more positive responses on advancement questions.

All People of Color Are Not Alike: Federal EEO-1 reports over the years have grouped employees under several basic categories for counting purposes (Black, Hispanic, Asian, Caucasian, Native American, etc.). This counting is so ingrained that one may be lulled into believing that these broad categories actually capture the reality of how employees view their points of difference versus other groups. Groups of African American employees may resent having their input grouped with Asian Americans (for example) even though they are both "minority" groups.

Even within an EEO category (such as Asian Americans), the nationality groups may view themselves very differently. My colleague Dr. Toshi Ki points out, for example, that individuals of Korean extraction may have negative attitudes toward individuals of Japanese heritage, an enmity that carries over from World War II. Mexican Americans recognize that there are stronger negative stereotypes about them than there are about Cuban Americans. Dark-skinned Latinos may feel more prejudice than fair-skinned Latinos, and so forth. (2) Remember, the broad EEO categories serve the accounting needs of government agencies. They do not capture the real world of differences, any more than the "white male" designation captures the rich differences between Howard Stern and Rush Limbaugh!

Break Out of the "Box": It is too easy to fall into the trap of conventional thinking. Diversity research offers the opportunity to tap relevant perspectives of those not even in the company. For example, one organization invited a diverse group of community leaders for a lunch and working session to identify how the organization was connecting with various segments of the community. Research could also include contacting a spectrum of customers to get their reactions on the importance of diversity in the company's representatives who serve their account.

Beware of a Tainted Environment: If you do the research at a time when the company is in the midst of a layoff, major reorganization or such, the data may be tainted by the reaction to such events. Try to find a window when "everything is cool" to do your research. In the absence of a sea of tranquility, expect some effect of surrounding events on your research data.

A great deal of material has been covered in this segment which should be very beneficial as you consider the need for diversity research and how to approach it. Subsequent chapters will deal with moving from the data to action plans and more examples of research results for specific subject areas.

IMPORTANT POINTS TO REMEMBER

1. Recognize that there are a number of reasons that a credible research base precedes your diversity action planning:
    - To counter the tendency to deny issues and results
    - To balance multiple agendas

- To treat diversity as a serious business issue
- To counter potential backlash in reaction to diversity interventions

2. Diversity research requires effective planning including a consideration of the following:

- Review the usefulness of data already available
- Determine numbers of employees to be included
- Preserve the anonymity of respondents
- Make sure people feel included, their voices heard
- Don't include so much information that the research ends up slowing down the process, rather than expediting it

3. There are at least six commonly used research methodologies:

- Written questionnaires
- Focus groups, sometimes by race and gender
- Individual interviews
- Diversity scan process
- Program and policy review
- Benchmarking

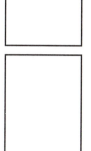

6 How to Establish Diversity Priorities and Develop Implementation Plans

The process of setting priorities and action plans is, for many organizations, the most challenging phase of a diversity change process. In this chapter we will identify some of the common stumbling blocks encountered in determining priorities and provide suggestions on analytical approaches that can be used for that activity. Also some suggestions for action plans to address the selected priorities are presented by way of two company examples. The activities described in this chapter form a critical link between issues and action.

ANTICIPATE UNIQUE CHALLENGES IN PLANNING AND IMPLEMENTING YOUR DIVERSITY INITIATIVES

In my diversity experiences, both on the corporate and consulting sides of the table, one of the most difficult tasks has been to identify the priorities that will serve as the focus of the initial implementation activity. In the priority setting/action planning phase, be ready to deal with the three issues described below:

Wide Range of Options: Diversity issues can involve virtually all aspects of the employment relationship. Therefore, the range of activities companies engage in has been very extensive. In Table 6.1 there are listed six groupings of diversity activities being carried out by organizations.

TABLE 6.1 Work Force Initiatives in Leadership Companies[1]

Communications
- Speeches by CEO/senior executives
- Video by CEO for employee showing
- Teleconferencing
- Closed circuit television
- Executive forum
- Corporate vision statement
- Diversity mission statement
- Diversity policy
- Diversity letter/memo from CEO
- Senior management behavior modeling
- Diversity brochure
- Employee handbook on diversity
- Employee newspaper/periodical articles
- Special diversity newsletters/status reports
- Second language communications
- New employee orientation
- New manager orientation

Education and Training
- Diversity briefings for senior management
- Diversity integrated into executive education
- Board of directors orientation
- Awareness training
- Diversity skills training
- Sexual harassment training
- New manager training
- Required core courses
- Mainstreaming of training into other training
- World-wide training
- Train-the-trainer programs
- Change agent seminars
- Cross race/gender training teams
- Partnering in-house trainer/external consultant

Employee Involvement
- Diversity task forces
- Task teams
- Issue study groups
- Focus groups

TABLE 6.1 Continued

- Diversity council
- Corporate advisory committee
- Business unit steering committee

Career Development and Planning

- Mentoring
- Identification of leadership potential
- Succession planning
- Expand job posting to V.P. level
- Career pathing
- Individual development plans
- Executive M.B.A. programs
- Developmental assignments
  - Lateral
  - Rotational
  - Special short term
- Internships
- Networking directories
- English as a second language courses
- Remedial education

Performance and Accountability

- Link diversity performance to other corporate objectives
- Develop quantitative/qualitative diversity measures
- Incorporate diversity in management by objectives programs
- Evaluate and reward behaviors that reinforce diversity
- Monitor and report progress
- Tie diversity performance to compensation and other rewards

Culture Change

- Conduct internal glass ceiling studies
- Incorporate diversity items in employee attitude survey
- Benchmark other companies
- Develop corporate diversity strategy
- Integrate diversity into total quality strategy
- Establish stand-alone diversity position
- Add diversity responsibilities to EEO/AA position
- Emphasize line management ownership
- Adopt flexible managerial style, not "one size fits all"
- Revise policies/benefits to support diverse needs

[1]*1993 survey results reprinted with the permission of the Conference Board, New York, N.Y.*

Analysis Paralysis: As described in Chapter 5, a diversity research study will often produce findings on 25 to 75 questions that were included in the study. Furthermore, the data may have been cut into perhaps 8 to 16 different race and gender groups. Additional data breakouts may be made by position (exempt, nonexempt and hourly), age or service breakdowns, and so on. Perhaps additional data cuts have been made by organization, e.g., headquarters and field sales. The data displays alone might require several hundred pages.

In addition to the numerical data, you may also have a number of pages of employee write-in comments from the written survey. Moderator reports on focus groups might generate additional dozens or hundreds of pages of text depending on the level of detail reported. All of this information coming in at once can bring the process to a stop while everyone is getting comfortable with the data.

Competing Constituencies: The data will typically show a number of areas where there is a commonality of interest. However, there will also be some aspects of change strongly desired by some groups (e.g., training and career development for nonexempt employees, dependent care assistance) that is of no consequence to others. The concern for "spreading around the goodies" to meet a wide variety of needs complicates the planning process, especially if it is being done in an environment of profit pressures and strict budget controls.

Let's now look at some of the analytical frameworks and productivity enhancing approaches that will enable you to deal with the unique challenges we have just described.

USE ANALYTICAL SHORTCUTS TO DEAL WITH THE DATA CHALLENGES

Each company has its own style for action planning and implementation. Some organizations that are very analytical and cautious will sift, sort and savor for months. On the other end of the spectrum is the intuitive, impatient organization that is comfortable with the "Ready, fire, aim!" approach. Some analytical steps that you can use to expedite your planning process are outlined below:

Sort Through the Data Based on Overall Scores: You should begin by looking for areas that have an overall low rating and need for improvement. For example, one organization developed a listing of the general areas of concern ranked from the highest to lowest overall scores, as shown in Table 6.2. As you can see, the planning group has selected for closer review from Table 6.2 the five broad areas having the lowest scores.

While this first step is a helpful start, you must refine your analysis further before you can draw any firm conclusions.

TABLE 6.2 Example of a Preliminary "First Cut"

	Summary of Overall Ratings* by Category		
Category	**Survey # Items**	**Mean Score***	**Highest Disagreeing Score/Group**
Compensation	4	78%	Minority nonexempt: 36%
Working Relationships	3	71%	White Female nonexempt: 27%
Performance Management	4	68%	White Female exempt: 31%
Quality of Supervision	7	58%	
Priority Areas: First Cut			
Supportive Culture	7	52%	White Female Exempt: 43%
Advancement & Development	8	51%	Minority Male Exempt: 51%
Environment for Females	5	50%	
Environment for Minorities	6	48%	Minority Female Exempt: 85%
Affirmative Action	6	46%	Minority Male Nonexempt: 100%

*A score of 100% indicates all employees express satisfaction with the status quo.

Take a Second Look Based on Respondent Group Characteristics: The high negative readings by a particular group may be a secondary level of analysis in priority setting (right hand column in Table 6.2). While overall scores provide a good starting point for analysis, you must be cognizant of the degree to which any one group predominates in the survey results. A high rating by the white males (or any other group that represents a large portion of the employee population) could disguise important differentials in perceptions. For example, one company was comparing the overall scores of studies done at five different manufacturing facilities. Production Facility number 3 appeared to have a slight edge on perceptions of the company, with an overall approval rating of 68%, versus 59% for the other facilities. However, in assessing the basis for higher score levels, some background data was developed for Production Facility number 3 that helped explain the basis for some of the differences:

- There was very little diversity in the workforce at Plant C (75% of the employees are white males)
- Of the minorities in the plant, the response rate to the survey was quite low due to confidentiality concerns.

- Furthermore, of the minorities who had responded, there were 21 questions for which *70% or more* of the respondents provided a negative rating.

In the instance cited, a data review that focused only on the *overall* positive numbers would overlook the intensity of negative perceptions associated with a specific group or groups.

Move From Broad Areas to Specific Issues: After you have selected some general areas for development, you need to peel back another layer of the onion to reveal the specific underlying core and any defects that may be imbedded therein. This step should be rather straightforward, as illustrated by the data in Table 6.3. Table 6.3 shows the scores for specific performance areas within an overall category of supervisory support.

The data having the overall lowest scores within the particular category (in this case, supervisory support) provide a logical starting point for your selection of target activity areas. You will want to look at some of the backup information on how different groups scored the issue to see if there is a particular group that drives the mean score, or registers scores somewhat different than the mean.

DEVELOP CRITERIA FOR ASSIGNING DIVERSITY PRIORITIES

After the preliminary screening steps described in the preceding section, you are ready to move the process forward one step further. There may still be too many issues to address after the first steps, and even if your list is small at this stage, you may need to set priorities within the list selected.

TABLE 6.3 Evaluation of Supervisory Support

Activity Area	% Favorable*	% Unfavorable
Having confidence in your ability	78%	7%
Treating you with respect as an individual	78	11
Dealing fairly with you	71	16
Below Are Priority Areas for Group Differential Analysis		
Acting on your ideas and suggestions	55%	24%
Telling you how you're doing	51	29
Keeping you informed	49	34
Showing you how to improve quality and service	40	37
Being a sponsor, mentor	27%	48%

Portion unaccounted for in the two columns were those responding "Undecided"

The objectivity of the process of setting priorities will be enhanced if the organization (through the diversity task force or other group) develops a list of criteria which takes diversity issues surfaced by the research and fits those in with other existing priorities and programs in the organization. As an aid to your analysis, you might consider the two lists of evaluation criteria shown below as a starting point.

Company-Centered Evaluation Criteria: The first list of nine evaluation criteria in Table 6.4 helps the evaluator to look at issues from the *company* or *senior management point of view*. Note that the criteria encompass both quantitative and subjective evaluation measures.

The criteria listed above may be tailored to fit the company's needs quite effectively, and the priorities can be shifted as some issues are addressed, new funding becomes available and so forth. However, those criteria may not fit the needs perceived by employees.

Employee-Centered Evaluation Criteria: The company-centered criteria may not answer the critical employee question, "What's in it for me?" Therefore, a second set of criteria may be needed to view the issues from the point of view of your employees. Some examples of those criteria are listed in Table 6.5.

The two lists of criteria in Tables 6.4 and 6.5 provide a comprehensive framework for determining your action plans. Now you need to plan on how to apply those criteria.

HOW TO APPLY THE DIVERSITY DECISION CRITERIA TO THE ISSUES IN YOUR ORGANIZATION

The criteria for setting priorities on diversity programming listed in Tables 6.4 and 6.5 may be used in several ways. The approach selected for your analysis will depend on a number of factors:

- The size and composition of the task force working on the diversity process (Larger groups may need more structure.)

- The nature of the diversity research supporting the effort (Is the input more quantitative or qualitative?)

- The preferred decision-making mode of the organization (For example, a high tech company said *"We have to put a number on everything, or we just aren't comfortable discussing the importance of the issue."*)

Let's briefly examine two approaches for developing the criteria into tools for analyzing the research data.

TABLE 6.4 Company-Centered Criteria for Evaluating Diversity Priorities

Criteria Category	Low Priority	Medium	High Priority

a. Dollar expenditures required
  • To implement change
  • To maintain as an ongoing program
	Major cost to put in place, maintain
	 e.g., company day care center
			Modest cost to put in place, maintain
			 e.g., communicate vision, create affinity groups

b. Cost avoidance due to improved performance	Little or no cost improvement can be identified e.g., mentor programs		Significant cost saving potential e.g., reduced turnover reduces recruiting and training costs
c. Consistency with other corporate priorities.	Runs counter to the theme of other programs, e.g., requires staff additions in midst of headcount reduction program		Consistent with, or complementary to other initiatives, e.g., improved working relationships support team management emphasis
d. Time required to implement and show results	Period of two to four years required e.g., recruitment initiatives at minority schools		Period of less than twelve months needed Change in leave policy to get more employee/mothers back to work following delivery
e. Number of employees who potentially are affected by the program.	Few employees, primarily in one ethnic group e.g., mentoring program for minority engineers		Many employees in nearly all race & gender groups e.g., improve performance review process to provide better developmental feedback
f. Amount of management time required to implement and/or maintain	Will require considerable time at all levels of the organization e.g., diversity training for all salaried employees		Will require limited amount of time from a few managers. e.g., dependent care referral program administered by external provider
g. Reduces risk of adverse legal or public relations exposure	Low risk of legal or negative p.r. exposure		Higher risk of legal or p.r. exposure e.g., sexual harassment training
h. Impact on revenues or operational effectiveness	Significant negative effect or minor positive effects e.g., scheduling diversity training during peak production period affects factory output		Significant positive effect or minor negative impact e.g., diverse markets team creates strategy for tapping new target markets
i. Previously demonstrated effectiveness of intervention in addressing issues identified	Examples drawn from your company's past experience, consultants' observations, or from external benchmarking study.		

TABLE 6.5 Employee-Centered Criteria for Evaluating Priorities

Criteria Category	Low Priority	Medium	High Priority
a. *Immediacy* of results as applied to employee needs	Impact will not be felt for several years e.g., change in the corporate culture to value more diverse input [requiring three years]		Some impact felt within six to twelve months of the start e.g., job posting introduced/ expanded to open the system for advancement
b. *Directness* of the impact on the needs of their interest group	Limited direct value on their personal agenda e.g., new hire mentoring program not open to current employees		Direct impact on the individual or their interest group e.g., broadened policy for return to work after maternity
c. Issue *intensity* to which change is directed	Expressions of concern by those affected are muted or stated with low emotional content e.g., desire to feature different cultural groups in company paper and cafeteria displays		Employee concerns are voiced with strong emotions which could affect: ▪ personal or group productivity ▪ filing of charges e.g., Complaints on racial or ethnic jokes and comments which are highly insulting to the targets of remarks and could lead to filing of formal complaints if not addressed promptly

Weighted Criteria Approach: Let's assume that the company involved is in the midst of an intense cost cutting program. Their concern is more about short term impact than long term effects. Thus the high priority items in this scenario are those that do not require large dollar expenditures, or which could contribute to avoidance of some future costs (e.g., costs of turnover, EEO charges). For this organization the criteria might be weighted as shown in Table 6.6.

If the evaluation is carefully constructed and rigorously analyzed, the criteria also can be used for communicating the basis for decisions taken. All employees may not agree with the programs ultimately developed on the basis of the criteria in Table 6.6, but at least they will understand the basis for the decisions taken.

Graphic Display Approach: You may find it useful to develop a visual display of the evaluation process, focusing on the two primary criteria for making priority assessments. Using those criteria, one can develop a simplified way both to assess

TABLE 6.6 Preliminary Weighting of Criteria for Priorities

	Points to be Awarded		
Factor	Low	Medium	High
a. Dollar expenditure required	10	5	2
b. Cost avoidance potential	2	4	8
c. Short term impact from the intervention on operations.	1	2	5

the priorities and to communicate the results to the various interest groups. An example of the process described is shown in Exhibit 6.1, with hypothetical ratings for a half dozen different programs. Note in this example, the cost criteria is represented on the left axis and the potential number of employees that might be affected is graphed on the horizontal axis. The criteria chosen would of course vary by the organization.

In Exhibit 6.1, a company could set whatever limits appropriate for each axis. For example on the left axis, $50,000 or less could produce the highest ranking, $500,000 or more the lowest ranking. A definition of "costs" is also needed,

EXHIBIT 6.1 Preliminary Assessment of Diversity Priorities—Example of Dual

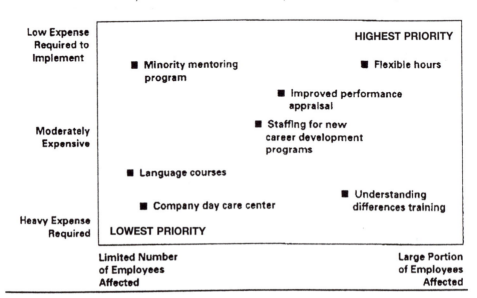

such as "Calculate on the basis of first year implementation costs and 3 years operating costs. Out of pocket costs only, does not include value of management time expended."

An example of scaling on the horizontal axis is "50% or more employees directly affected equals highest score, 5% or fewer employees the lowest score."

A large financial institution using the matrix approach for priority setting used the following criteria:

> **COMMITMENT** (horizontal axis)
>> **Reactive**—choosing to do the minimum to get by for compliance
>> **Active**—choosing to do what is expected by employees, the Board of Directors, the media and/or public
>> **Proactive**—choosing to see the issue as an opportunity to gain competitive advantage through leadership
>
> **EFFORT REQUIRED** (vertical axis)

The vertical axis was related to the degree of effort to implement the change, i.e., Low, Medium, and High effort. Each of the issues under review was placed into one of nine boxes on a chart that represented the way the issue was evaluated by the steering committee.

LINK DIVERSITY INITIATIVES TO OTHER EXISTING PROGRAMS

Diversity activities will be clamoring for attention along with other high profile activities competing for management time and energies. Therefore, it is important to establish linkages whenever possible so that the diversity issues get a fair share of attention and resources can be applied economically for the total benefit of the organization.

Anticipate Linkages to Broad Strategic/Tactical Efforts: Some typical broad corporate programs and linkages to diversity include those listed in Table 6.7, below:

The key point from Table 6.7 is simply that you should seek every opportunity to demonstrate that diversity activities are supportive of other priorities the company is pursuing. The linkage opportunity may provide the opening needed to weave diversity concerns into the fabric of the company, countering the notion that diversity is a tangential activity.

Human Resources Programs Provide Multiple Linkage Options: Many of the diversity issues will require adjustment of the various human resources policies and programs. Often the inter-connections are more complex than might appear on the surface. Let's take the example of the company who learned that 60% of its employees **perceived** that nonperformance factors were quite important to individual success and advancement opportunities. Nonperformance factors cited in the survey responses included who you know, member of the "good old boys'

TABLE 6.7 Creating Diversity Links to Other Concurrent Interventions

Concurrent Program	Possible Diversity Linkage
Total Quality Management	Performance of diverse work teams
Rightsizing/Re-engineering/ Downsizing	Preservation of previous progress in employment and advancement of women and people of color
Globalization	Awareness training in cultural differences, language barriers
Market Development/Diversification	Formation of diverse team for ethnic markets
Employee Feedback	Inclusion of diversity items in periodic surveys and other existing feedback processes
Delayering	Implement empowerment model of management focusing on results achieved, not on the incidental characteristics of the person.

club", golfer, Ivy Leaguer, under age 40, etc. Now *which activity areas might be adjusted or enhanced to address the finding?*

First there would be the primary linked activities such as developing and implementing balanced selection standards, succession planning, performance management and job posting systems. Secondly, you would consider less directly related programs such as mentoring, female/minority networking groups and efficacy training for those below the glass ceiling.

When the connections on the primary programs have been identified, you are in a position to develop an action plan that properly incorporates other related programs. The more that you understand the connections, the more you realize that managing diversity is not a discreet activity, but an integral part of effectively managing the human resources of the organization.

DEVELOP A CONCISE IMPLEMENTATION PLAN FOR THE EARLY STAGES OF THE INTERVENTION

After selecting priorities on which to focus, you need to develop a plan which specifies the activities to be pursued and the timetables for accomplishment. You should specify which individuals or groups have accountability for the successful completion of each activity. This schedule serves as the road map for the early phases of the implementation process.

The initial action plan for senior management approval should not be long and complex. Remember that not everyone has been immersed in the subject as you have, and may be intimidated or confused by a highly detailed document that runs many pages. You can cover much of the detail in the work that you do with subcommittees, HR specialists and the like. The level of specificity may also relate to the culture of the organization. Two examples are described below.

The Broad Approach to Action Planning: The *"Financial Federation Corporation"* example in Exhibit 6.2 covers two stages of a change effort: organizing for implementation and communication to employees. The FFC approach is to cover only the highlights, giving senior management a sense of the direction of the effort, yet leaving the Diversity Advisory Committee to work through the details.

EXHIBIT 6.2 Financial Federation Corporation:
Diversity Implementation Plan

I. Organizing for Implementation

Premise:
The effective development of a broad range of programs and the credibility of those efforts hinge upon the meaningful involvement of a diverse group of employees. The effort is too broad for the Diversity Action Committee [DAC] members to handle on their own in addition to their ongoing responsibilities. Specific activities and the accountability are summarized below. The appropriate group may select external advisors to provide technical or strategic perspectives.

Activities	By Whom	When
1. Expand the membership of the DAC. Add 4–5 members representing diversity dimensions not now incorporated, e.g.	CEO	6/95
• nonexempt		
• non-headquarters		
• more key functions		
• more non-traditional employees		
2. DAC continues to focus on broad policy and process issues. Appoint subcommittees to focus on particular areas of change. Each subcommittee is chaired by a member of the DAC and has diverse employees participation. Basic functions to be performed by the sub-committees are as follows:	DAC	7/95
• *Diversity Education & Training* Develop guidelines and recommended programs to provide employees with a basic understanding of diversity issues and how to deal with those issues in the FFC working environment.	DAC Subcommittee	9/95
• *Work/Life Programs Committee* Examine the issues raised regarding the balance of work requirements and personal requirements and recommend policies and programs to enable employees to balance each. Gather additional information needed, using available data whenever possible.	DAC Subcommittee	12/95

(continued)

EXHIBIT 6.2 Continued

Activities	By Whom	When
• *Policies and Practices Committee* Committee will delve into areas not covered by above sub-committees, and develop recommended changes for senior management approval. Focal areas include:	DAC Subcommittee	
a. Equity/recognition issues raised by nonexempt employees.		10/95
b. Development of mobility programs and systems.		11/95
c. Implement revised performance management system now under development.		3/96
d. Improved recruiting process		2/96
3. DAC mission, membership and objectives communicated as part of total strategy for achieving progress.	DAC	See Sched. II

II. Communicating to Employees

Premise:
During the data gathering phase some employees expressed doubt that any significant changes would result from the study. Prompt feedback of results is needed to reinforce management's commitment, to counteract any cynicism that may exist and manage expectations.

Activities	By Whom	When
1. Communication plan and budget developed.	Consultant	6/95
2. Plan review with DAC, including the following:	DAC	7/95
• Written communication piece on feedback of survey results and action plans.		
• Outline of brief presentation, Q & A for departmental meetings.		
3. Basic communication piece written and outline for departmental meetings readied. Issues to be incorporated include the following:	Consultant & FFC Mgr., Communications	9/95
• Explain business rationale for diversity		
• Define diversity in the FFC context		
• Reminder of objectives and techniques of the completed diversity research process, including actions to ensure confidentiality and candid input.		
• Describe about 8–10 key findings.		
• Describe possible action plans and time frame for completion.		
• Position the DAC and subcommittee roles		
• Reaffirm senior management commitment.		
4. DAC reviews and modifies communication materials drafted.	DAC	9/95

EXHIBIT 6.2 Continued

Activities	By Whom	When
5. Production of the feedback newsletter and materials for departmental meetings.	Consultant & FFC Comm.	10/95
6. Departmental meetings scheduled. Preliminary training session with key managers to prepare for meetings.	Consultant, HR & Comm.	11/95
7. Reconnaissance of employee comments and questions. Follow-up clarification or elaboration developed as necessary.	HR and line managers	11& 12/95

Detailed Approach to Action Planning: In this example the "Supreme Technology Company" has developed an action plan that fits the culture of the organization. In Exhibit 6.3 you can observe the penchant for detail and assumptions about the predictability of the timing for activities to be completed. Even the choice of the subject matter (measuring results) early in the process gives important clues as to the approach to addressing issues.

EXHIBIT 6.3 Supreme Technology Company: Diversity Action Summary

I. Diversity Measurement Team

Activity # — Activity Description	Start	Finish
I. A. Define the nature of the information desired by senior management.	3/1/95	4/15/95
A.1 Review current data available on human resources.		
A.2 Identify individuals and processes used to gather human resources data.		
A.3 Interview C. E. O. and direct reports regarding the diversity business rationale and data they seek to verify desired outcomes.		
A.4 Interview financial managers to assess potential needs and approaches to data gathering:		
▪ Mgr. Corporate Accounting		
▪ Mgr. Reporting Systems		
A.5. Meet with Corporate Planning to assess what information should be included in package for the long range planning cycle.		
I. B. Meet with other diversity teams to identify the anticipated activities, timing and outcomes from their principal initiatives.	4/15/95	6/5/95
B.1 Determine what issues are to be addressed by each team:		
▪ Performance of diverse work teams		
▪ Policies and programs		
▪ Recruitment and advancement		
▪ Work and family		
B.2 Review their action plan for completion, i.e., implementation of changes.		

(continued)

EXHIBIT 6.3 Continued

Activity #	Activity Description	Start	Finish
	B.3 Identify anticipated behavioral outcomes and their possible effect on operations.		
	B.4. Assess which outcomes may be subject to financial or statistical assessment: ▪ Through existing reports and systems ▪ Through new reports or systems		
	B.5 Determine the natural cycle for evaluating and measuring progress.		
	B.6 Coordinate meetings with each team and accounting reporting to determine nature and scope of data required.		
I.C.	**Conduct limited benchmarking to refine anticipated measurements and reporting.**	6/15/95	8/8/95
	C.1. Identify companies to be included in the benchmarking study.		
	C.2 Schedule site visits or telephone interviews.		
	C.3 Assign site visit team to prepare questions and data gathering format.		
	C.4 Conduct site visits.		
	C.5 Summarize the types of external data that are available.		
	C.6 Determine how external data needs to be massaged or reconfigured to provide meaningful comparisons with internal data.		
I.D.	**Provide recommended reporting package to senior management for approval.**	10/1/95	11/5/95
	D.1 Work with Accounting/Reporting to develop specifics of the package.		
	D.2 Present package for review with baseline data for selected segments.		
	D.3 Make adjustments to reporting package after senior management review.		
I.E.	**Develop first report and provide analysis to senior management.**	1/1/97	3/1/97
	E.1 Meet with teams quarterly to determine if plans are still on target for critical dates.		
	E.2 Support teams/accounting/reporting as needed to prepare first report for full fiscal year.		
	E.3 Meet with teams to assess the impact of the information and issues underlying the data.		
	E.4 Provide first diversity analytics/financial package to senior management.		

The differences in the approaches shown in Exhibits 6.2 and 6.3 demonstrate that there is no one right answer. In any event, it is worth remembering that diversity in many companies is a pioneering activity. Therefore, the rate of progress against action plans may not be easily predicted. Furthermore, empowerment of a task force implies that they will have flexibility to adapt to evolving needs without having to come back for approval on any little change in direction of the priorities.

DEVELOP YOUR SELLING STRATEGY

The fact that your senior management has let you go this far along in the process would seem to imply that they will be supportive of reality-based recommendations that result. However, there is a large distinction between having "permission" to do some research and planning versus having senior management "commitment." Even if the commitment words have been spoken, you have to test the level of commitment in the face of specific action steps.

In the chapter on communications there is a description of the various constituencies for diversity. You should review that material and determine what benefits you have to sell as a result of the diversity initiatives recommended. Tailor your sales approach to the probable concerns and needs of the various groups, senior management, advocacy/affinity groups, and diversity program resisters.

As pointed out at the beginning of this chapter, the action planning phase is critical and could cause delays for organizations that do not employ some structure in selecting priorities from among many alternatives, and then promptly moving ahead with a clear and realistic implementation plan. The guidelines described in this chapter should help you move quickly and decisively to address the needs identified through your diversity research.

IMPORTANT POINTS TO REMEMBER

1. Anticipate the unique challenges of diversity action planning:
    - Avoid analysis paralysis
    - Balance competing agendas
2. Use analytical shortcuts to focus on critical issues and move to selection of priorities.
3. Develop the criteria by which the alternatives will be evaluated.
    - Start with criteria focusing on the company point of view.
    - Balance the picture with criteria that relate to employees' perceptions of what is important.
4. Develop clear action plans that serve as both a road map for activity and a commitment to results.
5. Link action plans to other corporate initiatives and human resources programs.
6. Identify the decision makers and key influencers and develop a sales strategy that responds to their probable areas of concern.

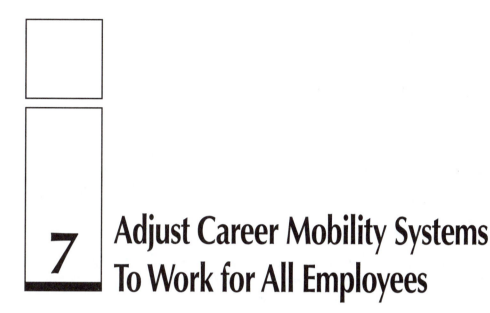

7 Adjust Career Mobility Systems To Work for All Employees

You have completed your diversity research and used the data to develop priorities and action plans. You are now ready to address some of the specific subject areas identified in the research. The first area we will examine is *Career Mobility Systems.* In this chapter we will do the following:

- Define and identify career mobility systems
- Describe why career mobility systems are important to managing diversity
- Identify six diversity issues associated with career mobility systems, and provide some specific suggestions for addressing those issues

In a number of instances, focus group comments from diverse employees are used to bring to life the general principles being discussed. Information from subject matter experts is introduced to provide perspectives that supplement the author's points.

DEFINING CAREER MOBILITY SYSTEMS

Career Mobility Systems (CMS) traditionally have been defined as the formal and informal programs which channel people into, and up through, the levels in the organization pyramid. In recent years, economic challenges have caused many companies to broaden the CMS focus from an upward mobility concentration, to include a whole range of lateral, circular or even downward moves. The most frequently observed CMS are illustrated in Exhibit 7.1.

In some cases the CMS are quite formal and well documented. Formal programs observed in medium-sized and large organizations include succession planning, performance appraisal, job posting and others shown below. These programs are often applied for management and professional employees on a company wide basis, complete with standardized forms and procedures, a specified timetable for completion of the process, and perhaps training of managers to use the system. In some organizations, there may be no formal system, but one operates nonetheless. After all, even if you don't have a manual on the subject, appraisals of performance will be made; decisions on who will be trained and promoted must be taken.

EXHIBIT 7.1 Career Mobility Systems in the Corporate Pyramid

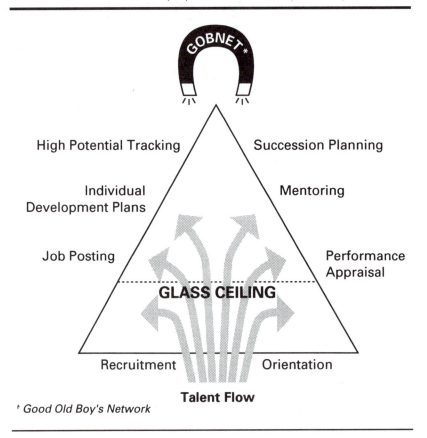

High Potential Tracking / Succession Planning

Individual Development Plans / Mentoring

Job Posting / Performance Appraisal

GLASS CEILING

Recruitment / Orientation

Talent Flow

ᶠ *Good Old Boy's Network*

Basis for Employee Concern About CMS: There are several reasons why effective CMS are important to your diverse work force, and essential to companies who seek to attain full utilization of that work force:

- CMS determine how far an individual will progress in an organization, the pace at which he or she will proceed and the development to be provided in support of his or her progress.

- Some of the systems, notably performance appraisal, have multiple applications. Thus, a mis-evaluation may affect salary, bonus, advancement opportunities, immediately and for a period of several years thereafter.

- Evaluations of individual performance and potential for advancement may reflect key assumptions about the corporate culture and characteristics of people who are presumed to be effective in that culture. Those assumptions may also result in a biased application by program administrators, and the preconceptions of employees will influence reactions to their treatment under the plans.

- CMS often represent the only formal record of how the individual is perceived in the organization. Therefore, the CMS have the potential to strongly influence the individual's sense of self worth, motivation to perform to expectations and commitment to his/her job.

- Weak or missing systems have a disproportionately negative impact on people of color and women employees. Informal approaches run a greater risk of becoming "buddy systems," with individuals moving more rapidly who look like, and/or act like the dominant group.

- Even with formal systems, employees perceive the strong magnetic effects of the *GOBNET*, or Good Old Boy Network. The GOBNET magnet, if not neutralized, can totally overwhelm the discipline of the formal systems.

- In the lean environment of the 90's there has been an important shift in emphasis by organizations. Instead of a paternalistic approach where the company felt responsible for development, the trend is to include a strong individual component in programs. Individual decisions on advancement paths and development needs are commonplace, but not all groups have had the preparation or guidance necessary to make informed decisions.

- As companies have delayered, reengineered and downsized, the processes by which decisions are made come under intensified scrutiny. The question is no longer who will get first choice of three promotions in the department. It is more likely a concern about who will get the **only** promotion, or who will be outplaced, and who will be retained.

In nearly all the diversity research projects that I have observed, CMS tend to get rather negative reviews by a broad range of employees. For example, one typical survey item reads as follows: *"Females and minorities have the same opportunities for advancement and recognition as white males."* (scale = strongly agree, tend to agree, tend to disagree, strongly disagree) The responses to this question for some companies that have gone through headcount reduction programs are summarized in Exhibit 7.2 below.

The pattern of responses illustrated in Exhibit 7.2 has been repeated on an overall basis for a list of twelve diversity research questions relating to advancement and development. Given the broad employee disappointment, particularly among people of color and women, it is no surprise that more and more companies have recognized the importance of the CMS and are addressing the diversity concerns associated with such programs.

HOW TO HANDLE SIX DIVERSITY ISSUES ARISING FROM CAREER MOBILITY SYSTEMS

In the remainder of the chapter, we will identify six diversity issues associated with career mobility systems. For each of the issues cited, we offer employee commentary to illustrate the nature of the issues, immediately followed by specific suggestions for responding to these issues. Application of this chapter will enhance the credibility and effectiveness of your Career Mobility Systems, so that they work well for *all employees.*

Issue: Individual Development Is Not Viewed as a Key Management Accountability: In many organizations, the development of the human resources of the organization is not viewed as a major management responsibility, and managers are not held accountable for development results. Or at least this is the way that the em-

EXHIBIT 7.2 Perceptions of Advancement Opportunities by Race/Gender/Level

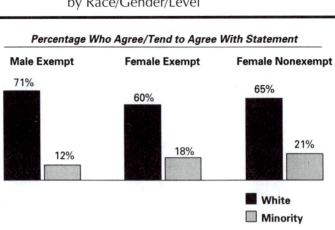

Percentage Who Agree/Tend to Agree With Statement

| Male Exempt | Female Exempt | Female Nonexempt |

71%
12%
60%
18%
65%
21%

■ White
□ Minority

ployees see the picture. It is not uncommon for only 25% of survey respondents to say that management in their organization is rewarded for developing employees.

When the question of support for development is brought down to the personal level, the respondents are more positive. When talking about their direct supervisor, around fifty per cent of all employees will give their supervisor credit for being concerned about their development. I interpret the differential in scores to an employee perception that their supervisors are willing to invest in development, but that employees perceive a lack of support provided through the corporate culture and programs that support development.

In some diversity research projects, participants can be quite vocal about their perceptions of insufficient company commitment. Comments illustrating the perceptions from a range of employees are as follows:

White Male:
"It's a sink-or-swim mentality here. There isn't a real defined training program compared with my prior employer where there was a constant emphasis on how you could further develop."

Asian Female:
"There is a reluctance of managers to spend the time and effort to help new employees with the transition to the Anonymous Company's processes and performance standards. Managers here are quick to judge and 'write off' people without giving them proper training."

White Male Senior Executive:
"This company is so focused on the numbers it cannot see the need and value of developing its people. I feel we are shortchanging them and the company. Even at my level I feel the need for some self development assistance, but my boss hasn't given me any moral support or specific guidance."

Employees also seem to be able to make distinctions between development systems or programs that work and meet their needs, versus those that are mere empty shells. Examples of these perceptions include the following:

Black Male:
"I know we have this succession planning and development program that they seem to be so proud about. However, from my experience it is simply an upward oriented exercise, primarily for the purpose of impressing the Executive Committee. I have never been given any developmental feedback relating to the paperwork that I have been asked to fill out, or from the meetings where my future was presumably discussed."

African American Female:
On job posting: "People who don't know [that there is already a person targeted for a job] are going to try to get an interview and set up their résumé. They're wasting their time because the selection was made before the posting went up."

There are a host of logical business reasons why companies have short-changed their development efforts. It is too expensive, too many irons in the fire, total focus on this quarter rather than the next five years, and so forth. Whatever the reason for the positioning of development, managers will certainly be aware of the organization's lack of commitment and turn their attention to activities for which they will be rewarded.

Corrective Actions for the Accountability Issue: The actions here are general in nature as is the issue toward which they are addressed.

ESTABLISH A COMPANY POSITION ON THE IMPORTANCE OF EMPLOYEE DEVELOPMENT: Commitment to the development of human resources should be one of the corporate principles, widely and repeatedly communicated. For example, the Quaker Oats Company has included information in shareholder reports about its commitment to development, plus information on some of the programs that it uses. The linkage of employee development with quantitative financial performance lends credibility to development as an important area of activity. The linkage also serves to subtly inform shareholders and the investment community that management is making strategic investments that go toward extending corporate success over the long haul. A public commitment also makes it difficult to back away when there is a temporary pressure on costs.

INCLUDE DEVELOPMENT OBJECTIVES IN PERFORMANCE REVIEWS: Every manager should have at least one objective for his or her own development, and objectives for the development of their subordinates. These can be very specific, or general. Some examples of development objectives are provided below which may represent agreements between the manager and his/her boss, or the manager and his/her subordinates.

- *"By the end of the third fiscal quarter, will attend the company seminar on 'Advanced Leadership Skills'."*

- *"Will seek assignment to the Profit Improvement Task Force to gain exposure to other parts of the company and to cost control techniques."*

- *"Will arrange for the preparation of an individual development plan focusing on leadership skills, based on 360 degree appraisal input on development needs."*

- *"Will work with internal OD group to gain awareness of cultural issues in my teams, and develop approaches to benefit from the diversity in our teams."*

Naturally if the development objective is included, there should be a performance discussion around that objective during the periodic reviews. If there is no follow-up on performance, the inclusion of developmental objectives will soon be recognized for what it is: an empty exercise for the record. For example, using a "training catalogue" approach (a listing of too many unrelated activities) will more likely serve as a source of frustration rather than a demonstration of commitment.

PROVIDE RECOGNITION TO THOSE WHO ARE GOOD DEVELOPERS OF THEIR EMPLOYEES: The provision of monetary rewards is often helpful in stimulating or reinforcing the specific performance or behaviors desired. I see no reason to assume that money would not be useful for the purpose of underscoring an organization's commitment to development. In this case, you don't need a finite formula for doing so. In one company, for example, a head of a division marketing group had been in his position a number of years. Although he had made some excellent contributions, for a variety of reasons he was never promoted to a division general manager role, which would be the next logical move. However, it was widely recognized by senior management that this individual's department did an outstanding job of selecting and developing employees. The diverse "graduates" of his department were heavily sought by other divisions and departments in the company. Each year at bonus time, his performance in development was an intangible positive factor affecting the size of his award, and it was communicated to him as such.

The recognition and reinforcement for development need not always be monetary. Executives are very competitive creatures, and they will be looking for opportunities to brighten their image and chances of success. If one of their number receives public praise from the company president for his development efforts, the message will be noted by those who are keeping score, and other upwardly striving managers will soon be competing for similar kudos for their own efforts.

What is required here are real senior management commitments, not just statements of intent. Your employees are adept at sniffing out the true degree of the company's commitment. Too often the organization will offer public praise for the developer of people, but at the end of the year they give all the money and promotions to "Mongo the Merciless"—who did not let development get in the way of making his/her numbers. Managers will readily conclude what the true underlying values and priorities of the company are. Empty platitudes are soon recognized as such.

Issue: Biases Intrude into CMS Design and Operation: Standards for recognition and advancement are often subjective, and thus prone to having cultural biases creep into their operation. Stereotypes may affect decision making on people, and overly rigid standards may create pressures for non-mainstream employees to assimilate to the dominant cultural norms.

It certainly would be difficult to prove that the disparity of results in advancement of different groups is *primarily* the result of biases that enter into the operation of the programs. However, biases are widely believed by employees to be a critical factor in their own advancement and therefore should be addressed as a serious issue.

In Chapter 2 we dealt in some detail with the psychological tendency to look favorably on the members of one's own group and less favorably on members of other groups. It seems virtually inevitable for each of us to bring some known or unrecognized biases to the work place, and in fact there is no law against it. Where the problem arises is when we knowingly or unknowingly combine our biases with institutional power (such as the power to hire, promote, reward) to work to the disadvantage of others. Then it is no longer simply a bias, it is racism, sexism, ageism, homophobia, etc. Table 7.1 shows some examples of biased attitudes which, if not dealt with, *could* lead to discrimination relating to advancement and recognition.

There is an interesting subtlety in the applications described in Table 7.1, for these managers profess and may be sincere in saying that they are acting in what (they feel) are the best interests of their employees. Thus, the male manager who will not put women in key line roles because it will be "too tough on them" is doing so to protect his female managers in this "father knows best" kind of organization. Unfortunately this misguided paternalism may deny opportunities, with accompanying risks, that the non-traditional candidates are quite disposed to endure.

TABLE 7.1 Potential Effects of Biases on Advancement & Development Decisions

Biased Assumption or Belief	Behavior Emanating from the Assumption or Belief
a. I have concerns about women being tough enough to handle difficult profit center turnaround situations.	Women are consciously or unconsciously omitted from candidate slates for high profile growth assignments.
b. I believe managers must use a strong "kick butt" approach to get superior results from their employees.	Managers attempting to use a team approach, with less authoritarian decision making, may be viewed as weak (regardless of results they achieve) and are not promoted because *"they will be eaten alive"* in higher level positions.
c. My personal values are that women should put families before careers. Thus, my expectation is that female employees will be less committed and less capable of handling the job pressures after they have had a child.	Females are not nominated for training/development assignments and are removed from the list of highly promotable employees. This spares them from having to make tough decisions on accepting transfers, adding responsibility and other actions which might make it more difficult to fulfill their family obligations.
d. I have heard some employees of ethnic group A, say that they would not want to work for members of ethnic Group B.	Members of Group B are directed into staff support positions where they will have few subordinates to supervise. This will limit their potential, but it is justified as sparing those ethnic managers from a situation where they are unlikely to succeed.

A second and related issue is that the standards used in the application of CMS are often quite vague, and on occasion may fall subject to career limiting stereotypes. Here is how some employees have perceived these standards in varying organizations:

Asian-American Male:
"You have to project yourself and sell yourself, be aggressive. You are told to talk loud because it shows confidence. But these are negative values in my culture, so I don't fit in."

African-American Male:
"I had one manager, when I first came here, tell me that he didn't know black people could write as well as whites. At least he was honest about it."

White Female:
"I think that if people were judged on an individual basis and not 'against the standard' there wouldn't be a problem. It seems as if Anonymous Company has in mind this mold of an employee in all positions. It wants the same thing time and again and it doesn't look for anything different."

Asian Female:
"As an Asian they stereotype me as competent, so that isn't a problem. However, as a woman I have to continually prove I am serious about a career, not overly emotional and that I put Anonymous Company ahead of my family. They can ignore that I am an Asian, but the stereotypes about women never go away."

Hispanic Female:
"They won't give you the benefit of the doubt, assume that you can do the job. It's like they think we just fell off the vegetable truck in front of the office."

Obviously the preconceptions of the evaluating manager usually work against people of color, and women, physically challenged and others who are different. However, there may be limited instances where the bias or stereotypes could work to their advantage, as illustrated by the following quotes:

Asian American Male:
"I think there might be a preconceived stereotype in that you're Asian, you come in, you work hard. You are graded well, regardless of whether you think you're doing that well or not."

African American Male:
"Sometimes we are given exceptional ratings for doing something that would be considered mediocre in a white male. They just don't expect a black person to be up to that standard, and so their shock gets registered on the form."

The positive bias may not be as beneficial as appears on the surface. Even where the bias seems to work in their favor, the individuals concerned are quick to point out that, *"It [the positive bias] still doesn't get us promoted, and the whites yell reverse discrimination."*

Corrective Actions for Bias Issues: If we are to progress toward the managing diversity vision, we need to chip away at individual bias, that unchecked, can progress to discriminatory actions.

BEGIN WITH YOURSELF: Each of us who are designers, controllers or users of CMS have the obligation to confront our own prejudices, and deal with them (at least to the extent of holding them in suspension in the work environment). Some actions for achieving this were covered in Chapter 2. In addition, various training and awareness activities were described in Chapter 8. There is much work that we all can do and need to do.

As the workforce becomes more diverse we will see new permutations of the effects of bias in the workplace. For example, employees of one organization expressed concern about an Asian "old boys' club" composed of Asian American key managers. These Asian managers were seen by non-Asians as more inclined to hire and promote people who looked like themselves. Alas, the cycle has the potential to repeat itself!

TRAIN YOUR MANAGERS TO UNDERSTAND AND VALUE DIFFERENCES: The same principles apply here as just described above. If managing cultural diversity has not been on the corporate agenda, we have no reason to expect our employees to have the knowledge and skills to deal with the issues. (The logic and approaches for diversity education and training are described extensively in Chapter 8.)

BE SPECIFIC AS TO WHAT YOU ARE LOOKING FOR—AND WHY: In addition to working at the personal level, you need to work the issue at the organization level. You should review the formal and informal standards for selection and advancement for evidence of stereotypical standards of performance, appearance or behavior. For example, the use of metaphors to describe desired characteristics *"able to quarterback the team"*, *"lean and mean"* have obviously limiting impact when applied to those other than the dominant group. Even within the same diversity grouping (white male on white male, female on female) these narrow prescriptions for success may be unfairly limiting as well as too open for different interpretations.

A number of organizations have gone through the process of providing more specificity in their requirements for advancement. An example of the two requirements being used by a high tech organization and a consumer goods company are listed in Table 7.2.

The development of standards like those shown in Exhibit 7.2 is just the first step. The next step is to train managers in the use of the standards. If efforts are

TABLE 7.2 Benchmarks for Determining Next Assignments

LEADERSHIP BENCHMARKS

High Tech Company
The individual exhibits the following characteristics:
- Leads by example
- Provides effective performance feedback
- Recognizes and rewards contributions
- Clearly models and communicates excellence as a standard
- Motivates employees, builds morale
- Listens, explains, answers questions
- Communicates vision, values and strategies in terms of the job at hand

Consumer Goods Company
Has the ability to influence others to perform a task effectively:
- Works cooperatively with a variety of peers and clients (can sell ideas, implement changes, face conflict, etc.)
- Works effectively with direct reports (able to motivate, delegate, organize, plan, etc.)
- Recognizes the needs and problems of others and treats them fairly

DECISION MAKING/THINKING/ANALYTICAL BENCHMARKS

High Tech Company
- Masters new technical knowledge, vocabulary and operating rules
- Provides clear analysis and actionable recommendations
- Generates good ideas for improvement
- Asks good questions, digs for answers
- Anticipates problems
- Well organized

Consumer Goods Company
Has ability to make timely and effective decisions on the basis of available information.
- Digs into situations and identifies real issues and problems.
- Considers all available information.
- Objectively evaluates alternatives and options.
- Selects appropriate courses of action and creates suitable implementation plan.

not made to "calibrate" the application of the system, the desired results will not be achieved.

At the Quaker Oats Company, Mike Cohen, Vice President of Management Development, developed a seminar for managers to develop skill and confidence in making assessment of individuals for future growth potential. Considerable emphasis was also provided to help managers work with their direct reports to prepare individual development plans. Specific case examples are used to illustrate what is meant by the general description of the standards, and group exercises are used to develop a *common understanding* of what the terms mean and how they should be applied and weighted for various positions. The case studies also enable the group members to observe the tremendously wide variety of ways in which their experience and preferences impact on their judgments on the case studies. Such training programs can be used to reinforce other diversity awareness training on the influence of biases and stereotypes in evaluations.

Employees may argue that some of the criteria listed in Table 7.2 are not valid or not useful, and that other potentially useful criteria are omitted. However, the criteria do provide *all individuals* in the company with a clear understanding of the characteristics that are being evaluated. No longer is this critical knowledge limited to a "chosen few," or left to inference by inquisitive "maze bright" managers. If someone feels that he or she is at a disadvantage in competing due to one or more of the factors, they now have some clear options, including the following:

- They can seek additional training or development to improve their skills in a given area, such as oral presentation skills.

- They can leave the company and go to another organization that is using standards with which they feel more comfortable.

- They can argue the relevance of the standard for the particular position or career path toward which they are aimed.

- They can seek a change in career path that better fits the mixture of company requirements and their own skill base.

AVOID APPLYING "NARROW BANDS OF ACCEPTABLE BEHAVIOR": Research on the glass ceiling by Morrison, et al. (1) documented that organizations tended to create overlapping circles of behavior deemed acceptable for men and women managers. As Exhibit 7.3 illustrates, the effect is to create a double standard for females.

As Exhibit 7.3 suggests, male managers customarily have a fairly large area within which they can operate and still be acceptable. Women also are faced with expectations of how they should behave in the work place. The females are expected to rise above the stereotypes of their group (e.g., women are too emotional) while adopting some, but not all masculine traits. Therefore, when require-

EXHIBIT 7.3 Narrow Bands of Acceptable Behavior

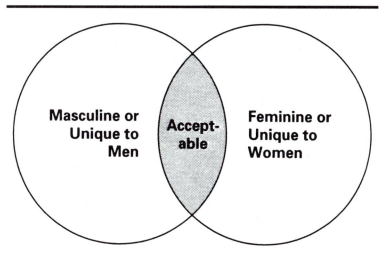

ments for both hoops are matched, women have to exhibit seemingly contradictory behaviors at the same time. They must pass through the overlapping portion of each pair of hoops as they are held side by side. Some of the specific narrow band constraints uncovered in the glass ceiling research included the following:

- *Take career risks, but be consistently outstanding.* Be willing to take nontraditional and failure-prone tasks, but don't dare fail in any of those risky ventures.

- *Be tough, but don't be macho.* Women were expected to make tough decisions quickly and be cool under pressure. However, swearing, wise-cracking or closing down plants might be viewed as unacceptable in a woman where it might be tolerated in a man.

- *Be ambitious, but don't expect equal treatment.* The woman manager should be willing to put her career in front of everything else. However, since she is assumed to have moved ahead due to affirmative action, she should not expect to be treated like male managers in compensation, authority, respect, recognition, and so on.

- *Take responsibility, but follow others' advice.* Women are told they are responsible for their own career advancement, but they should be more than willing to take advice offered by their male counterparts.

The narrow bands of acceptable behavior apply frequently to minority employees as well, and many minorities are well aware of the existence of the difficult standards and double standards they may face. Some companies provide "efficacy training" for their minority employees. One of the objectives of efficacy training is to learn the subtle, important and unwritten standards of behavior by which they will be judged. For example, minorities are advised in Cameron's *Minority Executives' Handbook* (2) that to reduce the risks of failure they must manage their corporate image through "the right attitude, the right clothes, the right speech, the right on-time habits, the right prose, the right presentation skills, and the right politics." Obviously a lot of energy can be focused on what should be viewed as peripheral issues. Furthermore, as previously discussed, individuals of all sorts are increasingly reluctant to go through the corporate assimilation/melting pot process.

The effects of the double standards and narrow bands can be reduced by the steps described in dealing with biases in Chapter 2 and Chapter 8. Progress will be more difficult where the setting of the standards and evaluation against the standards are both done by an organization's dominant monocultural group (as discussed later in this chapter).

DON'T LET PERFORMANCE STANDARDS CREATE AN ASSIMILATION TRAP: We have focused on the advantages of having clear standards. However, beware of defining your standards so narrowly that you create a "mold" that will be applied to bring everyone into conformance. Overly rigid standards can lead to a "crony" system that is antithetical to managing diversity. A contrast of crony standards and diversity supportive standards is summarized in Table 7.3.

The tendency for people to prefer working with people like themselves has been well documented through self identification. In addition there are those who would prefer working with their like kind, but are reluctant to admit it, even

TABLE 7.3 Advancement Criteria Under Crony vs. Diversity Approaches

Crony Standards*	Diversity Supportive Standards
1. Comfort	1. Contribution to results
2. Tradition	2. Creating a new vision
3. Homogeneity	3. Differential input
4. Evaluated as part of a group	4. Evaluated as an individual
5. Looks like me	5. Looks like himself/herself
6. Has experiences (work, education) similar to mine	6. Has some similar, but some very different exposures
7. Comfortably predictable	7. Generate electricity by introducing new approaches.

*Also known as GOBNET standards (Good Old Boy Network)

to themselves. Therefore it will be necessary to surface the issue and clarify that the GOBNET, "buddy system" and cronyism have not been effective in the past, and that those approaches will not even be an option in the future.

Issue: Missing or Weak Systems, Ineffective Communication: In some organizations some of the important CMS are missing entirely, or if in existence, are frequently bypassed in actual operation. Even where systems are in place, they may not apply to certain groups (for example, office and clerical employees), or may not be readily accessible by employees in a function that is not highly valued by the organization. Also the secrecy surrounding some programs and the basis for decisions may lead employees to view them as "closed systems," the secrets of which are available only to the chosen few.

Most of the systems listed earlier in this chapter are found in large sophisticated organizations. However, even among large companies there are wide variations in the breadth and quality of programs. For example, one Fortune 200 company has a culture that eschews organization charts, job descriptions, salary ranges, succession planning and other accoutrements of "modern" human resources management. The stated rationale for the absence of formal systems is that informality enables them to be flexible and treat people based on results rather than guidelines. Since the company [by financial measures] is highly successful, it is tempting to surrender the field of debate.

However, the particular organization described above also recognizes that it has a **very low** utilization of females and minorities at any management level in the company. The company culture and resulting informal "systems" have not worked well for all employees, and simply gearing up an affirmative action recruiting program is unlikely to bring lasting progress.

EXCLUSION AND THE COMFORT FACTOR UNDER INFORMAL SYSTEMS: The company described above is not necessarily an exception. Informal systems, such as mentoring or sponsorship activities, tend to work better for the dominant group in the culture. Women, gay/lesbian, minorities and others who are seen as "different" from the dominant group usually will lack "friends in high places" to informally guide them and advance their careers. The condition is not necessarily purposeful or insidious, but the simple reality of dealing with those with whom we feel most comfortable. The phenomenon is recognized by some as being, to some degree, inevitable, as captured in the words of an African American Female focus group participant:

"Look at two comparable people; one has nothing in common with you and happens to be black, the other is white like you. Who do you think you're going to feel more comfortable with? I don't necessarily think they're racist for feeling that way—it's human nature. They're gonna pick the person they feel more comfortable with."

Individuals are frequently aware of the missing CMS elements and the potential impact on their opportunities to develop and advance. They may not be able to articulate the specifics of a needed program, but they can certainly identify the general area of need:

White Male:
"My feeling is that having a mentor or sponsor could help a lot here. But managers don't want to take it on themselves to do that. They probably don't want to put their name on someone who might fail and reflect unfavorably on their judgment. It could do a lot of good, but until managers get courage, no real mentoring will take place."

African American Male:
"Nobody is developed in this company—even white males. So where does that leave us? The difference is, if you are a white male, you can rise without development, but we don't have a chance in hell of doing the same thing."

INAPPROPRIATE APPLICATION OF SYSTEMS: Even where well-designed systems exist, they do not necessarily operate in the manner in which they were designed due to the culture, lack of commitment and shortcuts taken by managers under pressure.

White Female:
"Job postings are a joke. The jobs are usually already filled, but the manager has to post it, just as a formality. If they have selected John Smith, they will write the description to exactly fit him."

Asian American Female:
"A white female may get a mentor as an exception, but I know of no instance where any Asian has had that benefit."

White Male:
"The Anonymous Company has this thing about hiring from the outside, even if there is talent right here. I think there is a bias against internal movement, a cultural issue. If you are good, your manager wants to keep you, so he doesn't want to see you promoted out of his area. You are stuck no matter what."

White Female:
"The promotional criteria are vague. There are no specific guidelines. If you were to ask five different people, you would get five different answers."

Hispanic Female:
"Sure we have a succession planning program that looks good on paper. But all you have to do is look around you to see that all the good jobs go to white males from Ivy League schools."

INEFFECTIVE COMMUNICATION OF EXISTING PROGRAMS AND PROCESSES: Another issue I have observed in some studies of companies which had development programs was that employees often did not have a good understanding of the existence of the programs, their intent, or both. For example, it is quite common to find half the employee population saying that they do not have sufficient information to make informed career management decisions, and/or they are not kept informed of available job openings for which they might apply. When confronted with this data, the human resources department may point out that two years ago they sent a memo to managers at a certain level describing this or that program. However, the information may not have gotten to all parties who have a legitimate interest in the information. Even if they did see it some months or years ago, it may not have been relevant to them at the time. Career desires and expectations change. The numerous programs are not usually brought together in a comprehensive and coordinated way, so that employees understand the purpose of each program element and the inter-relationships among the various programs.

Our reference has been primarily about larger organizations, i.e., having several or many thousand employees. In smaller organizations, the processes tend to be somewhat more informal, and the responsibility for the activity is not even clearly assigned.

Actions to Correct for Missing, Ineffective or Poorly Communicated CMS: In our research, people in the organization who are different voice skepticism about programs that are based on "unwritten rules." You may improve both the reality and perception of effective programming with some basic steps.

IDENTIFY GAPS IN YOUR CURRENT ARRAY OF CMS: Don't just look for the obvious—a missing system—but also evaluate how well the current CMS are meeting the needs of all your employees. Look for any groups that seem to be disproportionately sidetracked through application of the systems. The audit format found in Exhibit 7.4 on page 133 at the end of the chapter can be used to determine what you have and how well it is working. Remember that the acid test of the system in the eyes of people of color and women is "What are the results?"

DON'T SELL ANY GROUPS OF EMPLOYEES SHORT: Do not assume that nonexempt employees, employees over age 40, employees from the poorly regarded _____ department either lack capacity for, or interest in, career development and advancement. Certainly you may want to allow people to opt out of development activities at their own volition. Not all wish to strive for the top and be considered for transfers, or they recognize and accept characteristics which have limited their careers. However, to exclude individuals based on a group characteristic or stereotype, will send a clear, powerful and enduring message, and will result in under-utilizing a portion of the available talent pool. In many cases it would be illegal as well.

FIX OR DEVELOP THE SYSTEMS SO THAT THEY WORK NATURALLY FOR ALL EM-PLOYEES: Try to avoid the urge to tack on a set of programs designed solely for a particular group. An example would be a mentoring program or fast track program that applied only to minorities. The danger here is that the system will be viewed as affirmative action under the guise of diversity. Participants in highly targeted programs will be labeled as affirmative action beneficiaries and the whole effort will meet with a predictable level of white backlash.

Let's look at three examples of sincerely motivated diversity development efforts that did not have the intended impact because they were viewed as contrived and counter to the realities of the organization.

▪ Mentoring Example

A major processor of natural resources was concerned about the advancement of its minority employees. Senior management decided that it should create a mentoring program available to recently hired minority professionals. Senior officers and vice presidents were to serve as mentors, demonstrating the company's commitment to improving its diversity performance. In one instance an African American engineer recently hired at one of the plants was assigned for mentoring to a senior officer located at the corporate headquarters in another part of the country. This arrangement ignored some fundamental realities:

> There were about six management layers between the engineer and his mentor. The plant manager (who was three levels above the engineer) mused that with all of his responsibility, he rarely had an opportunity to interact with officers at the level provided to the young engineer.

> The differences in age, race, organization level and location made it difficult for the senior officer to provide practical and situation-specific guidance for the engineer, where the engineer was now in his career.

> Minority key managers who had been around for a number of years wondered why they were excluded from a program now, that clearly was not available to them earlier in their careers.

Mentoring programs can be a useful tool in the arsenal. However, as in any intervention strategy, care must be taken to avoid the pitfalls that have befallen some programs. (3)

▪ Interaction Examples

The CEO was anxious to do something to demonstrate his concern about diversity issues. Someone pointed out that, although he frequently took male middle managers to "get-acquainted lunches," he did not offer many invitations to the female managers at similar levels.

The CEO recognized the validity of the observation and was embarrassed by his oversight. Shortly thereafter he had his secretary schedule a half dozen lunches with female managers. The grapevine soon was operating, and the CEO's almost panicky zeal to bulldoze through a series of encounters led to many amused comments among the female participants, and they expressed doubts about the longevity of his interest in their development. It was simply out of character and too contrived.

In another example of interaction issues, a CEO, impatient with his human resources officer for the slow progress in developing a diversity program, decided to initiate a series of breakfast meetings with small groups of minority employees. He wanted to demonstrate his interest in diversity and reinforce the notion that he had an open door policy. However, the president had a reputation throughout the company of being brusque and impatient in meetings. Therefore, the minority employees kept their comments at a rather general and overly positive vein, for fear of being labeled as troublemakers, or having their boss "nailed" by the CEO as a result of their comments. After a few meetings, the president discontinued the program, saying it was a waste of his time.

Selection of the above examples is not to discourage specific activities addressed to the particular needs of one group or another. The key is that the activity should seem natural within the environment and be perceived as helpful by those for whom it is intended.

MAKE RELEVANT, EXTERNAL GUIDANCE AVAILABLE: In contrast to the examples immediately preceding, there are some practical, targeted activities that can be directly beneficial to women and people of color. There is an increasingly large body of research and publications dealing with issues and providing guidance that may be helpful to members of a particular group. Table 7.4 summarizes a study of black executives in major companies and findings regarding the key success factors.

There have also been numerous studies of the factors which impede or enhance the opportunities for females to advance in organizations. For example, in *Breaking the Glass Ceiling* (5), the research led to a description of six success factors that are helpful to the success of females. These factors include:

1. *Learn the ropes.* Understand the culture and unwritten rules necessary to survival.

2. *Take control of your career.* Don't wait for someone to take responsibility for your advancement. Anticipate resistance from peers, the organization, your family.

3. *Build confidence.* Be willing to take fair credit for your successes; convey your sense of self confidence to others.

4. *Rely on others.* Link yourself to people in the organization who can help

TABLE 7.4 Research Findings on Black Executives' Key Success Factors(4)

a. *Communication Skills*:

Articulate, clear and concise especially in the context of creative problem solving.

Why Important

In a less-than-supportive environment, need multilevel skills including oral skills, body language and ability to decipher unspoken meanings. Useful for bridging cultural gaps, overcoming racial obstacles, and gaining acceptance.

b. *Leadership Skills*:

Collaborative styles of leadership, power sharing and inclusion of all levels of corporate participants in making decisions.

Why Important

Unlike white males, blacks cannot be accepted as a leader based on shared culture, coercion, corporate political power, or other common forms of leadership seen as too "pushy" or aggressive.

c. *Interpersonal Skills*: communicated sense of self esteem, respect for others, patience and understanding, ability to make others comfortable with you.

Why Important

Overcome the natural barriers to someone who is "different," and recognize that much has to be accomplished through the efforts of others, over whom you do not have any formal organizational authority.

Note: Other key factors in predicting success as described in the report include hard work and ambition, understanding of the organization environment, strong personal values and ethics.

---

you get things done, get recognition for your work, to get good assignments, learn how the system works.

5. *Go for the bottom line.* Accept accountability for results; be tough minded in the pursuit of the objectives against which you will be measured.

6. *Integrate life and work.* Develop the balance that meets your needs and the needs of the organization; have backup systems during periods of overload.

Again, these guidelines are just examples of the kinds of information and training that are relevant to the needs of certain groups of employees at various points in their careers. They can readily be made available to employees and don't require large expenditures. The information can be useful, relevant and low key.

CHECK YOUR SYSTEMS FOR INAPPROPRIATE APPLICATION OR INSUFFICIENT COVERAGE OF ANY GROUP: Do your recruiting processes screen out disproportionate numbers of those who don't look like the dominant group? Are training opportunities well publicized and provided to a broad cross section of employees? For those who have an interest in an in-depth evaluation of their CMS, the audit guide at the end of the chapter (Exhibit 7.4) provides a format that can be used to work your way through the process of critically examining what is now in place (formally and informally) and the extent to which the systems are working for all employees.

INVEST IN COMMUNICATING DEVELOPMENT PROGRAMS IN PROPORTION TO THEIR VALUE TO INDIVIDUALS AND THE ORGANIZATION: Here is a simple exercise for you. First, pull together the information (booklets, letters, instructions, etc.) that relate to the various employee benefits that the company provides to its employees. Second, go through the same exercise for the career mobility systems of the organization. Now how the two types of information compare, along the dimensions of: a. Quantity of information; b. Quality of the materials; c. frequency of communication; d. numbers of employees reached, and so forth. Too often the information on advancement and development is a dog-eared and dated collection of woefully inadequate program descriptions. Communication in this area is all too often an afterthought.

Sometimes the reactions of development systems managers is that "We just covered that last year"; "Everybody knows how the system works"; "We are always here to answer their questions"; and so on. They just don't get it! Not only is more and better information needed, it must address the real questions on people's minds. If you want to improve the understanding, effectiveness and impact of your CMS, utilize the input of a diverse employee group. No matter what your position, your training, your diversity profile, there is no way to imagine the kinds of concerns employees will have.

Issue: Insufficient or Ineffective Performance Feedback: Corrective and developmental performance feedback may be withheld, understated or insufficiently specific to serve as a guide for change. The risk of ineffective communication is greater when the performance conversations involve individuals with significant cultural differences.

I believe that the adaptation of performance management systems should be one of the top priorities in a managing diversity change process, for the following reasons:

- Employees feel that valid and fair performance measures are quite important, but many also feel that in their current work place, their systems don't meet that need. In an American Productivity Center survey, the gap between performance appraisal importance and satisfaction was among the highest for any category of programs.

- There is a persistent pattern for older employees, females, and people of color to receive lower than average ratings. There is evidence to suggest that the disparity in results is an inherent limitation of single rater employee evaluation programs. Single evaluator programs are particularly susceptible to some of the biases that we have discussed earlier. For example, in one study it was determined that females tended to get lower than average ratings if they comprised 20% or less of their work group. However, when females comprised 50% or more of the group, females tended to get higher ratings. (6) From my point of view the "tyranny of the majority" is not a desirable condition, no matter whose majority it is.

- Performance appraisal is a "multiplier program." The most current evaluation may affect salary and bonus awards, eligibility for promotion or high potential lists. An inappropriate evaluation may carry over for a period of several years.

- Managers routinely express discomfort associated with providing performance feedback, especially if the feedback is negative. The discomfort occurs even when the communication is between individuals having similar diversity characteristics. So it is easy to see why the reluctance grows when the communication spans significant differences between the boss and subordinate. The reluctance may stem from a number of reasons:

    The individual may anticipate hostility in areas of potentially heightened sensitivity. Examples include a manager providing critique to someone 20 years his/her senior, a Hispanic female manager criticizing an Anglo male subordinate.

    There may be fear of an EEO complaint, or "getting in trouble with Personnel" if negative feedback is provided.

    The boss may be reluctant to record information that will discourage the employee or hurt the subordinate's future career opportunities.

Whatever the underlying rationale, the result of incomplete or ineffective appraisal feedback is to put non-majority employees at a further disadvantage. While females and minorities and others who are different may be more frequently shortchanged on developmental performance feedback, it is not unique to them.

African American Male:

"*Everyone feels that the performance appraisal process is a travesty. It just affects African-Americans more, because the appraisals are the only tangible means for advancement in money and position, whereas white employees have other avenues.*"

Hispanic Male:

"*Our formal appraisals only tell what we already know and it is too late to correct if not told informally before. We rarely get informal feedback, and I'm not comfortable asking for it, because you might be viewed as pushy or negative.*"

White Male:

"*For the last three years my annual performance appraisal discussion with my boss took an average of five minutes. [laughter] I swear I am not joking! You can appreciate how much developmental feedback I have been getting.*"

White Male:
"I had a very pleasant lunch with my boss, talking about a number of general issues in the department. As we left, he handed me the performance appraisal he had completed. I didn't realize that we had been having a performance review discussion at lunch, or I would have raised some issues of my own. Furthermore, the oral feedback did not match the negative comments on the written appraisal."

Actions for Fair and Effective Performance Appraisal: Providing fair and helpful appraisal feedback is a fundamental management responsibility. The suggestions below describe two basic approaches to address the challenges.

IMPLEMENT A MULTI-SOURCE PERFORMANCE SYSTEM TO SUPPLEMENT SUPERVISOR-ONLY EVALUATIONS: The supervisor-only evaluation system was probably not a good idea even when the workforce was not diverse. If you are prepared to commit to effective management of today's workforce, you will soon conclude that the supervisor-only model for evaluations is a weakness that companies can no longer afford. Let's begin with a description of a multi-source system, which also may be referred to as team evaluations, and 360 degree performance reviews. After familiarizing yourself with the concept described in Table 7.5, examine some of the potential benefits that may be associated with multi-source approaches.

Multi-source evaluation systems are a fairly recent phenomenon. However, where such rater systems have been used, there have been some documented improvements in the distribution of ratings compared with supervisor-only systems (7,8) that include the following:

REDUCED BIAS/PERCEPTION OF BIAS IN RATINGS
- Instead of performance ratings declining with age as typically happens, the ratings tended to increase slightly with age under the multi-source system.
- Instead of ethnic minorities receiving lower ratings as was occurring under supervisor-only evaluations, analysis of multi-source ratings showed no significant differences across ethnic groups.
- Performance ratings for females went from below average under supervisor-only evaluations to slightly above average on key dimensions of performance.
- Since the individual being evaluated selects the raters, it is difficult to rationalize away the results of the process.

EMPLOYEE ENDORSEMENT: In interviewing participants who had been through both single and multi-source systems, 80% preferred the multi-source system. Furthermore, in upward evaluations, 93% of subordinates say they wished to give input into the evaluation process, and 86% of supervisors stated a desire for subordinate input on leadership behaviors.

TABLE 7.5 Description of the 360 Degree Feedback Process

Objectives

- To improve the accuracy and utility of performance feedback by incorporating assessment information from the supervisor, work associates, direct reports, internal and external customers.
- To get a 360-degree view of the individual whose performance is being evaluated.

Methodology

Input may be provided in four ways, or in combinations:

- Traditional paper forms
- Scan forms—fill in bubbles on customized survey form
- Floppy disks to avoid paper work
- Electronic mail

The software provides the multiple assessments in a summary report for the individual being rated and his/her boss.

Feedback Process Key Steps:

1. Select and define feedback criteria and questions
   - Involve appropriate people
   - Identify and define critical individual or team behaviors

2. Select evaluation team
   - Raters have knowledge about the assessment target
   - Assured of confidentiality of input

3. Conduct survey
   - Train raters on project content and processes
   - Design, produce and distribute survey in the medium chosen [e.g., paper scan forms, disk]

4. Create reports
   - Rankings/profiles
   - Importance of activities weighted
   - Performance comments summarized

5. Analyze reports
   - Identify strengths and weaknesses
   - Identify target improvement areas

6. Intervention programs to improve targeted behavior
   - Communications among appropriate people
   - Select best possible interventions
   - Action planning and follow-up

Reprinted with permission from TEAMS, Tempe, Arizona.

OPERATIONAL BENEFITS

- The multi-source appraisal can be constructed to focus on validated competencies that are important to the job and the individual, linking the individual into the overall strategic objectives of the organization.
- Involvement of internal customers in the evaluation can be used to reinforce total quality or customer service initiatives.
- Re-positioning the supervisor from the role of judge to that of a coach permits early correction of performance deficiencies that impede total organization results.

IMPLEMENTING AN IMPROVED EVALUATION PROCESS: If the potential advantages of multi-source evaluations are so great, why isn't everyone already doing it? Tom Pawlak, who heads the Towers Perrin activity in this area, points out that there is a natural continuum along which companies may develop their performance management. He identifies three phases of the continuum as an organization moves from an administratively driven top-down process (*traditional appraisals*) to a strategically driven, multi-source process (*performance leadership*) as shown in Table 7.6.

Like any number of activities discussed, the benefits of improved performance management are not just limited to the diversity impact. Sound and innovative human resources practices can serve to benefit *all employees* as well as the organization.

TRAIN MANAGERS IN THE CULTURAL IMPLICATIONS OF PERFORMANCE FEEDBACK: The need is very basic: to improve the quality and consistency of feedback and to help the individual convert the feedback into a personal plan for improvement.

TABLE 7.6 The Performance Continuum: From Performance Appraisal to Performance Leadership

Factor	Performance Appraisal	Performance Management	Performance Leadership
Focus	Individual	Job	Link to business strategy
Supervisory Role	"The cop"	"The judge"	"The coach"
Communication Flow	One-way	Two way	Omni-directional
Driver	Supervisor Driven	Supervisor/Employee	Customer-Driven
Rationale	Administrative/Legal	Communicative/ Administrative	Developmental/ Communicative

This does not mean just training white managers to give feedback to females and minorities. It also includes helping females and minorities feel comfortable in dealing with the white males that they may be supervising as their careers progress and to recognize the biases they bring to the situation.

In recent years the amount of information regarding the understanding of the impact of cultural norms on appraisal processes continues to grow. For example, Gardenswartz and Rowe (9) provide a summary of how different cultural values can impact the expectations, and therefore the approach to be used, with "mainstream" culture employees, as compared with other employees. The differences start with the expectations for the process. Mainstream culture employees will see feedback as necessary for their growth, and the more direct the feedback the better. They have no difficulty separating their job performance from their perception of self worth. In other cultures, criticism may lead to feelings of personal disgrace. Criticism is taken personally, and viewed as an attack on them as an individual. Some of the specific cultural issues that may come up during the appraisal process are summarized in Table 7.7.

Perhaps the last thing you want to do is make your job more complicated by adding more things that you need to know how to do before you actually do it. However, just think of the situation as though you were learning to ski. You can rush out to the slopes and figure it out the hard way, just go barreling down the hillside. That may be exhilarating, but the more productive and safer way is to understand the basics before you make your first run.

Issue: Lack of Diverse Input into Career Mobility Systems: There may be a lack of diversity among the designers and controllers of the CMS. Those not in the mainstream may wonder if they can get a "fair shake" from people who are not like themselves.

As we have said repeatedly, all the criticisms of your CMS are not necessarily valid. Because individuals have personally been victimized by prejudice or have seen it happen to others, there will be a heightened sensitivity to actions and programs which seem to have a disproportionately negative effect on one's in-group. The credibility of the program will more often be in doubt if the rule makers and the rule administrators are monocultural. In several diversity research projects the human resources department was singled out for criticism for its lack of diversity. Employees felt that if HR itself had not made a commitment from a diverse workforce, perhaps it could not be trusted to be balanced in the administration of the appraisal process.

Aside from the credibility issue, companies can benefit from the richness that may flow from diverse input into CMS processes and decisions.

Actions to Include More Diverse Input: Until such time as you have established diversity throughout the corporate pyramid, you might consider some other steps to improve process validity and acceptance.

TABLE 7.7 Impact of Diversity-Related Variables on Performance Appraisals

Cultural Factors	Factor Impact on Appraisals	Possible Behavior
Avoiding loss of face	Anxiety, reluctance to accept or discuss any criticism	Smiling, laughter to disguise embarrassment. Delaying, stalling.
Respect for authority	Unwillingness to question the review or disagree with evaluator's assessment.	Lack of eye contact, reluctance to enter into dialogue with boss.
Emphasis on relationship rather than on the task	Relationship with boss, seniority and group status seen as more important than the details of the task.	Ingratiating comments, bewilderment
Emphasis on group over individual	Difficulty in separating performance from that of team. May feel disloyal to team for taking credit for successes.	Signs of discomfort, smiling, clamming up, minimization of their specific contribution.
Lack of common experiences	May feel misunderstood or unfairly judged if evaluator has not faced similar obstacles, [e.g., older worker, single parent, English second language]	Sulking silence or defensiveness.
Victim of previous perceived discrimination	Mistrustful and skeptical of the reviewer's objectivity.	Lack of participation, sarcasm.

Reprinted with permission from Lee Gardenswartz & Anita Rowe, Managing Diversity, *p. 198, Business One Irwin, Homewood, IL, 1993*

FORCE SOME DIVERSE INPUT INTO THE SYSTEM: If you have a succession planning process that ends up looking monocultural at the upper levels, dip down to include diverse input even though the individuals might not normally be included. For example, adding a minority director to a group of VP's doing evaluations may enhance the perspectives of the group as well as provide a very useful development experience for the ad hoc participant.

PROVIDE FOR "VIRTUALLY DIVERSE" INPUT: Some companies will not be comfortable using the preceding approach in succession planning processes; it is just too different. One company tried to get some semblance of the value of diversity by asking its white male director of development to observe the meetings in which the performance and advancement potential of managers was reviewed each year. In his observations he focused on differences in the way that commentary varied, based on the ethnic or gender groups of the individuals being discussed. The Director of Development observed and pointed out that when the evaluators were discussing other white males, the individual's potential for advancement was the focus rather than his shortcomings. However, conversations about people of color and women tended to focus more on their current deficiencies which were barriers to their advancement, with relatively less focus on their potential for moving upward. This detached perspective of the observer enabled the evaluating group to recognize an inadvertent behavior pattern and the knowledge enabled them to monitor themselves for evenhanded discussions.

Issue: Narrow Definitions of Diversity Limit Improvement: The examples and case studies in this and in other diversity books and studies tend to focus on race and gender issues. This is where most companies are feeling the pain, and where the research is most readily available. However, you should not get trapped into limiting all your thinking and planning along race and gender lines.

In some work done in a major chemical company, the development staff noted the productivity of boss–subordinate relationships was heavily affected by the decision making approaches that the individuals used. A manager (of any race or gender) could have a series of successful assignments under different managers. Then he or she is assigned to Manager X, and for no apparent reason hits a brick wall career-wise.

Having too frequently observed the phenomenon described above, the company began using a management style assessment tool to test for potential style compatibility. The questionnaire collects data on individual preferences for operating in areas of data collection, analysis, decision making and presentation of findings. After the boss and subordinate go through the style self identification, they are given training which helps them better understand his or her own style, how it differs from the boss's style, and how the two might better work together.

Self evaluation instruments serve a useful and legitimate analytical objective and can be used to enhance the productivity of a working relationship. Furthermore the use of such instruments underscores the fact that the appreciation and management of differences often have nothing to do with race, gender, nationality and other primary diversity dimensions. The white male manager trained as an engineer may well have some difficulty working with a white male subordinate who happens to have a liberal arts education. However, the minority female engineer he supervises presents no problem because they are more alike in their approach to the job. The obvious diversity dimensions of race and gender do not get in the way of the working relationship.

SUMMARY

The establishment and effective management of a diverse work force in all levels of the organization is a process that may take years of diligent effort. Progress will require challenges to some of the basic assumptions of the characteristics that are valued in the organization. The basic human resource systems also must be challenged, upgraded or restructured so that they will work for a diverse group as well as they have for white males. The Career Mobility Systems are among the more critical of those that you should examine, challenge and improve.

IMPORTANT POINTS TO REMEMBER

1. Establish development as a company commitment and hold managers accountable for results. Recognize successes and failures appropriately.

2. Recognize the potential for bias in the operation of career mobility systems. Be specific on job requirements so all can be measured against the same yardstick. Provide employees information to help understand the issues of a specific group and how to deal with them.

3. Introduce formal programs to better respond to the needs of all employees. Where programs now exist, assess their effectiveness in meeting the needs of all employees.

4. Improve performance feedback by introducing multi-source evaluation systems, and training employees on the effects of cultural differences in evaluations.

5. Provide for diverse input into the operation of career mobility systems.

6. Don't get trapped into viewing diversity issues as simply related to race, gender and other primary diversity dimensions. Consider leadership and decision making styles, communication and problem solving approaches.

EXHIBIT 7.4 Audit of the Diversity Implications of Anonymous Company Career Mobility Systems

---

TABLE OF CONTENTS
INTRODUCTION

INTRODUCTION
AUDIT OF CAREER MOBILITY SYSTEMS DIVERSITY EFFECTIVENESS

Career mobility systems are those programs which bring people into the organization and determine the rate and ultimate level of their career progress, and the paths utilized en route to their ultimate destination within the corporate hierarchy. In some cases the programs may not be formalized, but operating nevertheless. For example, in one limited employee survey the company received praise from employees on its mentoring program, but the company does not have a mentoring program in place. In other cases the company may have a formal system in place but the system may be bypassed in actual practice. For example, focus group comments may suggest employees perceive the "Good Old Boy Network" or crony system as principal means of advancement, despite the fact that an elaborate succession planning process was instituted several years ago.

The principal systems to be discussed are listed and described on the following pages. To ensure a balanced and comprehensive review, the evaluation team will be meeting with a range of individuals that view the systems from different perspectives. The interviews will be conducted among members of the following groups:

- *System Keepers*: Those who design, control and seek to maintain the integrity of the systems. Typically the system keepers are in human resources.
- *System Users*: Those key managers who rely upon the systems to provide the talent necessary to meet their organizational objectives.
- *System Participants:* Employees who have been on board long enough to have a clear impression of how the systems work. Should include fast track and slow progress employees at various levels, as well as incorporating the more obvious aspects of diversity.

The general questions following will probably be among those addressed for the first two of the above groups, plus some additional specifics relevant to each department and division.

I. PLANNING FOR STAFFING

This activity involves the correlation of key elements of the company's strategic plan [e.g. growth rates, geographical expansion, structure] which should have an impact on the types and numbers of people who are hired. Sample queries:

1. Are senior human resources managers involved in developing significant plans and changes of direction in corporate strategies that might affect the

number and type of employees required? If not, what sources of data should they seek out?

_____

_____

_____

2. Is HR input sought on issues regarding the availability of necessary talent before the annual operating plans are locked in place? If so, does the HR input find its way into plans, or result in modifying the original plan?

_____

_____

3. What kinds of data are available for planning staffing?

_____

_____

4. Are affirmative action goals linked to overall staffing projections in the planning process?

_____

5. Is there a clear identification of employees who are surplus or who may become surplus? Are efforts made to link their availability to the overall staffing needs of the organization, or does each operating unit handle its needs autonomously?

_____

_____

II. RECRUITMENT AND SELECTION

This activity involves the actual process of going out to find people to fill jobs and the procedures used in deciding which of those people to hire. The standards for hiring for various positions are also an important part of this review.

Internal Recruitment

1. Is there a readily accessible data bank containing the information on individuals from within the organization who may be candidates for openings? Does the data include:
   - Skills and education
   - Experience with current/previous employers
   - Performance information
   - Personal career objectives

2. Can the internal talent data system provide 24-hour turnaround on the availability of candidates for openings?

_____

_____

3. What approvals are required before passing over internal candidates and starting an external recruitment process?

_____

External Recruitment

1. Is there a comprehensive description developed which identifies the key requirements of the position, and the skills and experiences necessary to master it?

_____

_____

2. Are there clear guidelines as to which positions will be filled by:
   - Internal recruitment staff _____
   - Contingency search firms _____
   - Retainer Executive Search Firms _____
   - Target opportunity search/employment firms (For example, specialty in a given industry, function or candidate group, i.e., engineers, minorities) _____
   - Are external providers reviewed for their effectiveness in developing diverse candidate lists? _____

3. Where advertising is involved, which media vehicles are most frequently used to advise prospects of the opportunities which the company has available? Do these media reach a diverse target audience?

_____

_____

4. What messages does the recruitment/selection system communicate to future employees about the nature of the organization and its approach to people? (For example, provide a feel for the culture, its opportunities and the company's position on diversity)

_____

_____

5. Do any elements of the program discourage segments of the applicant pool? [For example, pictures, examples used]

_____

_____

6. Which steps are taken to include currently employed females and minorities as full participants in recruiting processes?

_____

_____

III. INDUCTION, SOCIALIZATION AND INITIAL TRAINING

After the employee has been hired, there is a period during which he or she learns the ropes, learns how to get along in the organization, how to work, how to fit in, how to master the particulars of the job, and so on.

1. What role models are used to inform about productive behavior in various parts of the organization?

_____

_____

2. Are any particular steps taken to ensure that non-traditional employees receive adequate guidance?

_____

_____

3. Are individuals assigned sponsors or coaches to help them quickly learn the ropes?

_____

_____

4. Are there subtle or overt suggestions as to how individuals should adapt themselves to the organization? (clothing, decision making, speech, associations to form)

_____

_____

5. Does the employee get a brief "break-in" period, or is the pressure intense from the outset?

_____

_____

6. Are newer employees given prompt and constructive feedback on their behaviors which run against organization norms?

_____

_____

IV. PERFORMANCE APPRAISAL AND COACHING

Performance appraisal seeks to objectively identify the level of the individual's performance in his or her current responsibilities. It may also serve as an opportunity for boss and subordinate to identify the key task and behavioral objectives to be achieved during the coming performance period. It is an extremely important system as it may strongly influence both career and pay progress as well as perceptions of self worth; and may be the only written record of how the company judges the individual.

1. Are there standards for performance for most positions? If so, how are those standards communicated?

   _____

   _____

2. Do ratings and development needs tend to be communicated candidly or guardedly?

   _____

   _____

3. Is there training for managers on how to do appraisals and give feedback? Does the training include cross-cultural communication awareness and skills?

   _____

   _____

4. Are appraisals consistently done on a timely basis and the basis for ratings clearly documented?

   _____

   _____

5. Has analysis been done to determine patterns of ratings variance when comparing white males to non-mainstream employees? When unexplained variations are identified, are actions taken promptly to correct the problem?

   _____

   _____

6. Is performance input solicited on a confidential basis from individuals other than the employee's direct supervisor, such as peer level employees, internal clients, external clients, 360-degree appraisals?

   _____

   _____

7. Is comprehensive and written feedback given at least annually? Is additional feedback provided on a more frequent basis?

_____

_____

V. POTENTIAL APPRAISAL

This activity is aimed at determining how far in the organization that the person might advance and at what pace the advancement might take place. Coupled with other programs, the potential appraisal process can provide the company with an inventory of management talent and assist the individual to shape his or her personal development planning and career expectations.

1. Is there a formal procedure for appraisal and recording of potential for advancement?

_____

_____

2. If appraisals of advancement potential are provided, are they done in conjunction with performance appraisal or at another time? If at the same time, how is spillover prevented?

_____

_____

3. Are there written standards or competencies for the various functions and position levels? If there are standards, are they communicated broadly?

_____

_____

4. Has there been diverse input into the development of existing standards?

_____

_____

5. Is the appraisal of potential documented with specific behavioral or performance evidence?

_____

_____

6. Who receives the information on potential? How is it used in placement and advancement decisions?

_____

_____

7. Are managers trained how to do the appraisal and provide feedback to individuals for future development needs?

_____

_____

8. Are individual development plans generated (with employee involvement) to systematically address development needs and to prepare individuals to achieve their full potential?

_____

_____

9. Are managers held accountable for the development of their subordinates? Are they rewarded for successes and critiqued on their failures?

_____

_____

VI. MENTORING

A mentor relationship exists when a more experienced or higher level employee provides guidance to the newer or lower level employee. The guidance may cover a range of issues beyond basic job responsibilities, such as helping the employee fit in, and navigate through the subtle unwritten rules which may help or impede an individual's progress in the organization. The relationship may be informal and develop naturally as a result of the interest and positions held by the two parties. Mentoring may also be part of a formal program that provides criteria for selection of mentors and mentees, training of mentors, and so forth.

1. Is the program formal or is it an informal practice driven by the initiative of the participants?

_____

_____

2. Who serves as mentors? Do mentors self select or are they chosen?

_____

_____

3. How does an employee get a mentor? Must he or she take the initiative?

_____

_____

4. Is mentoring exclusively or primarily reserved for females, minorities and other disadvantaged groups?

_____

_____

5. Is there a balance of diversity among the mentor group?

_____

_____

6. Is there a company policy, performance standard, or cultural support for managers to assume responsibility for helping others become successful in the organization?

_____

_____

7. Do employees who are not provided mentors understand the basis for inclusion/exclusion in the process?

_____

_____

VII. SUCCESSION PLANNING

Succession planning involves the systematic preparation for management replacement. In formalized systems there may be elaborate records, charts and review meetings to plan for management turnover and to clearly identify those individuals who may be ready for advancement to the vacant position, if and when it becomes available. Typically there would be a series of discussions in which various management tiers are reviewed, and replacement needs and sufficiency of backups explored. Such reviews might start at the top and cascade downward, or may begin at the entry level ranks and culminate in board level review of senior management.

1. Is there a formal program in existence for the primary purpose of planning for management succession and development? If not, how does succession planning happen?

_____

_____

2. Are the criteria for advancement clearly spelled out?

_____

_____

3. Are discussions of potential exclusively centered on performance dimensions, or are management style issues discussed as well? Does one dimension usually dominate advancement decisions?

_____

_____

4. Is there a systematic attempt to include females and minorities on replacement rosters?

_____

_____

5. Is the diversity of the upper management ranks included as part of periodic reviews of talent planning?

_____

_____

6. Are any assumptions made regarding members of a particular group where their advancement is evaluated by assumptions as a group [e.g., working mother's willingness to transfer, previous failures of a given group in certain positions, general managers must come from _____ function, etc.]

_____

_____

VIII. JOB POSTING SYSTEMS

In order to open up career advancement systems, many companies maintain a policy of "posting" planned or current job openings so that internal candidates may "bid" or express their interest in being considered for the open positions. Usually management discretion is reserved to not select from among bidding candidates, should they feel that the bidders do not meet the job specs. Some organizations include only the clerical and entry level exempt jobs under the job posting system.

1. Is a job posting system in place? If so, which levels of jobs are covered? In which parts of the company?

_____

_____

2. Does the rate of applications/hires through the bidding system show any disproportionate representation of members of any given ethnic/gender group?

_____

_____

3. Are unsuccessful bidders given developmental feedback to aid them in enhancing their chances for future opportunities?

_____

_____

4. What do employees who have used the posting system say about their experiences? Do perceptions vary by function/job level or diversity grouping?

_____

_____

5. What do hiring managers who have used the system say about their experiences?

_____

_____

6. What steps are taken to ensure that managers don't bypass the system through various techniques such as:

- Defining job specifications so narrowly that only a pre-selected candidate could fill the needs?
- Getting the word out that, although a job is posted, a given candidate has "a lock on the position"?
- Emphasizing different pluses and minuses of the job depending on the bidder, so that different groups of candidates for the position come away with varying perceptions of its attractiveness?

_____

_____

7. Are jobs posted widely enough, and long enough for interested parties to nominate themselves?

_____

_____

IX. LEADERSHIP TALENT TRACKING

Especially in large corporations, there is a risk that individuals of exceptional promise are overlooked or simply "lost in the system." To assure proper development and exposure to senior management, a list of individuals with significant potential for advancement into leadership positions may be generated. Inclusion on the list usually entails special development efforts tailored to the needs of the individuals.

1. Is there a list for individuals showing high leadership potential? What are the criteria for getting on the list?

   _____

   _____

2. Is there a separate system for females and minorities, or are they included with others in the base system?

   _____

   _____

3. Are detailed development plans prepared for the individuals, with their involvement and the commitment of their supervisors?

   _____

   _____

4. Have results of previous identification efforts been assessed? For example, are they useful predictors of success, or is advancement probability like rolling the dice?

   _____

   _____

X. FORMAL TRAINING AND DEVELOPMENT PROGRAMS

Many companies provide their employees with an exposure to a variety of formal training and development courses. These may include programs formulated and conducted by internal staff, or the programs might be provided by various universities, consulting firms, professional groups, etc. Subject matter could include the following:

1. *Functional skills* (advertising, finance for non-financial managers, personal computer utilization)
2. *General managerial skills* (communications, negotiation skills, giving performance appraisals)
3. *Company programs* (for example, total quality management, affirmative action)

These programs constitute one form of development, and are often the most visible sign of the organization's commitment to development of its human resources.

Another form of development would be the establishment of a planned progression of assignments to prepare individuals to move up through the entry level ranks of the organization. Development through work assignments could include geographic, functional, divisional, field/headquarters and other variations of work experience. There is an underlying assumption that the planning and monitoring process is in place, and that the assignments are not made simply to fill an opening that happens to be available.

1. Does the company have in place a formal training and development program and philosophy?

   _____

   _____

2. How are individuals selected for development or training opportunities?

   _____

   _____

3. Is participation monitored to assure balanced representation of all employee groups in the development processes?

   _____

   _____

4. Have diversity subject modules been incorporated into the ongoing management training programs?

   _____

   _____

5. Are development opportunities publicized, so that individuals may self-nominate for programs, events, assignments?

   _____

   _____

6. Is the development system monitored to ascertain that all individuals have the opportunity to participate in the appropriate programs at the right time in their careers?

   _____

   _____

7. Has senior management made clear their support of the development program and processes? Do they hold managers accountable for development of their subordinates?

   _____

   _____

Create Awareness and Motivate Behavior Change Through Diversity Training

8

The point has been made several times that many of our attitudes toward others are developed very early in life. Is there any hope of reversing or neutralizing some of the attitudes that have been part of us for so long, and that have been reinforced by associates, the media, and our experiences? I fervently hope the answer is yes, because one of the most frequently utilized tools in a diversity change process is education or training. The percentage of companies using diversity training ranges up to 63%. (1,2) The demand pull for training has spawned a cadre of diversity training providers, using a wide variety of techniques with even more widely varying degrees of effectiveness. Unfortunately diversity training has become controversial in some quarters, either because of its cost, unanticipated side effects or doubts about its long term effectiveness. In this chapter you will find both strategic and tactical guidelines to prepare you for the following activities:

- Define the strategic objectives that may cause you to include or discard diversity training as a change element.
- Understand potential subject matter of the typical diversity training programs, and a sampling of the techniques used.
- Review the issues in the debate about efficacy and ethics of diversity training.

• Identify safeguards which should be incorporated into your planning process to develop and execute diversity training for maximum positive impact.

This chapter alone will not prepare you to lead a training session. However, it will prepare you to develop and evaluate diversity training strategies and programs.

WHY TRAINING IS FREQUENTLY A KEY ELEMENT IN A DIVERSITY CHANGE PROCESS

There are four reasons why organizations include training as a key element in a diversity change process.

1. Employees Identify the Need for Diversity Training: A frequent outcome of diversity research is a widely expressed need on the part of employees for a better understanding of diversity issues and a familiarity with means to deal with those issues in the work setting. Typically 75% of the focus groups comprised of women and/or people of color cite the need for awareness training, providing numerous examples of what they considered rude or insensitive behavior or discriminatory treatment directed to themselves or persons like themselves. In many cases the targets of the behavior are willing to grant the perpetrator the benefit of a doubt, that is, assume that the problems are due to ignorance or insensitivity on the part of the offending party, rather than being based on a deep-seated animosity toward themselves. Those individuals who feel aggrieved see training as a necessary bridge to a change in awareness and behavior.

Occasionally white male respondents in diversity research will identify some training need, such as how to communicate with the new and different worker. However, as a rule white males are less likely than other groups to come to the conclusion that diversity training is necessary.

2. Training Provides a "Cool" Environment for "Hot" Topics: The mere mention of frictions and misunderstandings that arise from differences can create apprehension in some people. The issues may be deemed too sensitive and laden with underlying emotions. Furthermore, fear that a well-intended comment could lead to a discrimination complaint may discourage employees from plunging right in to deal with differences at the workplace. Establishment of a training venue breaks the "code of silence" on diversity and signals that it is o.k. to put the subject of differences on the table. When done in a structured training environment, led by qualified facilitators, progress can be made without undue risks for the company or any of its employees.

3. Diversity Training Can Provide Efficacy and Efficiency: There is a wide variety of information and skills that need to be absorbed and mastered by participants in a diversity change process. The breadth and the nature of the issues requires a variety of training approaches. Yes, some of the information can be gleaned individually from books and videotapes. However, many aspects are best covered by sharing different experiences or hearing different reactions to the same experiences.

4. *Diversity Training Can Be Used to Motivate Behavior Change:* As we saw from the survey examples earlier in the book, a significant number of people don't acknowledge the existence of diversity issues in their work place, and thus are likely to be unmotivated to change their behavior. An intense personal experience can open them up to the need for behavior change in themselves and others. Success in a structured setting can motivate them to move forward to apply their learnings in the work place.

UNDERSTANDING THE THREE I'S OF DIVERSITY TRAINING

There are dozens of diversity training organizations working in hundreds of companies. So you would not be surprised to learn that the training offerings are, dare I say, quite diverse. In an attempt to provide an overall guide to the many options available and the purposes they serve, I borrow the framework used by Ken Boughrum, Director of Education and Training for Diversity Consultants Inc. (3)

Ken starts with the premise that the role of educational activities is to build awareness and understanding as a foundation for behavior change which will follow. There is more effort given to the awareness and understanding phase in diversity, than typically found in other company training activities, simply because the material usually has not been covered in the participants' previous educational experiences. Training, on the other hand, aims at providing individuals with specific skills that they might apply in the work setting. Within this framework, we can describe the activities colloquially as the "Intellect," "Insights," and the "Implementation" of education and training.

The "Intellect" Component: In this range of activities we are appealing to the intellectual capacity of the participants, simultaneously attempting to build a knowledge base and a sense of urgency for change. Some of the materials covered in this phase include the following:

- Workforce changes that will affect your organization
    - Demographic shifts in the composition of the workforce; age, gender, ethnic, marital status blend.
    - Skills gaps among those entering the workforce that could have strategic implications.

- Values shifts among current and future employees that may affect their choice of occupations and employers, as well as influence their on-the-job behaviors.
- Changes in the business environment
    - Market place impact of demographics, e.g., consumer and customer profiles that are somewhat different from what the organization has experienced in the past.
    - Changes in management approaches, e.g., total quality and team management concepts.
    - Competitive implications that might arise if the organization does not effectively deal with the issues.
- Results of previous efforts at dealing with diversity (for example, turnover cycle, clustering below the glass ceiling, lost productivity).
- Definition of terms and concepts, such as differentiating affirmative action from diversity management in its broader context, describing prejudice versus racism, etc.
- Description of some of the primary and secondary dimensions of diversity, and their importance to our behavior.

The *intellect* training materials provide a framework for action such as developing the business rationale, and assessing what sort of priority to give to diversity efforts in your organization as compared with other competing business needs.

Throughout this chapter are examples of exercises that can be used for each of the three components of diversity education and training. These are intended to describe some specific applications and reinforce your understanding of the approaches and concepts.

Some Examples of "Intellect" Exercises

- *Identifying the Business Rationale* for your organization's diversity efforts; review the assessment exercise at the end of Chapter 3. It will help you sort out potential diversity implications for company success based on eight dimensions. (The Panoply Products Corporation case in Chapter 15 also provides an opportunity to develop a business case for a diversity effort.)
- *Work Group Cohesion*: Managers are introduced to the concept of "process loss." Process loss identifies the variables that cause efficiency to drain away from group problem solving and decision making. Examples may include a collectivist culture (e.g., African American, Hispanic) in conflict with an individualist culture (Anglo American) or age and tenure differences.

Managers learn why it is important to be mindful of the conditions under which process loss can occur. Organizations may bring diversity in, but when they require conformity with the goal of minimizing process loss, they lose out on the unique value that diversity can bring. Participants will also learn how difficult it is to develop group cohesion when dissimilar individuals are unable or unwilling to conform to the organizational values that demand assimilation as a condition of acceptance.

The "Insight" Training Component: The "insight" activity segment is targeted at building awareness and insight among participants. It creates an environment for introspection on your attitudes toward others and raises consciousness on how others may react to those attitudes. The goal is to foster empathy and develop an understanding of cultural differences and how those differences may show themselves in the workplace. Some of the subject matter covered in the "insight" segment includes examples such as the following:

- How an organization creates pressure for non-traditional employees to assimilate to the dominant group's expectations and the effect of those expectations on individuals and the organization.

- Exclusionary behaviors—work patterns, communications or social circles that indicate to individuals that they are not accepted or valued members of the team.

- The traps of stereotyping; how we all fall into those traps, the impact on members of the stereotype target and how we can work around those prejudgments to build effective working relationships.

- Understanding parenting dilemmas, the dynamics of balancing work and family responsibilities and the impact on productivity.

- Recognizing the narrow band of acceptable behavior or double standards.

- Introducing the notion of unearned privileges and unearned abuse in the work place. For example, the white male manager may be assumed to know his field and have strong career aspirations. He, therefore, is nurtured through formal and informal methods. The female manager may be assumed to have gotten her position through affirmative action efforts, just putting in time until she quits to have children, so development and mentoring are held back. The assumption of competence and commitment accorded the white male has not been earned by the individual, nor the abuse earned by the female.

In addressing the issues described above, the training activities occasionally focus on blatant displays of bias or purposefully malicious behavior. These conditions do exist in some organizations. However, with increased sensitivity to legal pitfalls and politically correct behavior, today's problems are more frequently those of the subtle impact of unintended or insensitive actions and comments.

Some Examples of Insight Exercises: For a refresher, review exercises previously described including the following:

- Develop understanding of how early experiences helped develop our attitudes toward members of other ethnic and gender groups (Tracing Our Cultural Roots, Chapter 2).

- Understand how conscious and subconscious attitudes shape your behavior and how others react to it ("The Johari Window," Chapter 2)

- How to surface stereotypes we hold about people with whom we work who are different from us, and activities that we may use to minimize the effects of the attitudes on developing effective working relationships. ("Great Expectations" exercise, Chapter 2)

In addition to those referred to, two additional Insight exercises are provided.

EXERCISE 8.1 Diversity Associations Exercise

Objective
To heighten awareness of the perceived impact of individual diversity dimensions on the development and outlook of the individual.

Exercise Set Up
Pages from an easel pad are taped on walls around the room. At the top of each page will be a short diversity descriptor, e.g.

- White male   - Education   - Age
- Black   - Family   - Female

The number and selection of dimensions would be adjusted to fit the characteristics of the group.

Working the Exercise
Each person is to look at the terms at the top of the sheets posted around the room and determine the three most important influences on who they are, what they think and how they have conducted their lives. The participants are asked to gather around the sign that represents the third most important influence. Those gathered there share with one another why they feel that particular factor has been important. For example, those gathered under the age sign might represent the extremes of the group. Older employees might talk about their sense of time running out on their careers, being overlooked or having a sense of satisfaction from having contributed to the success of the organization. Younger employees might express frustration with their contributions being discounted for lack of experience and with the resistance to change in the organization.
The cycle is repeated a second time, and then the third time everyone should be at the sign representing the most important influence on their lives.

Possible Learning
Generally the third round will find women and people of color clustered around the sign that describes their particular group (for example, Asian-American). The ethnic-based identification is made because they see it as a key part of their own personality but also as the source of being differently viewed and treated in their organization. On the other hand, white males will rarely think to select the white male sign as the principal influence on their development. Their position, status and advancement opportunities are assumed to be earned solely on the merits of their performance.

The discussions ensuing from Exercise 8.1 will enhance understanding of how one dimension may have a similar impact on one group of individuals, and a very different impact on others. For example, a discussion under the Family banner might cover the impact of child or elder care responsibilities, and unwillingness to transfer and the impact of that on the person's career potential and so forth.

Other exercises help participants understand the dynamics of being "different" within the organization. Exercise 8.2, for example, illustrates how powerful the insiders can be, and how frustrated the outsiders may become.

EXERCISE 8.2 Insider/Outsider Exercise

Objective
Provide individuals with an understanding of the feelings that accompany being excluded from the work and social pattern of a group.

Exercise Set Up
Two members of the group are asked to leave the room. The remaining members are divided into two groups. They are told that the "outsiders" will come back into the room and try to join the groups. The groups are to physically arrange themselves and behave in such a way that makes it difficult for the outsider to become part of their group. The outsiders waiting in the hall are simply told that they are to return to the room and attempt to become participants in the discussions that their group is having.

Working the Exercise
The in-group may arrange themselves in a circle with their backs to the outside. When the outsider comes to try to break into the group they will ignore the intruder, avoid eye contact, refuse to respond to comments that individual makes, etc.

The outsiders may try to physically push their way into the group, and attempt intrusive comments to get the group's attention. The activity is permitted to go on for only five minutes or so, because the frustration can build quickly.

Possible Learnings
The in-group understands how easy it is to make someone feel excluded. They also understand the sense of power that comes with being in control and making the rules of the game. The outsider quickly understands how frustrating it is to be in proximity, but not part of a group. The sense of rejection and being devalued can be acutely realized.

In any of the Insight exercises the value of the experience is usually heightened when there is a diversity of participants to compare their reactions to the situation they have just experienced.

The "Implementation" Training Component: Referring to the diversity change model described in Exhibit 1.1, all of the activities in a diversity process are directed toward influencing changes in the behavior of your organization's employees. The behavior must incorporate some new skills in day-to-day execution of supervisory responsibilities to make managing diversity an operational reality. Skills needed include the following:

- Providing performance feedback and coaching to someone who is not like you, and whose cultural norms result in different reactions to the experience (candor, use of words).
- Developing effective teams comprised of a mixture of ethnicities, genders, age, and culture.
- Resolving and avoiding conflicts that arise from different cultural expectations and use of language.
- Rewarding behaviors in a culturally sensitive way.
- Determining performance standards for advancement that focus on what gets done while minimizing the influence of the individual's characteristics in the evaluation process.
- Organizing people from different backgrounds and different skills to generate creative solutions to the work challenges the group faces.
- Communication sensitivity when the other party has a primary language other than English.

The implementation segment is the key test point for diversity training. If managers are not equipped to behave differently in the work place, then all the preceding education and awareness-raising efforts will have been in vain.

Examples of "Implementation" Exercises: As your diversity process progresses you will try to make diversity an operational reality. Therefore, you will want to find opportunities to incorporate diversity-focused exercises in your ongoing employee/management training. Some examples are described briefly below.

RESOLVING DIVERSITY-RELATED CONFLICTS: Managers brainstorm diversity-related issues from their experiences that have caused conflicts that they felt ill-prepared to resolve. The group reaches consensus on the issues they want to work on. They are introduced to conflict resolution techniques and are provided an opportunity to practice the techniques in a scenario that each participant brings to the table.

ESTABLISHING RAPPORT WITH SOMEONE DIFFERENT FROM YOU: A key to developing a supportive environment for managing diversity is fostering open communications. Managers need to demonstrate by their actions that they support open communications, are personally willing to break the "code of silence" and discuss diversity-related issues. Managers learn how to overcome protective hesitation and engage in meaningful, yet non-intrusive, conversation with their employees and co-workers. Participants will be introduced to some of the key cultural aspects of communication such as language, location, personal space, touching, etc.

STIMULATING CREATIVITY IN A DIVERSE WORK GROUP: Managers participate in exercises to encourage idea generation while avoiding the discounting of input based upon the stereotyped labels that might apply to a given group, or due to their lack of perceived power in the group. Skills at consensus building and drawing out alternative viewpoints are practiced.

TAKING A STAND: To fully support managing diversity commitment, managers need to close any "say/do" gap and align rhetoric with their actions. They are encouraged and have the opportunity to practice challenging counter-productive actions such as racial, ethnic, or sexually derogatory comments, or promotional decisions that perpetuate the status quo.

Create a Balance of Intellect, Insight and Implementation Training Experiences: A total diversity education and training strategy requires a blend of the "intellect, insight and implementation" experiences. The relative emphasis varies according to the way in which the participants will use the information. To illustrate how the blend of training may vary by organization level, Exhibit 8.1 provides a conceptual view of the balance.

The thoughts underlying Exhibit 8.1 are as follows:

Senior Management: The emphasis on the "intellect" activities recognizes that the big task here is to get their rational acceptance of diversity as a legitimate business issue, worthy of the application of the organization's resources. The im-

EXHIBIT 8.1 Training/Education Balance

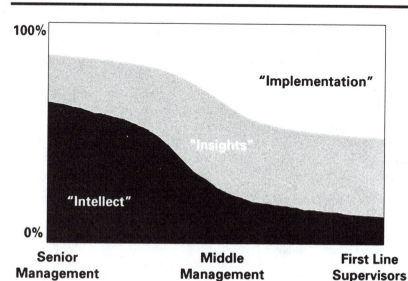

pact of corporate culture on diversity management must also be understood by this group, as well as their own role in defining and perpetuating that culture. Less emphasis would be placed on skill building, since the managers they supervise are not very diverse.

Front Line Supervisor: The front line supervisors are less concerned about cultural roots of the organization, and demographically segmented marketing strategies or other concerns of the executives. They will be interested in how to give performance feedback to persons of a different culture, how to communicate with a workforce whose first language may be Spanish, Tagalog, Chinese, Polish or whatever.

Front line supervisors will be focused on acquiring skills that help them get out that day's production. However, the "intellect" activities can't be ignored entirely for this group. It is quite important, for example, that the front line supervisor have some understanding of why the company is putting diversity on the agenda, and just what senior management plans to do to set the proper example and establish accountability.

Since diversity concepts have not been taught in our high schools and colleges (until very recently), there is usually a lot of work to be done to build the knowledge base before moving into skills application training.

HOW TO ANTICIPATE AND OVERCOME THE CHALLENGES OF DIVERSITY TRAINING

During the early '90s many companies rushed into diversity training as a means to solve a wide range of issues. A diversity training cottage industry quickly developed to meet the needs perceived by various organizations. Under that scenario, it is not surprising that there have been some negative repercussions falling out of education and training efforts. Unfortunately the media have chosen to focus on a number of extreme examples to cast doubts upon the value of any kind of diversity training. Individuals within organizations who were resisting diversity from the outset have been provided with convenient ammunition to justify their resistance or lack of support. To prepare for planning and decisions on diversity training, let's briefly examine some of the principal challenges, followed by guidelines for planning around those potential or real problems in your own efforts.

Challenge # 1: How to Shape Realistic Expectations for Training and Deliver on Promises. Many organizations have embraced training as though it were the **total** strategy for approaching diversity issues. No matter how diligent these efforts might be, their impact is usually limited to improving understanding and appreciation of the most obvious differences among people—race, gender, ethnicity and so on. After the training is completed, the individuals go back to the work place and find that nothing has really changed. Senior management who approved the program and participants who went in with high expectations are all disappointed that the miracle cure did not take place.

In some case the company may have jumped the gun on diversity training. In response to urging from the CEO or to complaints raised by employees, the company quickly names a diversity task force. Over a period of months, the task force finds it difficult to define its mission and accountabilities or to get consensus on priorities. In response to escalating pressure to "do something" a series of understanding differences training seminars is provided. By the time the scheduled training is half completed, attendance begins to fall off and the lasting value of the effort is limited.

STRATEGY: POSITION EDUCATION AND TRAINING AS PART OF A TOTAL DIVERSITY STRATEGY. Training to enhance awareness of differences is an important program element and can lead to real breakthroughs in self awareness and cross cultural understanding. However, any behavior changes motivated by the training will be short lived if not accompanied by changes in the culture. The organization's cultural root establishing the "mold" (desired physical, behavioral characteristics) for the organization and the accompanying requirement for assimilation are the two most powerful aspects of culture affecting diversity. Long term progress must include review and adjustment to the corporate culture.

In addition, the systems and policies (especially human resources systems and policies) should be tested to see if they are working for all people. A focus group participant observed: *"This is great. Now my boss understands some of the differences about being black. It doesn't mean much, though, as long as we all are stuck down here in the bottom of the organization."* Diversity training is a key change intervention and its mere presence on the corporate agenda will send a strong message to the organization. However, education and training should not be the only important initiative.

STRATEGY: START YOUR TRAINING WITH A THOROUGH NEEDS ANALYSIS. The issues of diversity may be present in any aspect of the employment relationship. The issues may also vary by organization levels, function, geography and industry. The needs of the shipping department manager in San Antonio are probably somewhat different from the needs of the accounting manager in Minneapolis. Don't fall into the trap of buying what is readily available simply to respond to the pressure for action.

Much of the information required to identify training needs can be gleaned from your basic diversity research process (Chapter 5). Written questions can provide the hard data, and focus groups and employee advocacy/support groups can fill in the flavor and context for what is needed.

STRATEGY: MEASURE THE EFFECTS OF DIVERSITY TRAINING AS YOU WOULD ANY OTHER DEVELOPMENT PROGRAM. Some critics attempt to install a tougher standard for evaluating diversity programs than they would other HR activities. I have encountered training managers who are looking for irrefutable proof of tangible benefits for diversity training. My response to them is "Do you have a similar level of proof for the benefits of other types of training?"

Certainly you should always attempt to measure the value of each activity—but you should also beware of the double standard and be realistic of the kinds of "metrics" that can be generated for any activity. In the case of training the measures are likely to be somewhat subjective.

Challenge # 2: Avoid Allowing Your Diversity Training to Become Divisive or Counter-Productive. Criticisms of the content and impact of diversity training tend to raise issues regarding the balance, for example:

- Focuses too much on "shame and blame," and white male bashing. The origins of our assumptions are important and the recognition of ineffective or unfair practices is a prerequisite to correction. However, an attempt to assign guilt to any given group can create barriers rather than gateways to improved understanding and behavior changes.

- Training can be divisive and widen rather than bridge the gulf in understanding. Some trainers rely upon highly confrontational training techniques. A manager described an example of a confrontational approach (that is perhaps extreme) where the trainer shouted at some participants and cursed, belittled their race and religion, and generally made them extremely uncomfortable. The ostensible objective was to make the participants understand how it felt to be degraded as some minority groups had been in this country. However, for a number of participants, they experienced more anger than empathy.

- The training can inadvertently reinforce stereotypes and labels. By putting some of the issues of stereotyping on the table, we may give the view undue credence and reinforce the victim status of the stereotype target.

STRATEGY: USE A PARTICIPATIVE DESIGN PROCESS. The process of developing diversity training is an opportunity to put the concepts of diversity to work. You must avoid what is sometimes referred to as the traditional "BOWGSAT" design process [that is a *Bunch Of White Guys Sitting Around a Table*]. Your input should include the gamut of diversity dimensions, including by the way, some white males.

The inclusion of different viewpoints will help to keep the end product balanced, that is

- Candid, yet not divisive
- Constructive rather than destructive confrontation
- Solution focused rather than blame focused

Some degree of issue confrontation is necessary to create awareness and to get participants to internalize the issues. Like salsa, companies should decide among the mild - medium - hot varieties. Better yet, create a blend that fits your organization's needs. Keep in mind that "mild" programs may allow participants to skirt the real issues. By themselves mild programs create comfort but may not motivate change. On the other hand, the "hot" variety of program may be seen as inappropriate for your organization, especially as a first step. After laying the proper groundwork, the employees may be ready for the more difficult challenges.

As you go through the design process you will find that it is very difficult to find a "one size fits all" solution to your diversity education and training needs.

STRATEGY: TEST THOROUGHLY BEFORE ROLLOUT. Given the sensitive nature of the subject matter it is critical to obtain participant reactions to a pilot program before rolling it out to the masses. Although the actual instances are rare, there have been anecdotes related about a participant taking offense to material covered in a program. Some of the more sensitive aspects of the education and training activity that need to be tested include the following:

Balance: Does the material incorporate discussion of what **everyone** brings to the party or does it slip into an extended white male bashing? A great deal of time may be spent on the issues of non-majority employees. Will white males be given a chance to raise their issues as well? Several companies have established separate venues for white males, but that practice remains controversial. (4)

Degrees of Confrontation: To what degree is it necessary to get people rather "stirred up" to gain the insights and awareness enhancement that is the target of the program? Is it ethical for an organization to beat up on any group of its employees? You should have a sense of how that confrontation will play out in your culture. The confrontational approach will not work well in many environments, and it may run counter to one of the themes you probably will be fostering, respect shown for everyone.

On the other side of the spectrum, some organizations have complained that *"the trainers were too nice"; "they were too easy on us."* The material may look right in printed form but was covered with such style and grace that it didn't grab the attention of its tough-minded audience and did not force issues on the table for discussion.

Perpetuating Stereotypes: Inclusion of a diverse participant group will help to identify material that crosses the line into stereotyping. Any exercise must be started with the caveat that the objective of highlighting stereotypes is to make it "o.k." to talk about them as a step on the way to understanding and behavior change.

Depending on the mix of attendees at a program and the dynamics that develop, you may find very different group and individual reactions to the same material. You may wish to test fly your program with a variety of different groups to develop an anticipated range of responses:

- Members of employee advocacy groups
- A broad diversity council
- Human resources professionals
- A diverse body of "just folks"

While pilot testing is both prudent and productive, don't get trapped into too many pilot programs. Every group will have some differences in reaction that are different from the previous group who saw the same material. The makeup of the group, the effectiveness of the training leaders and other factors can lead to too many ideas for change. You can spend too much of your budget in endless tinkering that has an impact only on the margins of the program.

Try to get a senior management group to go through diversity training prior to or upon rollout of the broad program. Senior management involvement will speak volumes about the level of commitment and how serious the organization is about addressing these issues, and it will be of value to them as individuals as well.

Challenge # 3: How to Assure the Quality and Objectivity of Diversity Trainers. The meteoric rise in demand for diversity training created a lot of instant experts. Unfortunately, not all consultants, trainers, college professors, organization development specialists and the like are well prepared or sufficiently skilled to deal with the challenges and interpersonal dynamics of diversity training.

Most of the diversity trainers I have met express deep personal commitment to the work that they are doing. In fact, I don't see how you could be effective without bringing some passion to the training experience. However, a small handful of trainers may slip into zealotry, causing them to both lose their neutrality and create barriers to acceptance from some training group participants.

STRATEGY: INCORPORATE QUALITY CONTROL IN SELECTION OF TRAINING CONSULTANTS. Many organizations choose to conduct their diversity training through a mix of internal staff and external trainers. There are dozens of diversity training consultants to choose from who have track records you can evaluate. One thing you will learn is that there is no one "perfect" program or trainer for any organization, or perhaps for any group of participants in its entirety. In Exhibit 8.2 are summarized some key screening criteria to use for evaluating potential training consultants so that you can choose the one that best fits the training requirements developed through your internal research.

EXHIBIT 8.2 Guidelines for Selecting Diversity Training Consultants

1. Will the nature and size of the organization allow them to meet your planned training needs? (This is especially important if there is a large group to be covered within a specified time frame.)

    a. How many trainers are available for your project?

    _____

    b. What is the home base of the trainers? (Expense control issue)

    _____

2. Of the training content capabilities that we require, in which ones can they demonstrate competence? (In alphabetical order)

Subject Matter	Our Need?	Their Capability?
a. Age issues	_____	_____
b. Assimilation requirements and effects	_____	_____
c. Communicating across cultures	_____	_____
d. Cultural impacts on negotiations and relationships	_____	_____
e. Demographic trends	_____	_____
f. Diversity/business linkage	_____	_____
g. EEO/Affirmative Action	_____	
h. Empowerment management	_____	_____
i. Exclusionary behavior	_____	_____
j. Gender issues	_____	_____
k. On-the-job application	_____	_____
l. Performance appraisal across cultures	_____	_____
m. Performance of diverse work teams	_____	_____
n. Physical/disability issues	_____	_____
o. Prejudice and discrimination, nature of	_____	_____
p. Sexual harassment	_____	_____
q. Sexual orientation issues	_____	_____
r. White issues/backlash	_____	_____
s. Work and family issues	_____	_____
t. Other areas relevant to our needs	_____	_____

3. What design capabilities can they demonstrate?

    a. Primarily off-the-shelf?

    b. Primarily custom programs?

    c. Combination of standard and custom?

    _____

    _____

(continued)

EXHIBIT 8.2 Continued

4. What are their primary instructional techniques?
   a. "Talking heads"?
   b. Experiential exercises?
   c. Videotape package?
   d. Case studies?
   e. Group problem solving?
   f. Opportunity to observe?
   _____
   _____

5. What degree of confrontation is included in the design?
   a. Highly intense?
   b. Mild, non-threatening?
   c. Mix of high intensity and mild activities?
   _____
   _____

6. What are the relevant credentials and experiences of the individual trainers doing the work?
   a. Ethnic and gender diversity?
   b. Maturity? (Intelligence versus wisdom)
   c. Credibility with broad range of employees?
   d. Evidence of personal commitment?
   _____
   _____

7. What is the fee structure for curriculum design?
   a. For basic design and testing?
   b. Licensing for client internal usage?
   _____
   _____

8. What are the fees for conducting programs?
   a. One-of-a-kind programs? _____
   b. Multiple programs? _____
   c. Train-the-trainer? _____

9. What is their track record with organizations in similar circumstances?
   a. Industry experience? (For example, banking)
   b. Location experience? (Plant vs. headquarters)

10. Other issues relevant to our organization?
    _____
    _____

In addition to the factual responses to the questions in Exhibit 8.2 you must assess the "chemistry" of those who would do the training with your organization. It all takes time, but these steps increase your probabilities of a successful training experience.

STRATEGY: INCLUDE ADMINISTRATIVE AND LOGISTICAL CONSIDERATIONS AS PART OF YOUR QUALITY CONTROL. The arrangements made for the conduct of diversity training can impact the effectiveness of the training, which can probably be said about any kind of training. However, for diversity training the impact of seemingly minor details can be quite dramatic and send messages about the importance of the activity as well. For example, the issue of who attends the programs will be interpreted by employees as a sign of senior management commitment. Exhibit 8.3 is a summary of the key logistical/administrative decision areas to be considered. Going through the checklist as you develop your training strategy should be a good exercise for you.

EXHIBIT 8.3 Diversity Education and Training: Administrative and Logistical Considerations

Issue	*Pluses and Minuses of This Option*
A. Attendance	
1. Voluntary	+ Participants will bring a more open mind and positive attitude to the experience if attendance is voluntary.
	– The persons who could most benefit from the experience may elect not to participate.
	– If participants are permitted to self-select, it may be interpreted as a sign that the company does not think the training is really important.
	– Unpredictable attendance could complicate planning and staffing the training sessions.
2. Mandatory	+ Communicates that senior management is committed and views the activity as important.
	+ Ensures that all who need the training experience actually receive it.
	– May stir resentment among those who resist the premise of diversity training or who don't personally feel the need for the training.
B. Rollout Of the Program	
1. Top down	+ Senior management involvement at the outset of the program sets the right example for the rest of the organization.
	– A negative reaction from senior management could spell an early demise for the program.
	– Senior management may be too remote from the day-to-day issues to effectively judge whether or not the training meets the needs of the troops.
2. Bottom up	+ Addresses issues at levels where most of the diversity in the company now exists.
	– Will not be taken seriously by many until there is clear evidence of a senior management commitment.

(continued)

EXHIBIT 8.3 Continued

Issue	*Pluses and Minuses of This Option*
C. Group Size	
1. Small (under 10)	+ Allows for intensive experience and individual practice of behaviors.
	+ It is easier to build openness and trust in a smaller group.
	− Increases the number of training sessions required to cover the target population, thus raising training cost.
	− Extends the time period necessary to cover the target population.
	− May not get sufficient participant diversity in smaller groups, reducing the learning value of the experience.
2. Large Group (20 +)	+ Less costly to cover the target population for training.
	+ More likely to include a broad diversity among the participant group.
	− Larger groups may inhibit open discussion and opportunities to practice new skills.
D. Participant Mix	
1. Limited to one or two levels (e.g., hourly, senior mgt.)	+ More comfort in speaking openly, asking questions, taking risks.
	+ Material can be tailored to the particular needs of that group.
	− Upper management sessions may have limited participant diversity, reducing the value of the experience.
2. Multiple levels	+ Participants gain understanding of diversity issues at levels other than their own.
	+ Easier to schedule for diversity among the participants.
	− A wide range of organization levels may inhibit participants to speak out for fear of looking bad in front of employees at levels somewhat more senior/more junior than themselves.
3. Intact work groups	+ Allows the participants to focus on issues relevant to their own group.
	+ May allow for an easier transfer of learning to the work setting.
	− If discussion of sensitive issues becomes uncomfortable or heated, relationships could become strained in the work setting as well.
4. Build in minimum diversity among participants.	+ Avoids homogeneous groups assembling that could limit the learning value of the experience.
	− If available diversity is limited, may require participation at multiple sessions by some diverse employees, causing resentment.
E. Program Length	
1. Short, for example, one day or less	+ Limits program cost and has immediate impact on productivity.
	+ May leave the door open for subsequent refresher courses.
	− Could be too short a time to bring meaningful knowledge gain.
	− Participants may infer that the activity is not important enough to devote much time to it.
2. Medium, for example, two days	+ Recognizes the complexity of the subject matter and challenges inherent to changing attitudes and behaviors.
3. Longer, for example, 3–5 days.	+ Sends strong message of the importance of the activity.
	+ Permits in-depth exposure to concepts and practice in the application.
	− May be too expensive or have a negative impact on operations.

As you consider the issues raised in Exhibits 8.2 and 8.3, you can see that diversity training is not an activity that can be taken casually. On the other hand, most of the issues are straightforward and well within the skills of most organizations to deliberate.

Challenge #4: Diversity Training Must be Integrated into Other Training Programs to be Viable Over the Long Term. Some organizations have learned that a free-standing diversity training activity is predestined to fail. It may be dismissed as a fad if seen as unrelated to the real "business at hand," unrelated to other developmental experiences the company provides and inconsistent with the culture of the organization.

STRATEGY: INCORPORATE THE DIVERSITY TRAINING ACTIVITIES INTO YOUR CORE DEVELOPMENT CURRICULUM. If diversity progress is to be sustained in your organization, it has to become a natural part of the way the company operates. If your diversity training and educational efforts are seen as a one-time program, the long term impact on the culture of the organization and the behavior of individuals will be minimal. It is true that an intensive "catch up" diversity training experience may be necessary to establish a knowledge base and focus people's attention. Eventually, however, diversity components should be blended into existing programs for orientation, supervisory skills, sales training, performance management, communication skills, general management development and so on. In the ideal world we will not need to have a separate training activity with a "diversity" label attached to it, because it will be seen as a natural part of managing people. However, most organizations are far, far from that stage of development.

During your needs analysis and design process be alert to opportunities to consolidate related training activities to provide natural linkages, reduce overlap and limit expenses. For example, you may have separate programs available in affirmative action, valuing differences, working with women, team building, and sexual harassment. Re-assess the continuing need for each program. Then for efficiency and consistency of message look for ways to combine related programs under one diversity training umbrella.

IMPORTANT POINTS TO REMEMBER

1. Training is often a key diversity intervention based on needs identified by employees, which can provide efficient learning about potentially sensitive issues.

2. Diversity education and training can be described under three primary headings:

- Intellect: issues of strategic necessity, objective raising of issues
- Insights: understanding how people different from us feel about us, and what and why we feel about them
- Implementation: Learning to apply new knowledge and skills in the work setting

3. Various strategies can be utilized to increase the impact of diversity education and training.

- Position it as part of a total diversity strategy
- Start with a thorough needs analysis
- Measure effects
- Use a participative design process
- Incorporate quality control in selecting trainers
- Incorporate quality control in planning the logistical aspects of training

9 Energizing Affirmative Action Programs

You must have diversity within your organization before worrying about managing it. Therefore, a typical diversity research finding is that a significant number of employees will cite the need for additional affirmative action progress as an important priority for the future. In this chapter you will gain insights into the following:

- The genesis of affirmative action/equal employment opportunity programming, and how its history is both a strength and a weakness for accomplishing results.
- The distinctions between traditional affirmative action and the broader vision of managing diversity.
- The success factors that are the key to sustainable affirmative action results.
- Dealing with resistance to affirmative action that is likely to be found in some parts of the organization.
- The specific kinds of activities you might consider as you attempt to improve your affirmative action performance.

This chapter will prepare you to develop and execute an important element of your broad diversity strategy.

THE ORIGINS OF AFFIRMATIVE ACTION

The first section of this chapter is intended as a brief summary of *affirmative action (AA)*. Readers who are already well grounded in the principles can skip the first few pages if they wish. Affirmative action is a term that stimulates strong feelings and sometimes unproductive debate. Let's start with a brief working definition: *Affirmative Action is taking extra steps to assure equal access to the employment processes of the organization, e.g., hiring, advancement, compensation.*

Unfortunately, in many organizations affirmative action evolved into a numbers-driven compliance exercise to satisfy externally imposed requirements. There is good reason for seeing AA as being externally imposed, since there is a significant legislative history pertaining to equal employment opportunities and affirmative action, including the following:

1. Civil Rights Act, 1866, Section 1981
2. Equal Pay Act, 1963
3. Civil Rights Act, 1964, Title VII
4. Executive Order 11246, 1965
5. Age Discrimination in Employment Act, 1967
6. Rehabilitation Act, 1973
7. Vietnam Era Veteran Readjustment Assistance Act, 1974
8. Immigration Reform and Control Act, 1986
9. Americans with Disabilities Act, 1990
10. Civil Rights Act, 1991
11. Family and Medical Leave Act, 1993

In addition to legislation and executive orders at the national level in the U.S. that are cited above, there are a number of state and local statutes and contract compliance regulations, court cases and rulings of various agencies which may affect employers and employees.

The legislative approaches starting in the 1960s were in recognition of the pervasive discrimination in the work place and society in general. There was also tacit recognition that prevailing attitudes would limit the pace of change unless certain behavior was legally mandated.

In Canada, a similar pattern is evident. Employment Equity legislation affecting federally regulated employees has been in place since 1986 and provincial legislation has also been passed. Compliance activity is still at a low level. However, Canadian managers anticipate an increase in the stringency of the requirements over time. Indeed, Canadian HR managers have exhibited a keen interest in the U.S. experience with diversity. The interest, however, is not to replicate our experience with AA/EEO, but to learn from our past mistakes.

EVALUATING AFFIRMATIVE ACTION RESULTS

Before you prepare to fix the mechanics and processes of your company's affirmative action programs, you should fully realize the strong emotions and opinions that may accompany the mere mention of the word. On the national level the debate continues regarding affirmative action's effectiveness as a socio-economic intervention strategy. Within each organization that is practicing affirmative action, the debate continues on a more personal level. Let's briefly review some of the positions and issues that surround the debate.

The Case for Affirmative Action: There seems to be wide agreement and significant substantiating evidence to suggest that affirmative action as a national strategy has been enormously successful in bringing minorities and females and other protected groups into the workforce. In support of the "yes" point of view, let's look at the numbers for the black population. I select this group since those in the workforce now are primarily native born, and have been present in considerable numbers during the period when most of the legislation was enacted. As shown in Table 9.1, increases in black professional employment in the categories shown range from 253% to 479% during the last 20 years. (1) During this measurement period the total U.S. black population increased by only 42%.

The employment results shown in the table have also brought economic progress to the participants, suggest the AA proponents. Black purchasing power in the U.S. totals $300 billion a year, a figure which equals the total of the twelfth largest nation in the world. (2)

TABLE 9.1 Measuring Black Progress in the White Collar World

Job Type	Number Employed		Percentage Change
	1972	1991	
Accountants	19,000	110,000	+ 479%
Engineers	16,000	66,000	+ 313
Lawyers	5,000	19,000	+ 280
Managers & Administrators	243,000	858,000	+ 253
Total U.S. Black Population	21,064,000	29,986,060	+ 42%

The many advocates of affirmative action say that broad data such as that shown above is ample evidence that the legislation has served the mission for which it was intended, and the progress would not have been achieved without the weight of legislated support. There are also some studies which demonstrate a positive linkage between financial performance of an organization and its affirmative action record. (3)

Some Generic Criticisms of Affirmative Action: The numerical progress in employment that has accompanied AA is recognized and welcomed by many. However, the skeptics continue to raise doubts about the value of affirmative action, offering a variety of reasons for their ambivalence or opposition. Some of the principal questions raised by AA detractors are summarized below:

GOOD START—LONG WAY TO GO? Despite the seeming progress there are lingering gross disparities in the treatment and economic status: (2)

- In 1950 the unemployment rate of blacks was double that of whites; in 1990 it was triple.

- While many minorities have progressed economically, Euro-Americans still own a disproportionate 97% share of the stocks, bonds and business properties in the U.S.

- Periodic studies have demonstrated that minorities are discriminated against when companies make employment decisions (4)

AFFIRMATIVE ACTION IS REDUNDANT AND/OR MISTARGETED: There is a view, particularly among some conservative thought leaders, that affirmative action hasn't worked for those for whom it was intended. Those who have succeeded would have made it on their own anyway, but now they carry the "AA Baby" stigma, that is, they had to have special help to make it. The young, the disadvantaged, the undereducated who needed help the most in breaking into the job market are worse off than ever. (5)

NUMBERS DO NOT EQUAL CLOUT: Critics contend that the progress portrayed by the numbers is misleading. Although many females and minorities indeed have entered the work force, they remain clustered below the glass ceiling, with little power and small hope for advancement to the upper levels. For example, only 6.0% of the officers of corporations are women and 2.3% are minorities. (6) After decades of activity, how can this performance be considered satisfactory?

AFFIRMATIVE ACTION MEANS QUOTAS/THAT'S UN-AMERICAN: A significant number of people will maintain (at least among themselves) that affirmative action is unfair on the face of it, and runs counter to the meritocratic principles upon which this country supposedly was founded. The "guidelines" which are part of the process are viewed as quotas that interfere with our freedom of association. The "anti AA" attitude is more frequently expressed by individuals in the lower organization levels who will be most directly affected by increased competition for employment and advancement.

DISCONTENT WITH AFFIRMATIVE ACTION AT THE INDIVIDUAL LEVEL: The criticism of AA flows freely at a societal level, and issues are raised at the company level as well. In diversity research probes, women and people of color frequently note in interviews and focus groups that, after decades of promises and programs, there are very few of their kind in positions of importance in the organization.

Because performance is viewed as the acid test for commitment, employees need to see more results before they will accept their employers' statements of support at face value. Comments from focus groups illustrate the lingering doubts about how well the organization has done:

Black Female:
"I'd like to see black people in the positions which are Anonymous Company's core business, instead of just being stuck in the support departments."

White Female:
"This is not a good place for a female to work. Just look at the key management positions; there are very few women in prestigious positions."

Hispanic Male:
"We are underrepresented up at the top . . . I think we should be on the executive floors where the decisions are made."

Asian Male:
"I referred some of my friends to the company for jobs. They felt they were not given a chance . . . it was very embarrassing for me to be working for a company like that."

Black Female:
"Look at the human resources department. There is not one minority in a position of importance. Doesn't that set a great example for the rest of the organization?"

White Male:
"I agree that we have brought a lot of minorities and women into the organization over the years. But doesn't it strike you as a failure on our part that we have never had a minority, and only one woman on the 30th (executive) floor?"

Diversity research within a company will often show that there is not unanimity for the need for enhancing AA programs. In response to questions regarding the need to upgrade affirmative action activities, a preponderance of the white respondents often will not favor more AA efforts, and even people of color express ambivalence on the desirability of expanded affirmative action, as shown in Table 9.2.

Each of the groups of respondents may have very different reasons for withholding support for affirmative actions. Comments from minority and female focus groups are along these lines:

"I can make it on my own with special help if the policies and practices are even-handed, non-discriminatory."

"The bad thing about affirmative action is that it puts too much of a spotlight on something that should be handled quietly. It's like special ed in school—you get tagged as coming in on the short bus."

"Members of my group don't really benefit from affirmative action. All the attention goes to [other group] employees."

(For example, blacks may perceive that Asians and Hispanics advance more easily because they are less discriminated against on the basis of skin color or negative stereotypes. Asians or Hispanics may claim they don't get fair treatment because of their accents or because they are not as outspoken as other groups, and so forth.)

The debate on the value of affirmative action will go on but will probably have no significant effect in terms of national policy. AA is a way of life, and many employee organizations perceive much work to be done to raise the level of performance. At the same time, resistance to increased affirmative action can be anticipated for a wide variety of reasons as covered in more depth later.

TABLE 9.2 Example of Employee Attitudes Toward Enhancing Affirmative Action Programs

Statement: Anonymous Company should significantly expand its efforts to provide opportunities for females and minorities. (Agree/disagree)

Group	% in Agreement
African American	51%
Asian American	45%
Hispanic	41%
White	21%

HOW TO EVALUATE YOUR AFFIRMATIVE ACTION PROGRESS

Stripping aside the jargon and the regulations, there are at least three key areas of evidence for assessing how well your past affirmative action efforts have succeeded.

- Judge your success through hierarchy analysis.

- Determine how **all employees** perceive the environment, not just the few who file formal charges or lodge complaints.

- Determine how current employees may be mobilized in support of improved AA performance.

Each of these points is covered briefly below.

Apply the "Pyramid Power" Test to Your Organization: The method for recording the numbers for the various gender and ethnic groupings has been firmly established by the standardized format for government reporting commonly referred to as EEO-1 reports. The groupings on the current reports include the following:

Job Categories
1. Officials and managers
2. Professionals
3. Technicians
4. Sales workers
5. Office & clerical
6. Craft workers (skilled)
7. Operatives (semi-skilled)
8. Laborers (unskilled)
9. Service workers

Race/Gender Breakouts
Male   Female
A. White [not Hispanic]
B. Black [not Hispanic}
C. Hispanic
D. Asian or Pacific
   Islander
E. American Indian or
   Alaskan Native

Federal reporting formats serve a macro purpose but the categories in these reports are so broad, that they may not give a clear picture of where the individuals are in a given corporate pyramid. To illustrate the limits of measuring progress on the basis of federal reports, let's examine the sales division of the mythical "Really Good Products Corporation." Really Good Products has been subject to the requirements of federal contractors and has had an affirmative action program for several decades. They have steadily increased the inflow and percentages of females and minorities. Company management knows they have more work to do, and yet they are not displeased with the progress to date. Data on the organization are shown in Table 9.3.

What does data in Table 9.3 tell you about the company's affirmative action successes? Not much, I'm afraid. Even if you break the data down further into the EEO-1 categories of *Officials and Managers, Professionals, Sales Workers,* and so on and compare with area availability for individuals in various groups, you still may not have a picture as to what is going on. Comparisons of like companies in your industry or area might be helpful. However, a more useful analysis, is to see where those individuals are located in the corporate pyramid. Let's look at Exhibit 9.1 which shows the sales department of Really Good Products Corporation in the pyramid context.

The pyramid analysis reveals that people of color and women are stuck at lower levels where they have little power. It is verification for many employees that, despite the company's pronouncements of support and its affirmative action efforts over two decades, *"The white guys still have all the good jobs."* Each organization has its own characteristics that can be used to dramatize the current profile. For example, the senior human resources officer of a multi-national company used a series of slides showing the race/gender representation of the occupants on an elevator as it progressed toward the upper executive floors in the company headquarters tower. At the lower levels of the tower, the occupants of the elevator were diverse. By the time the elevator reached the top floor, the only remaining occupants, of course, were white male senior executives. Now those senior executives cannot ride those elevators without being aware of the diminishing diversity of the occupants as they proceed from the "trenches" to the executive suite.

Some organizations are reorganizing their human resources systems to provide clearer tracking of the progress of employees up through various career channels. They start with the realization that the traditional EEO-1 counting provides data but not actionable information. Diversity must be built into all the career mobility systems of the company.

TABLE 9.3 Really Good Products Corporation: Employment Profile

Category	Employees		
	Number	Percentage	
Total Employees	1,000	100%	
Males	700	60%	
Females	300	40%	
Minorities	150	15%	(exceeds area availability%)

EXHIBIT 9.1 Really Good Products Corporation: Sales Pyramid Power

Power		Percent of Incumbents	
		Female	Minority
	Region Managers (5)	0%	0%
	District Managers (50)	4%	2%
	Sales Agent (450)	18%	8%
	Customer Support and Administrative Services (200)	45%	20%
Numbers	Clerical and Secretarial (300)	85%	30%

Determine Employee Experiences/Perceptions: In your diversity research process it will be extremely helpful to ask some rather direct questions regarding the perceptions about the environment. As we discussed earlier, the perceptions do not necessarily equal the reality, as the responses may be strongly influenced by cultural pre-conditioning. Nevertheless, the data can be both quite useful and quite surprising. In the tables below we have provided some examples of questions that might be posed, and how some employees have responded in a sampling of companies that have not had exceptional affirmative action programs.

Data in Table 9.4 on page 176 would indicate that jokes and comments of a sexual nature are common among exempt employees, since less than half agree with the statement. However, the 63–64% approval rating given by the nonexempt females seems to indicate that they are more likely to be spared jokes and comments of a sexual nature.

The perceptions of minority employees about ethnic jokes and comments shown in Table 9.5 are somewhat lower than for the white respondents for two of the groupings.

The last set of data, in Table 9.6, demonstrates a pattern we point out in a number of places in the book: females give lower ratings than their male counterparts, and minorities give lower ratings than non-minorities.

Often managers will express both surprise and disappointment about their data. Perhaps they have assumed that the relatively small number of formal EEO charges or open complaints is indicative of the true feelings of employees. However, the number of formal discrimination charges may bear only a slight resemblance to employee feelings. Filing a charge is a last resort, and even if the charg-

TABLE 9.4 Statement: Jokes and comments of a sexual nature *are not tolerated* in my department.

Race/Level[a]	% Who Strongly Agree/ Tend to Agree	
	Males	**Females**
White Exempt	50%	47%
Minority Exempt	43%	53%
White Nonexempt	b	64%
Minority Nonexempt	b	63%

[a]*FLS designation, Exempt usually includes managerial and professional, Non-exempt clerical, secretarial.*
[b]*insufficient number of responses in this category*

ing employee "wins" he or she recognizes the possibility of losing more in the long run by coming forward.

Company managers often are distressed to see data such as that shown in Tables 9.4 through 9.6. In most cases they strongly feel that they are doing a better job than the data would indicate. In fact, there is some evidence in employee feedback that the situation is not as bad as it would appear. Perhaps employees are simply using the opportunity to send a clear message to management. While they are disappointed, their overall support of the organization may be stronger than one would assume from the data alone.

TABLE 9.5 Statement: Jokes and comments of a racial or ethnic nature *are not tolerated* in my work area.

Gender/Level	% Who Strongly Agree/Tend to Agree	
	White	**Minority**
Male Exempt	54%	35%
Female Exempt	60%	57%
Female Nonexempt	66%	49%

TABLE 9.6 Statement: The manner in which Anonymous Company
employees are treated *is not influenced* by their gender, ethnic
background (age, sexual preference, disability, etc.)

	% Who Strongly Agree/Tend To Agree		
Race	**Male Exempt**	**Female Exempt**	**Female Nonexempt**
White	59%	36%	47%
Minority	36%	22%	22%

Mobilize Current Employees to Move Ahead: If you want to improve the affirmative action performance of the company, one of the best places to start is to harness the energies and good will of those already on board. Testimony from a like person will be taken more seriously by a potential recruit than trite statements in the company recruiting brochure. To help develop an overall perspective of satisfaction of your employee groups, you can include several questions in your research which call for some summary judgments on the desirability of the employer, such as shown in Tables 9.7 and 9.8.

The typical spread in evaluations between white respondents and others is again demonstrated in Table 9.7. The low approval rating given by minority employees poses a challenge when enlisting their aid in helping to attract other minorities to the company.

As the data in Table 9.8 indicates, the female employees are not happy with the environment that they perceive to exist.

In total, the data in Tables 9.4 through 9.8 suggest that your female and mi-

TABLE 9.7 Statement: I would recommend Anonymous Company
as an employer of minorities.

	% Who Strongly Agree/Tend To Agree		
Race	**Male Exempt**	**Female Exempt**	**Female Nonexempt**
White	64%	52%	52%
Minorities	30%	27%	35%

TABLE 9.8 Statement: I would recommend Anonymous Company as an employer of women.

Race/Level	% Who Strongly Agree/Tend To Agree	
	Male	Female
White Exempt	65%	47%
Minority Exempt	47%	37%
White Nonexempt	*	51%
Minority Nonexempt	*	33%

insufficient number of responses

nority employees (in particular) may view the environment with ambivalence. Less than a third of the minorities would recommend the company as a place for other minorities to work. Less than half the females would recommend their employer to other females. You have some work to do to build credibility before you can count on employees to help recruit their ethnic/gender counterparts into the corporation.

PREPARE TO NEUTRALIZE THE RISKS OF ENHANCED AFFIRMATIVE ACTION

When the need for enhanced affirmative action has been identified, there are three areas of general concern that should be addressed in your strategy planning. Each of the risk areas is spelled out below, along with a strategy for dealing with the risks.

Recognize the Potential for Message Confusion: When adopting the broad vision of managing diversity, there may be a reaction from females and people of color that a broad diversity program will result in a reduced commitment to affirmative action hiring and promotions. They may question whether affirmative action is still an integral part of the basic strategy.

On the other side of the coin, if the diversity program has not been clearly differentiated from affirmative action or if the affirmative action portion is seen as the only result, skeptics will say that managing diversity is just a new and more palatable name for hiring and promoting on the basis of race and gender quotas. Or as expressed by one white male, *"I hate to break the news, but numbers is what it's all about. Diversity is just affirmative action for the 'kinder, gentler' '90s."*

Steps to Minimize Message Confusion: To counter the misconceptions on the relationship of managing diversity to traditional affirmative action, you must communicate the diversity vision clearly and repeatedly. The distinctions are real, but they are also unfamiliar to many.

For those concerned about abandonment of affirmative action programs, reinforce the commitment to continue progress and point to new interventions and success. Be straightforward in recognition that the AA job is not finished. Anticipate continuing skepticism until the progress extends to the higher levels of the organization.

For those who dismiss MD as a refined version of affirmative action, continue to highlight differences between the two. Exhibit 9.2 provides a concise summary of the principal differences.

- Underscore the benefits to all employees that may come from diversity programs. Communication should be through channels where the company says what it really means, for example, financial communications to shareholders, etc.

Don't assume that everyone will "get it" the first—or second—time around. Resistance is natural and self-centered. Continuous and consistent communications as described in Chapter 12 are necessary for success.

EXHIBIT 9.2 Differentiating Affirmative Action from Managing Diversity (6)

DIMENSION	AFFIRMATIVE ACTION	MANAGING DIVERSITY
Emphasis	• Women • Minorities	All groups, including white males
Assumptions	• Members of protected groups have deficiencies • Most "different" employees wish to emulate a dominant group	• Members of all groups have potential • Individuals may be reluctant to assimilate away key differences
Change Required	Individual adapts to existing culture and systems	Both the individual and the organization adapt
Results	• Diverse workforce at lower levels of the organization • Repetitive cycles of hiring and turnover • Dominant culture orientation	• Competitive advantage • Full utilization of all employees • Multicultural orientation

Anticipate and Neutralize Backlash: The flip side of the demand for more and better affirmative action is the potential backlash from employees who perceive it as unearned preferences given to others. The backlash comes most frequently from white males.

Some Examples of Backlash: Underlying concern and resentment is represented by comments such as the following (taken from white male focus groups):

"What I found really annoying was seeing a lot of white males let go and then re-placed with minorities and women. It all seems political, and morale has been shot to hell as a result."

"More work is being placed on fewer people and when the minorities can't handle it, it's thrown on us. They'll cry discrimination if we try to distribute it equally, so we just bite the bullet and do it ourselves."

"They don't have to work hard, even to get promotions. They know they can get it by just being black and waiting for the numbers to be right to get where they want to be."

"I don't see minorities as a problem (competing for advancement), but I do see women making life difficult for white males. They are on the lower levels, and they are just waiting for the slots to open. Then we've had it! They had a bad deal, but it wasn't our fault. Now we have to pay for it."

Speaking more broadly, nearly half the white males in the country feel they are paying an unfair penalty for the advantages that they had in the past (7). Attitudes like those cited above might be dealt with through awareness training and issue clarification. However, a more fundamental force that is stirring up resistance is the reduction in job security and job opportunities that has been the by-product of frequent downsizings. Secretary of Labor Robert Reich said that "Even if you have a job, your chance of not having a job a year or two from now is increasing. There is a greater degree of job insecurity these days, no matter where you are in the corporation, than we have seen at any time in the post World War II era." (8)

In group after group I have seen the preoccupation with job security harden attitudes. In some surveys up to half the minority employees do not favor more affirmative action hiring. Job insecurity pits one group against another, newcomer against veteran. A comment that captures the spirit was *"The issue isn't whether females and minorities will have better opportunities here. The issue is whether any of us will have a job in two years!"* Over the next several years this fundamental economic issue may be one of the toughest impediments to affirmative action acceptance.

Some Approaches for Reducing Backlash: A significant degree of resistance or backlash seems inevitable, no matter how carefully you communicate about the differences from affirmative action. You can work around it, or run over it, but it

cannot be ignored. Some activities that might be used to neutralize the anticipated resistance include the following:

- Communicate the business rationale as a reason to change behavior and
  company affirmative action performance. Remind doubters why the organization sees a business necessity for the activity and why it is in their interest
  to support progress toward the business goals of AA.

- Include resisters in the planning and problem solving. Involvement of key
  individuals in the identification and resolution of issues will heighten their
  awareness of the legitimacy of the issues and concerns, increase acceptance
  of the validity of the effort and deepen their personal commitment to improving the situation.

- Point out that many diversity motivated initiatives will help white males as
  well as others. For example, improved appraisal and development programs can benefit everyone.

- Provide structured opportunities to ventilate their feelings and frustrations.
  The diversity training that takes place should allow individuals who see
  themselves being disadvantaged by affirmative action to openly address
  their issues. The differences of opinion will not magically disappear, but the
  ventilation of deeply held attitudes is a necessary step toward mutual understanding.

- Recognize at the outset that you will not get one hundred percent buy-in.
  The combined forces of deep-seated bias and perceived threat to one's own
  security will always result in a significant degree of *passive* resistance. However, eventually action must supplant debate, so you must be clear that *active resistance* is unacceptable. There should be negative implications for
  those who attempt to undermine the program, just as there would be for the
  attempt to undermine other valid corporate programs. Eventually the senior
  management of the organization must establish a *"Lead, follow, or get out of
  the way!"* standard of behavior throughout the organization.

Build a Foundation for Affirmative Action Success: Many companies have gone
through repeated cycles of affirmative action hiring where females and minorities
were brought into the organization, only to be underutilized and devalued
through the pressures for assimilation to the prevailing company mold. Disappointment and departures from non-majority employees soon follow.

In analyzing affirmative action triumphs and failures, I have developed a
view of the necessary components of long term success in affirmative action.
*These components are the foundation and the pillars of effective affirmative action pro-
grams,* as illustrated in Exhibit 9.3.

The component and characteristics of the foundation and pillars are summarized as follows:

EXHIBIT 9.3 The Foundation and Pillars of Effective
Affirmative Action

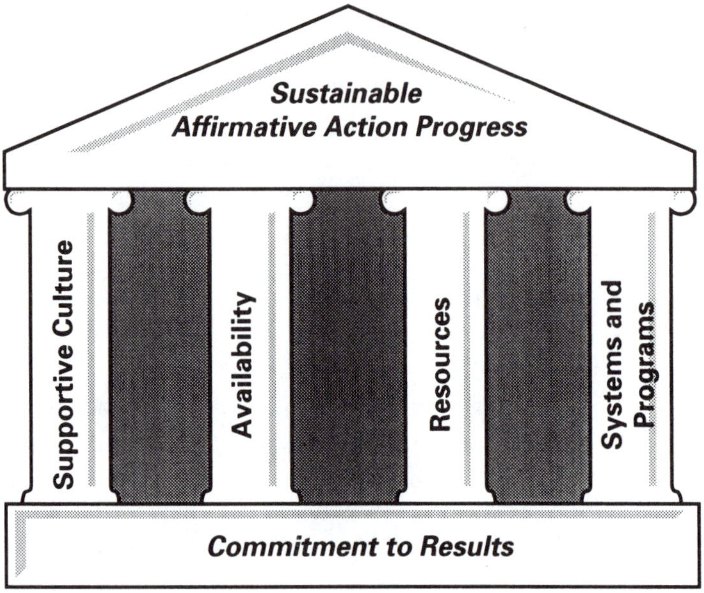

**Sustainable
Affirmative Action Progress**

Supportive Culture

Availability

Resources

Systems and
Programs

Commitment to Results

1. **Commitment to Results—The Foundation for Success**

    An organization is unlikely to achieve sustainable progress in affirmative action unless there is clear and deep commitment, characterized by the following conditions:

    • The company has had a longstanding policy of commitment to establishing and developing a diverse work force, as evidenced by its hiring, advancement and development programs.

    • The company has determined that there are specific business benefits which might accrue as a result of having a diverse work force.

    • The policy has strong and unwavering support from the chief executive officer of the organization, and from the persons in charge of the local operating units.

    • The company's policy and senior management commitment has been clearly and consistently communicated through all levels and locations of the organization.

    • Progress against diversity objectives is measured. Line managers are held accountable for performance shortfalls and the successes are celebrated and rewarded.

Once the *foundation* is in place, the *pillars of support* must be erected and stabilized. The four pillars are described below:

2. Corporate Culture that is Supportive of Diversity

Individuals hired into the organization will be prone to turnover if they do not feel that the environment is supportive, and that differences are welcomed and utilized.

- Females and minorities can be found in all levels and in all departments in the organization, and serve as role models for success.
- There is no rigid model of physical or behavioral characteristics used for screening potential employees or for determining the pace and ultimate level of their career progress.
- Individuals are valued and respected based upon their contribution and input irrespective of their diversity dimensions (e.g., age, function, college, etc.).
- The skills for effectively managing people are valued, appraised and rewarded by senior management (e.g., performance management, team building, coaching, communications).
- Jokes, put-downs or other disrespectful comments based on diversity characteristics (such as race, gender, religion, sexual orientation, etc.) are not tolerated.
- Managers are encouraged to mentor and develop all employees and those who do so are recognized for the efforts.
- The predominant management styles focus more on obtaining productivity through empowerment of employees, rather than from control and close monitoring.

3. Availability of a Diverse Labor Pool

While labor availability has not been an issue for most companies recently, there have been geographic areas and occupational fields that have not had the benefit of a diverse labor pool.

- A diverse population exists in your recruiting areas, from which the company may draw its work force.
- A significant portion of the job candidates have the job-related skills which the company reasonably requires, or the applicants can be readily trained to such level.
- The competition for diverse talent has not driven competitive pay levels out of reach for your organization.
- The time and/or distance from candidates' living areas to your location do not exclude a given target group from considering your employment opportunities.

4. Financial and Staffing Resources

What gets supported, gets done. Commitment goes beyond dollar expenditures, but the financial resources are still an important part of the equation.

- An individual has been designated to plan and manage the affirmative action programs and activities of the organization, and has been empowered to apply the resources of the organization toward the goal. Adequate support staff exists as well.

- The diversity/affirmative action function is consistently funded to include:

  - Research to identify potential needs and solutions.

  - Training in the basic knowledge and skills to meet the legal and operational requirements.

  - Programs which address the needs identified through employee research efforts.

  - Communications to provide clear statement of the company's commitment and inform individuals of supporting programs available.

- Funding is provided for positive employer-community relations activities positioned to reach target community groups.

5. Systems to Create/Monitor/Develop a Diverse Workforce

Missing or ineffective human resources systems and programs can impede the development of all employees. However, employees who are not "mainstream" feel the impact of weak systems disproportionately.

- Recruitment processes incorporate non-traditional channels that produce a diverse applicant flow.

- The processes used to screen prospective employees have been tested to minimize the intrusion of biases.

- The input of diverse employees is used to enhance recruitment processes and the interviewing teams are reflective of the diversity which the company hopes to attract.

- New hires are provided training and orientation to increase their comfort level in the new environment and to learn some of the "unwritten rules."

- A human resources information system exists to track the presence of diverse employees in the various departments, and their progress through the organization.

- Comprehensive employee climate surveys are conducted on a periodic basis. Results analyses include breakouts of data and differential analysis on a race and gender basis.

- The organization makes available a broad range of training programs to foster the development of all employees, including

- technical skills
- management skills [goal setting, leadership, etc.]
- understanding differences
- There is a formal performance management program in place that incorporates the following features:
  - performance objectives are mutually agreed upon
  - feedback on progress is ongoing, candid and specific
  - multiple inputs are utilized
  - boss and subordinate are trained in the process
- There is an open job posting process which enables individuals to become aware of, and to compete on equal terms for advancement opportunities, without the necessity of having a "sponsor."
- The organization recognizes the potential for dependent care demands on employees and supports them through a variety of policies and programs such as:
  - flexibility in working hours
  - flexibility in holidays, vacations
  - assistance in developing day care and elder care options
  - surveys to assess local employee needs
  - involvement of working parents and others with dependent care obligations in program review and planning.
- There is a confidential complaint process which permits the airing of diversity-related concerns while maintaining confidentiality.

The foundations and pillars of successful affirmative action just described are summarized in an assessment tool, Exercise 9.1, at the end of this chapter. The tool can be used to obtain a preliminary read on the internal aspects of your organization that should be strengthened prior to, or in conjunction with enhanced affirmative action programming.

HARNESSING THE ENERGY AND IDEAS OF YOUR EMPLOYEES

All too often human resources managers are reluctant to fully engage their current diverse employees in the development of winning affirmative action strategies. Employee involvement can produce a broad range of activities that they will suggest for the company. For example, Exhibit 9.4 continues a lengthy list of affirmative action activities that have been suggested by participants in various client studies.

EXHIBIT 9.4 Employee Recommendations: How to Strengthen Your
Affirmative Action Foundation and Pillars

Commitment to Results
- Incorporate diversity comments into every internal and external CEO speech.
- Incorporate AA comments in company credo, annual report and other publications.
- Include AA planning in the business planning process.
- Include affirmative action objectives in individual performance goals and objectives.
- Include updates of AA progress in regular performance discussions.
- Relate a portion of annual bonus to AA progress.
- Have line managers rather than the HR group provide reports of AA progress.

Supportive Corporate Culture
- Make high profile appointments of qualified non-traditional employees.
- Critically evaluate the written and unwritten list of characteristics used to screen for hiring and promotion. Eliminate or weaken those characteristics that are not specifically tied to performance.
- Include people management skills, empowerment management as criteria for advancement and provide training in these areas as part of the company management development programs.
- Provide programs to raise awareness of cultural differences and develop a climate of mutual respect.

Increase the Diversity of Your Applicant Pool
- Locate facilities (or a portion of them) in localities that incorporate a diverse population.
- Work with schools to interest diverse student bodies in career opportunities, and provide the necessary skills.

Financial and Staffing Resources
- Increase the AA budget, even in the face of cuts elsewhere.
- Have a high potential manager rotate through the top AA position, empowered to bring about change.
- Have the AA director report to a senior officer of the company.
- Provide funding for outreach and community activities
  - Significant portion of corporate contribution program allocated to groups supporting the development of females and minorities (for example, NAACP, Hispanic MBA Association)
  - Have senior management directly involved in high impact community experiences.

Human Resources Systems and Programs
  Strengthen College Recruiting
- Expand the base of schools for recruiting beyond the traditional sources that the organization has used, e.g., add historically black colleges, major city universities.
- Establish cooperative work/study programs primarily directed at female and minority prospects [e.g. Inroads] and for the physically challenged.
- Strengthen the campus recruiting efforts:
  - Good advance reading materials
  - Minority recruitment social activity

EXHIBIT 9.4 Continued

- Use current minority employees for information meetings
- Develop relationships with placement offices and heads of relevant departments
- Develop relationships with ethnic campus groups [e.g. black Greek associations]
- Maintain summer internship program for college and graduate students to build skills, provide two way assessment opportunity and create a bonding.

Improve Recruitment Processes

- Include women and people of color on every recruiting team.
- Include candidates who do not precisely fit the "mold" that the organization has traditionally used to expose managers to realistic options.
- Provide a mentor/contact of same race and gender to provide support through the recruitment process and in the early days of an individual joining the company.
- Use diverse focus groups to identify obstacles in the recruitment process and enlist their support.
- Use internal job posting to ensure internal candidates are considered before external recruitment begins.
- Follow up appointments with periodic "how's it going?" assessments.

Develop Outreach Programs

- Support employee involvement in the Black and Hispanic and Asian MBA associations.
- Develop working relationships with the NAACP, LULAC, etc. and other national and local groups.
- Develop working relationships with schools that have heavy minority populations.

Expand Recruitment Sources

- Utilize qualified recruitment firms concentrating in minority and female hiring.
- Advertise in minority/female-focused professional and general interest publications.

"Open up" advancement processes

- Include higher level positions [e.g., officer group] in job posting process.
- Define skills and abilities needed for advancement in principal job families; provide information to employees.

Improve planning and tracking

- Develop career ladders for primary job groups. Identify diversity present at each level, and set goals for improvement.
- Use a committee to monitor the impact on diversity progress as the organization goes into a downsizing mode.
- Provide annual report of turnover levels to senior management, differentiated on a job level, race, gender and other relevant bases.

Provide for improved communications

- Repeat surveys including diversity items; provide reports on results and action plans to employees.
- Train supervisors on cultural differences in communication and listening patterns.
- Include all employees in information regarding important company developments that may affect them.

The items in Exhibit 9.4 are just a sampling of the kinds of information that your employees will be more than happy to share with you. The beauty of it is that you not only get the information, you get their commitment by involving them in the process. The assessment tool at the end of the chapter can provide a framework for that involvement.

Affirmative action has been a way of life for decades; yet many companies recognize it has not fully achieved its full potential. Before embarking on another round of targeted hiring, you should assess all the aspects of the organization which impact on the probable success of affirmative action programs. Exercise 9.1 is a good starting point for energizing your affirmative action programs.

EXERCISE 9.1 Assessment of Diversity/Affirmative Action Success Potential

Anonymous Corporation Base Line Assessment

Success Factor	Current Assessment Here		
	Strong	Acceptable	Needs Improvement
1. COMMITMENT TO RESULTS:			
a. Strong position, emanates from senior management.	1.a	1.a	1.a
b. Longstanding policy, practiced down thru middle management ranks.	1.b	1.b	1.b
c. Commitment clearly, repeatedly communicated.	1.c	1.c	1.c
d. Managers held accountable for shortfall/rewarded for success.	1.d	1.d	1.d
e. Position on issue linked to strategic/competitive rationale.	1.e	1.e	1.e
2. SUPPORTIVE CORPORATE CULTURE:			
a. Females and minorities now in all levels of the organization to serve as role models.	2.a	2.a	2.a
b. Individuals valued based on their contribution and input irrespective of group membership.	2.b	2.b	2.b
c. Jokes and comments disparaging a group are not tolerated.	2.c	2.c	2.c
d. Mechanisms exist for resolution of diversity-based problems.	2.d	2.d	2.d
e. No rigid model of physical or behavioral characteristics used for screening or for advancement.	2.e	2.e	2.e
f. Managers encouraged to mentor a diverse group of employees.	2.f	2.f	2.f
g. People management skills are valued and rewarded.	2.g	2.g	2.g
3. AVAILABILITY OF DIVERSE TALENT POOL:			
a. Diverse population exists in your recruiting areas.	3.a	3.a	3.a
b. Major portion of candidates have required job-related skills or can be readily provided such.	3.b	3.b	3.b

EXERCISE 9.1 Continued

		Current Assessment Here	
Success Factor	**Strong**	**Acceptable**	**Needs Improvement**
c. Competition not bidding wages beyond your reach.	3.c	3.c	3.c
d. Commuting patterns do not exclude a given target group from interest.	3.d	3.d	3.d
4. FINANCIAL/STAFFING RESOURCES:			
a. Clearly designated head of affirmative action activities and processes.	4.a	4.a	4.a
b. Funding available for • research • training • programs • communications	4.b	4.b	4.b
c. Community relations programs provide positive positioning with target employee groups.	4.c	4.c	4.c
5. SYSTEMS TO CREATE/MONITOR/MAINTAIN:			
a. Recruitment processes incorporate non-traditional channels for applicants.	5.a	5.a	5.a
b. Screening processes tested for minimization of bias.	5.b	5.b	5.b
c. Company interviewing teams are diverse.	5.c	5.c	5.c
d. Upfront training/orientation to provide comfort and understanding of basic survival skills.	5.d	5.d	5.d
e. HRIS tracking & analytical capability • Primary data on individuals • Differential analyses	5.e	5.e	5.e
f. Comprehensive employee climate surveys conducted: • on a regular basis • feedback differentiated by race and gender	5.f	5.f	5.f
g. Formal management/technical training programs to develop all employees.	5.g	5.g	5.g
h. Documented performance appraisal program in operation: • mutually agreed upon objectives • feedback more than annually • multiple inputs • user training	5.h	5.h	5.h
i. Policies and programs which accommodate the needs of working parents.	5.i	5.i	5.i
j. Confidential complaint process exists and is effective.	5.j	5.j	5.j

███████

IMPORTANT POINTS TO REMEMBER

1. Develop an understanding of the strengths and weaknesses of affirmative action at the societal level and the personal level before moving into action plans.

2. Test the degree of affirmative action progress within your organization through pyramid power analysis and by seeking confidential input from employees.

3. Prepare for possible resistance to enhanced affirmative action efforts through communication and management leadership.

4. Firmly establish the foundation and pillars upon which successful effort will rest:

   - Commitment to results, the "foundation"
   - Corporate culture that is supportive of diversity
   - Availability of a diverse labor pool
   - Financial and staffing resources
   - Systems to create, monitor and maintain a diverse work force

5. Harness the energy, and benefit from the suggestions of current employees to make your programs successful.

10 Linking Work/Family and Diversity Strategies and Programs

In many organizations the work/family programs have been developed prior to, and independently of, the overall diversity strategy of the organization. On the surface, the needs addressed appear to be different, and the support activities often report through different channels in the human resources department. This characteristic separation of activities may contribute to underachievement in both diversity and work/family areas. In this chapter you will gain an understanding of the similarities and potential linkages between work/family issues and broader diversity change processes. With that understanding you will be in a position to improve the power and momentum of both activity areas. Suggestions for shaping your work/family programs for 2000 and beyond are described, along with a brief case study which illustrates how programs can be linked to corporate strategies.

FOUR REASONS WHY YOU SHOULD LINK DIVERSITY AND WORK/FAMILY INITIATIVES

Organizations that have separate diversity and work/family programs should understand both strategic and tactical reasons for positioning work/family programs as a key element of a diversity umbrella strategy. The four reasons for such linkage are described below.

1. *Similar behaviors are experienced in the workplace.*

     People of color, women and persons with significant dependent care responsibilities are the subject of biases and stereotyping that can limit their recognition and advancement. For persons with heavy dependent care responsibilities, the bias may include assumptions about the individual's commitment to the job, willingness to work overtime, travel or relocate. They may be viewed as a stereotype (e.g., member of the class "working mother") rather than on basis of their contributions.

2. *The similar behaviors yield similar effects.*

     Women, people of color and working mothers are often disproportionately clustered at the lower ends of the corporate pyramid. After getting tired of bumping up against the glass ceiling they tend to leave in greater percentages than do white males, as they seek an organization and environment that more strongly values and accommodates their points of difference.

3. *Both diversity and work/family programs encounter similar risks to survival.*

     Too often diversity and work/family programs are seen as "program du jour," driven by the fad-conscious human resources department rather than by business necessity. If the programs are seen as "nice to have" rather than a source of competitive advantage, they stand the risk of being axed in the first cost-cutting action. The risk may be exacerbated by the fact that senior management is seldom diverse, and they more frequently have a spouse who works at home. Thus, senior executives simply don't have the same experiences as employees at lower levels in the organization.

4. *Inclusion of Work/Life programs positions diversity initiatives beyond "doing things for the minorities."*

     As pointed out in other chapters, white males often see diversity as a clever new name for affirmative action, which, in turn, they associate with benefits intended solely for women and minorities. On the other hand, nearly all employees *at some time in their career* can benefit from work/family programs in their employment life cycle. For example, in work/family focus groups, men are becoming more vocal about their desire to share more in their children's growing up.

     Work/family programs provide a legitimate opportunity to broaden the base of support for the total diversity program. For example, at Rochester Telephone, white males, particularly union members, were reluctant to support the diversity efforts because it seemed to be affirmative action which produced no benefits for them. Michael O. Thomas, the recently hired Director of Diversity and Staffing, addressed the resistance by expanding the diversity initiative to cover job sharing, career planning and other issues that go beyond race and gender. The more inclusive approach is drawing more support from those who were previously resisting or distancing themselves from the effort. (1)

Some Cautions About Linking Diversity and Work/Family: Despite the apparent logic for close linkage of work/family and diversity initiatives, many organizations have not attempted to integrate the two. In some cases, it may simply be a matter of inertia, or that they hadn't thought much about it.

A potential impediment to linking diversity and work/family initiatives, is that some groups will raise concerns that inclusion of too many activities under the diversity umbrella will diffuse the impact and focus on the "real issues." For example, people of color have commented that the problems are still *"racism and discrimination—plain and simple!"* They may be concerned that the addition of work and family in total diversity strategy will be a ruse to sidestep taking on the more difficult issues. These concerns can be ameliorated by including diverse input into the strategy planning and priority setting, and by actions which demonstrate that there is no basis for their concern about tackling tough diversity issues.

ACTIONS YOU CAN TAKE TO INTEGRATE DIVERSITY AND WORK/FAMILY INITIATIVES

As more organizations recognize the logic and value of linking diversity and work/family programs, they will take action to bring about the specific potential benefits of such linkage. Some of the activity areas where the linkage is natural are described below.

Include Work/Family as Part of Your Diversity Vision: The Introduction provided a definition of effective diversity management as creating *"an environment . . . that seeks to tap the full potential of all employees, in pursuit of company objectives, where employees may progress without regard to irrelevant considerations."* (2) Certainly the dependent care responsibilities that the individual has should be an irrelevant consideration when determining the performance and advancement potential of the individual. Therefore, this should be part of your diversity vision and definition.

Include Work/Family in Organization Plans: If you have a diversity task force, include a subcommittee to focus on work/life issues. Make sure that within the human resources department, the support of work/life and diversity activities is closely coordinated, either informally or through specific organization efforts. Coordination will assure that resources are allocated to best balance competing priorities, and that the organization is not overloaded with a flurry of programs vying for attention simultaneously.

Include Work/Family in Employee Research: A diversity survey can benefit from the inclusion of some work/life questions. It would not be feasible to include a detailed evaluation of a number of work/life program options such as what types of dependent care are needed and at what locations, how much are employees willing to pay out-of-pocket, etc. However, key issues can be covered as a means to assess priorities, for example:

- Does the company have policies and programs that support the balance of work and personal life?

- Is the culture accepting and supportive of the needs of individuals who have dependent care responsibilities?

- Does maternity/paternity leave have an impact on an individual's advancement opportunities?

- Are supervisors carrying out company policies in the way the policies were intended?

Include Work/Family in Communications: The linkage can be reinforced, and economies realized by combining work/family communications with other diversity communication activities. Whether the communication is to express a corporate commitment, announce a research project, report on research findings, or describe new policies and programs, the inclusion of work/family programs can yield efficiency, cost effectiveness and greater visibility.

Include Both in Your Education and Training Activities: Diversity education and training aimed at raising awareness on race and gender issues can be broadened to include the issues associated with balancing work and personal life. This includes information about the changing demographics of dependent care, the business case for addressing the issues, and prejudices that we may have toward people with significant dependent care responsibilities. The combination of the subject matter may make the best use of the training budget and participants' time away from the job. The issues to be addressed in work/family training may be determined from the research data. For example, a high technology company found in a diversity survey that there was wide disagreement among employees regarding the quality of the company's work/family policies and programs. In the focus group sessions which followed the survey, it became clear that the work/family policies were not clearly understood by supervisors and were administered differently from division to division, and sometimes there were variations among departments within the same location. These deficiencies could be readily addressed through some specific training modules in the diversity effort.

Evaluate the Career Mobility Systems: Career mobility systems generally do not work as well for women, people of color and working mothers. The absence of friends in high places, and underlying bias can result in these individuals being left out of the informal mentoring and sponsorship systems that determine who will advance at what pace. A particular issue with regard to working mothers are the assumptions that might be made regarding their future advancement potential. If females are bumped from the "fast track" list after becoming pregnant, or if development efforts are withheld, you will simply be reinforcing the glass ceiling that is already in place in many organizations.

Tie in Culture Change Efforts: Extended working hours is one aspect of corporate culture that heavily affects the balance of work/life. Some organizations generate such pressure for face time that even officer-level employees will describe it as a "sickness." In one closely held company, the Chairman said he stayed late at the office on a regular basis because he felt guilty leaving while so many people were still at their desks. However, a middle manager said that there was usually a huge traffic jam in the parking lot five minutes after the Chairman left! Senior management can promptly change the time aspects of culture simply by changing their own behavior and clarifying their expectations.

Measure Results Over Time: As with diversity initiatives you should be prepared to demonstrate the impact of your work/family programs on the operation of the business. In fact, the tangible impact of work and family interventions is often more readily measured than some other diversity activities such as training (see Chapter 14 for a discussion of measurement). The greater measurability of work/life program results is extremely important to its support, because it overcomes a frequent senior management resistance to what they might view as expensive giveaway programs.

If organizations follow the guidelines described, the operation of diversity and work/family programs could, over time, become a seamless entity. The end result will be strategic clarity and economies in planning and execution.

DESIGN WORK/LIFE PROGRAMS FOR 2000 AND BEYOND

During the past decade there has been a burgeoning of work/family programs. The commitment has reached the stage that many companies engage in heated competition for recognition in *Working Mother* magazine as one of the ten best companies for mothers to work. At the same time there has been an evolutionary development of the work/family activity, as you would expect in any relatively new field. In observing the recent past and talking with work/family program managers and senior human resources officers, I have developed a perspective on the several recognizable stages in the history of work/family programming. As we look into the late 1990's and beyond, I see evidence of a new and slightly altered stage, as shown in Table 10.1.

To maintain competitive and effective programs in this evolving arena, there are three particular strategies you should incorporate into your future work/family planning:

TABLE 10.1 Stages of Work/Family Evolution

Program Dimension	Late 80's →	Early 90's →	Late 90's
Area of Concern	Child care	Dependent care	Balancing time demands of work/life and dependent care.
Target Population	Working mothers	Working parents & those with elder care responsibility	All employees
Companies Providing Programs	Large, sophisticated e.g., IBM, Johnson & Johnson, Aetna	Large, medium-sized companies, hospitals, government bodies.	Employers of 100 or more
Typical Program Intervention	child care providers resource/referral	Child care center/ support flexibility for maternity leaves, elder care referral	Flexibility, building supervisory awareness and support
Motivation	Right thing to do, may yield collateral benefits	Reduce turnover, absenteeism, ease productivity deterrents	Become employer of choice.
Effects Sought	Positive employee reactions	Listed as "100 Best" in *Working Mother* magazine.	Measurable impact on bottom line

Extend Programs Beyond Working Parents: Nearly 25% of companies have broadened the descriptions of their work family programs to be more inclusive, moving well beyond the original child care focus. (3) The first evolutionary phase recognized that elder care in some organizations could be as important a concern as child care. (4) The evolution progressed naturally and with little fanfare driven by better understanding of employee needs, and recognition that earlier efforts had, in fact, delivered some of the positive benefits that had been envisioned. Also, as companies increased the level of dependent care support, they began to encounter a "singles backlash." (5)

The singles backlash occurs among employees who have neither child care nor elder care responsibilities at the moment. They may feel that they are missing out on benefits. Companies began to realize that they needed a way to think strategically about these benefits, and at the same time communicate the intent in a way that appealed to as many employees as possible. As a result, the types of programs being offered to meet work/life needs has been gradually increasing, and the wide variety of programs now available has been documented in a 1994 Towers Perrin survey. The Towers Perrin survey categorized practices in six categories:

PROGRAM TYPE:

1. Employees taking care of dependents
2. Making work more flexible
3. Saving employees time
4. Creating the right environment
5. Support for employees through financial life cycles
6. Keeping employees physically and mentally fit

The practices were further categorized according to prevalence as **Baseline** (40% or more of the companies providing), **Progressive** (10–40%), **Leading Edge** (up to 10%), and **Emerging Issues** that involve ideas still in the consideration or prototype stage among a handful of companies. This data presents a comprehensive perspective of where companies are now and what can be anticipated in the coming years. Highlights are included in Tables 10.2 through 10.6.

Build Programs Around Life Cycle Events: Many work/family program planners utilize the concepts of employee needs that change during their life cycle with the organization, from new hire to death.[1] Ultimately the life cycle perspective may lead to all employee benefit programs being assessed from a more strategic perspective than has often been the case for benefits generally. Companies are beginning to structure and communicate programs in terms of employee needs. For example, in 1992, Allstate Insurance Company created a very effective employee communication piece based on life cycle events in the form of a cardboard dial. The employee can turn the dial to a particular life event such as: 1. New Employee, 2. Marriage, 3. Pregnancy and Adoption, 4. Child Rearing, 5. Divorce, 6. Elder Care, 7. Retirement, and 8. Death. Upon dialing the appropriate number the employee can read a list of all the company programs that are relevant to that life event. The programs are summarized under the headings of Financial Assistance, Programs and Services, Counseling and Information and Time. Michael Snipes, Director of Compensation and Benefits at Allstate (who developed the life cycle wheel), reports that it has become very popular with employees. Mr. Snipes suggests that "Employees appreciate a communication piece that links company programs to their immediate and particular needs, rather than being driven by some ERISA disclosure requirements."

Margaret Regan, a Towers Perrin principal, notes the developing interest in an all-inclusive *"Life Cycle Account,"* a package of nontraditional benefit options with an employer subsidy that's limited to a specific dollar amount. The em-

---

[1]Dana Friedman, Wendy Gray, *Life Cycle Stages and Company Programs,* Human Resources Monthly Briefing, May 1989, The Conference Board.

TABLE 10.2 Helping Employees Take Care of Dependents*

1. Baseline Programs
   - Dependent care spending accounts
   - Child care resource and referral
   - Well-baby care covered under medical plan
   - Dependents of part-time workers eligible for health plan coverage
   - Expanded unpaid family leave
2. Progressive Programs
   - Use of sick days for dependents
   - Wellness program for family members
   - Financial assistance for adoptions
   - Dependent care assistance program
   - Long-term care insurance for family members
   - Elder care resource and referral
3. Leading Edge Programs
   - Company-owned or supported child care centers
   - Child care vouchers
   - Sick child care center, voucher or service
   - Employer match on dependent care spending account
   - Child care expense reimbursement account for overtime/business travel
   - Medical benefits for domestic partners
   - Paid parental leave of absence
   - Paid family leave
   - Working parent support groups
   - Elder care fairs presenting community resources
   - Elder care support groups
   - Summer/holiday child care
   - Adoption resource and referral
   - Accommodation for nursing mothers
   - Employee discounts at local child care centers
   - Grants/contributions to local centers
4. Emerging Issues
   - Consortium child care centers with other companies
   - School day work schedule

*Tables 10.2–10.6 from *1994 Work/Personal Life Benefit Survey,* reprinted with permission of Towers Perrin, New York, N.Y.

TABLE 10.3 Making Work More Flexible

1. Baseline Programs
    - Flextime (narrow band)
    - Gradual return to work
    - Prorated benefits for part-time workers
    - Vacation days carryover
2. Progressive Programs
    - Flextime (wide band)
    - Compressed work week
    - Job-sharing
    - Telecommuting
    - Employer-provided office equipment for work at home
    - Full benefits for part-time workers
    - Paid time-off program
3. Leading Edge Programs
    - Voluntary reduced time
    - Midday flextime
    - Summer hours
    - Part year/School day work schedule
    - Equivalent head count system
    - Vacation day buying/selling

TABLE 10.4 Saving Employees' Time

1. Baseline Programs
    - On/near-site banking
    - Company medical services
2. Progressive Programs
    - Subsidized lunches
    - Travel ticketing/discounts for personal travel
    - Company convenience store
3. Leading Edge Programs
    - Cafeteria take-out suppers
    - Onsite dry cleaning, barber/salon
    - Concierge service

TABLE 10.5 Building the Right Environment

1. Baseline Programs
   - Employee attitude surveys
2. Progressive Programs
   - Employee focus groups, surveys on work/life issues
   - Training in work/life sensitivity issues
   - Work/life workshops
   - Work/life coordinator manager
3. Leading Edge Programs
   - Work/life newsletter/handbook
   - Work/life committee/task force
   - Work/life resource center on site

TABLE 10.6 Support for Employees Through Financial Life Cycles

1. Baseline Programs
   - Closing cost assistance
   - Paid time-off for relocation
   - Housing resource and referral
2. Progressive Programs
   - Spouse relocation placement assistance
   - Downpayment loans or grants
   - Post secondary school scholarships
   - Mortgage rate subsidies
   - Long-term care insurance for employees
3. Leading Edge Programs
   - Life cycle account
   - Direct employee loans
   - Cancer insurance
   - Tuition assistance for dependents
   - Group auto insurance
   - Financial planning for nonexecutives

ployer allocates a specific lifecycle amount to each employee, say $10,000. Employees receive reimbursements against this account as they incur eligible expenses. Certain benefits may be subject to annual maximums (e.g., tuition assistance) or frequency-of-use limits. The approach can help employees by providing a flexible menu that fits their needs, while putting limits on the extent of the company's financial commitment.

COMMIT TO WORK AND FAMILY LEADERSHIP AS A CORPORATE STRATEGY: THE HELENE CURTIS STORY

Work/family programs should be linked to corporate strategies, but practitioners often are at a loss as to how one goes about achieving that linkage. A good strategic model is Helene Curtis Industries, Inc. Helene Curtis is one of the nation's major producers of brand name personal care products such as shampoos, conditioners, styling aids, anti-perspirants, deodorants, and skin care products. The company markets its consumer products through supermarkets, mass merchandisers and drugstores.

In 1993 Helene Curtis sales were $1.2 billion. The company employs 3200 people worldwide, 2800 in the U.S. The largest concentration of employees is in the greater Chicago area.

Helene Curtis is traded on the New York Stock Exchange. The current President and CEO, Mr. Ronald J. Gidwitz is known in the community for his civic leadership and philanthropic activities.

In 1991, two related but separate initiatives at Helene Curtis were started, which ultimately led to a significant commitment to work/family as a strategic corporate issue.

Senior Management Strategy Initiative: In 1991, the senior management group formalized a new long range strategic plan for the company and developed a mission and values statement that was supportive of the directions in which the company needed to move by the year 2000.

The senior management exercise resulted in a new vision statement that incorporated the overriding characteristics that would guide the company during the '90s. The values statement was printed on a card for all employees, and introduced in a communication program. The Vision Statement incorporates a business mission and set of core values. The values have been identified with the involvement of all Helene Curtis employees through their participation in a company-wide survey. Selected statements from the vision document are reprinted in Exhibit 10.1. The portions that I have highlighted for emphasis are those values relating to promoting the welfare of employees' families and creating and fully utilizing a diverse workforce.

EXHIBIT 10.1 Excerpts from Helene Curtis Vision Statement**

- We will foster the *well-being of our employees, their families* and our communities.
- We *value the contributions of all* employees.
- We will *create an atmosphere of respect,* openness and trust that builds enduring relationships among ourselves, and with our consumers, customers, suppliers, and communities.
- We will foster an environment in which we enjoy and are *fulfilled in our jobs.*
- We will *promote diversity* in our organization to *fully utilize differences* in background and perspective.

**Emphasis added by this writer

Employee Initiative Emerges: Simultaneous to the development of the Helene Curtis Vision, an informal employee committee was formed to share experiences regarding work and family issues and to try to develop some suggestions for the company. The company was supportive of the group, because they were beginning to see turnover of valuable employees as they gravitated to other organizations that were more aggressive in addressing work and family needs and who used their programs as recruiting stimulants.

The committee, working mostly with human resources, developed a survey to assess employee needs and preferences. They also did some external benchmarking to learn about successful programs in other companies.

The Program: Working with Felice Cota-Robles, Supervisor EEO/Family Programs, the committee finalized a work/family program which they called "Family to Family." Program elements were built around the life cycle approach, addressing issues of the new worker, marriage, pregnancy and adoption, child rearing, divorce and elder care. A proposal was developed for Helene Curtis senior management review that incorporated the following elements:

Resource and Informational Assistance

- Adoption resource service
- Child care resource and referral program
- Elder care consultation and referral program
- Employee assistance program[†]
- Lunchtime seminar program
- Pre-retirement planning program[†]
- School Smart education service

FINANCIAL ASSISTANCE

- Adoption expense assistance program
- Dependent care voucher program[†]
- Health care flexible spending account
- Paid medical leave of absence[†]

FLEXIBILITY IN THE WORKPLACE

- Family care leave assistance
- Flextime
- Flexible work arrangements—part time employment

[†]Previously in existence, incorporated into the overall program.

Mr. Robert K. Niles, Helene Curtis Vice President of Human Resources, said that the proposal for expanded work/family programs was readily adopted by senior management, since it was a "natural fit" with the vision and values of the company.

Results of the New Program: The "Family to Family" programs were very well received by employees. The impact on employees' feelings about returning to the workforce after a maternity leave were particularly significant and resulted in measurable behavior changes. For example, the percentage of mothers not returning from maternity leave was 31% at the start of the programs, and declined to 7% three years later. Turnover was reduced from 13.4% to under 9% during that same time frame.

Ms. Felice Cota-Robles, Supervisor EEO/Family Programs, reports that the performance improvements represented in the above data more than pay for all the costs of the programs. It has turned out to be a self-funding system, while yielding strong kudos from employees. The programs are now featured as part of the company's recruiting program. This is an important element, as prospective employees have become more knowledgeable about the types of programs available and will inquire as to what you have to offer.

In October 1993, Helene Curtis was selected by *Working Mother* magazine as one of the 100 best companies for working mothers. However, the company is not content to rest on its laurels. It has established a work/family advisory committee of sixteen employees representing all position levels, functions and locations. This group is now considering possible additions to the existing core programs, such as the following:

- Mothers' room for lactation
- Reimbursement of child care expenses resulting from company travel

- Sick child care
- Manager flexibility training

The company also plans to examine if there are ways in which it can link its efforts and recognition to its marketing image. Mr. Niles comments that "We are proud of the recognition by *Working Mother* magazine. However, we are even more pleased at the response of employees and their families, and the effect the programs have had on behavior. The programs positively impact productivity and help to more strongly position ourselves as an employer of choice for the diverse workforce that we seek."

Mr. Niles also notes that the credibility established through the work/family programs is an important base as they move toward working on other diversity issues that are supportive of the company vision statement.

IMPORTANT POINTS TO REMEMBER

1. Because of similarities in issues and approaches, you should attempt to link diversity and work/family strategies and programs.
   - Both are addressing bias and stereotyping in the workplace.
   - Both address issues of glass ceiling and excessive turnover.
   - Linkage of the two programs positions the total strategy as going beyond the interests of a specific gender or ethnic group.
2. Take action to integrate diversity and work/family strategies and programs.
   - Include work/life as part of the vision for diversity.
   - Include work/life in your organization planning.
   - Include work/life in diversity communications/research/training.
   - Include work/life in your education and training programs.
   - Include work/life in your culture change efforts.
   - Measure the operational impact of the programs over time.
3. Design your work/family programs for 2000 and beyond.
   - Expand programs beyond working parents.
   - Plan work/family programs for employee life cycle needs.
4. Tie corporate commitments to work/life programs to the core values and strategies of the organization.

11 Design Compensation for a Diverse Workforce

Having spent a part of my early career as a compensation benefit consultant, and as a compensation director at the corporate level, the subject is dear to my heart. However, as a practical matter, compensation issues have seldom loomed large in diversity studies in which I have been involved. The relatively modest emphasis on the compensation dimension may be attributable to the fact that the organization is feeling more pain in other programs or corporate culture areas, and focuses its efforts accordingly. Or perhaps the organization may not see compensation as having diversity dimensions. However, as you look into the future, a number of compensation issues relating to workforce diversity can be identified.

Therefore, this chapter will be brief, focusing on the following:

- Reviewing some examples of diversity research findings on pay equity and the linkage of pay with performance.

- Identifying some aspects of contemporary compensation practices which no longer fit the new workforce.

- Examining in detail the advantages of linking diversity performance to compensation as a means of instilling commitment.

IDENTIFYING AND CORRECTING GROUP-BASED PAY DIFFERENTIALS

We have all read about the differentials in pay that have traditionally existed between males and female workers in the United States. The persistent gender-pay gap has closed slightly over the years. In 1979, women earned 63% of the median weekly wage of men. By 1992 the gap had been narrowed to 76% of the males' wages (1). Given the national pattern represented by those statistics, we should not be surprised to see a disparity in perceptions of pay equity when responses are reported on a gender basis. Exhibit 11.1 shows data from a small sampling of companies in a diversity change process.

Statement: I am paid fairly compared with others in similar positions.

The survey composite data in the following graph indicates a slightly lower level of pay equity satisfaction among females, with the most significant levels of discontent among female nonexempt employees. There is a wide range of equity issues that are raised in focus groups by nonexempt employees, such as those identified below:

Hispanic Males:
"If you are promoted to level 3, you can get only the minimum of the range. If they are hired in off the street, they come in at the midpoint. You have the knowledge, he gets the pay."

EXHIBIT 11.1 Perceptions of Pay Equity: Gender-Based Differentials

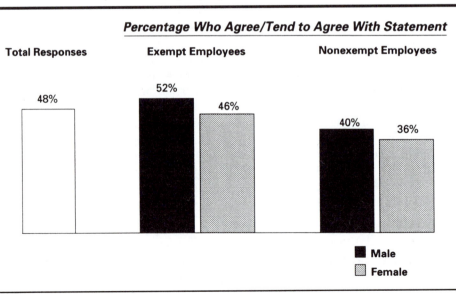

"They say they will bring us up to the minimum slowly, which usually means several years. In the meantime everyone is passing us by."

Black Female:
"Black employees are limited to mid points, but white employees are allowed to go to the top of the salary range."

Asian Female:
"There is a rule upstairs that degreed people get paid more regardless of experience and performance. That is sad and demotivating."

White Female:
"We are paid by (secretarial) job titles. They don't give credit for all the added responsibilities we pick up as we get to know the department better. The position descriptions haven't been changed in years."

Black Male:
"I said why am I being paid below the minimum and below the white guy who is doing the same work? My supervisor said 'It's the best I can do for you right now. Don't raise any trouble.' Right there that's telling me there is something wrong."

Hispanic Female:
"Men are paid more regardless of their position or job performance. Men have the advantage of networking and bonding with other men in decision making positions."

As you might gather from the comments above, the range of issues is fairly wide, and varies from specific examples of a perceived inequity to some very broad culturally based assumptions (e.g., networking comment).

A second key issue in determining individual satisfaction with pay is the perceived relationship between pay and individual performance. As shown in Exhibit 11.2, there are differentials on the scores for this sample, but no overwhelming pattern of ratings assigned by the groups.

Statement: My pay is related fairly to my performance.

Exhibits 11.1 and 11.2 illustrate that the differences in perceptions analyzed by race and gender groups are much less dramatic than, say, the differences recorded for the career mobility systems or for concerns about affirmative action and the corporate culture. The lower levels of differentiation [along diversity dimensions] I believe are caused by several factors:

Compensation levels (at least in medium and larger companies) tend to be better analytically supported and quantitatively driven as compared with other HR systems and programs. Detailed job evaluation plans determine internal comparative job worth, the external market is surveyed in detail, and so forth.

EXHIBIT 11.2 Perceptions of Pay/Performance Equity

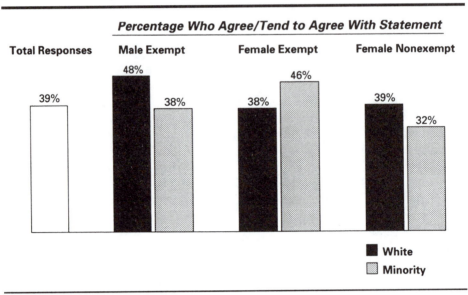

Percentage Who Agree/Tend to Agree With Statement

Total Responses   Male Exempt   Female Exempt   Female Nonexempt

39%   48%   38%   38%   46%   39%   32%

■ White
▨ Minority

There may be more checks and balances in the compensation systems. The manager in a given department will be constrained by systems and guidelines in determining the job evaluation level, the starting salary, the amount of the annual increase in relation to performance, and so forth. Many companies routinely audit the operation of their pay programs. Some perform multiple regression analyses to test the relationships between pay level, performance, race and gender. While bias still can (and does) creep into administration of pay, the system strictures make it more difficult for a manager's biases to drive pay decisions very far off course.

If employees sense inequity they can test their thesis in the market place. If they feel their pay is out of line, they can seek to peddle their services as a test.

While companies might be pleased that scores don't fluctuate widely between the groups, the fact is that the evaluation pattern exhibited is for *universally low scores*. Consider the following:

In the first chart above only **48%** of all employees felt they are paid fairly relative to other positions in the company. Only **39%** feel that their pay is closely related to their performance on the job.

On another question, two-thirds of the respondents perceived that *merit increases* were not merit increases at all. They viewed their annual salary increase as driven by budget considerations, not the individual's performance. White employees' scores hovered around the 70% range in that perception, with a little less than 60% of minorities maintaining that position.

In another piece of bad news, survey respondents were asked to identify potential impediments to their contributing all that they could on the job. The lack of incentives and rewards was consistently among the top three most frequently mentioned inhibitors of performance.

If I were still a compensation practitioner, the data shown above would be like living my worst nightmare. I have put out all this information about how thorough our system is, how important merit increases are, how carefully we track market place pay levels, and so forth. However, if the results shown are reflective of general conditions, the folks receiving the pay simply aren't buying the program! But this is more a broad strategic issue than it is a diversity issue.

HOW TO POSITION COMPENSATION PROGRAMS FOR 2000 AND BEYOND

In addition to the general lack of confidence in the pay systems, there are some other compensation issues which become more important with the increase in work force diversity. Let's review some of those issues in a summary fashion, and speculate about what might be the implications for planning compensation for the remainder of this century and beyond.

Compensation Issue: Trust: Diversity research often indicates a general distrust of HR systems and a perception that they don't work as well for females, minorities and others who are "different."

POSSIBLE STRATEGY IMPLICATIONS

- Open up systems for all to see how they work. For example, expand and rotate membership in position evaluation committees, share information on company pay levels versus the competitive set, provide information on the relative rankings of similar positions within the company.

- Provide for diverse input into the design and administration of compensation programs, including level, function, ethnic and gender diversity.

- Formalize systems to reduce the opportunity for inadvertent bias in assigning job evaluation levels and individual pay levels.

- Review the system for the impact of pressure from "sponsors" or "squeaky wheels." Make sure employees who do not have strong negotiating skills or limited organization power don't get left behind their more aggressive counterparts when rewards are doled out.

- Conduct formal audits to verify system fairness, for example, multiple regression analysis to detect inequities, followed by corrective actions, even if budgets are exceeded.

- Triple check evaluation and pay levels for positions where female and minority employees are concentrated. Use a knowledgeable third party to challenge any unexplained variations in pay levels.
- Use multisource performance appraisal techniques to provide a credible basis for a pay and performance linkage.

Compensation Issue: Variable Needs: Changing family patterns and the variety of personal interests and needs makes obsolete some of the traditional assumptions on compensation planning.

POSSIBLE STRATEGY IMPLICATIONS

- Senior management and HR presumptions of what employees want may no longer be valid. Design of effective programs will entail considerable employee input at all levels.
- Flexible compensation and flexible benefit programs that employees can adjust to their own needs will be seen as a "must," rather than as a "nice to have" program enhancement.
- Compensation/benefit data base should include diversity dimensions (age, gender, race, dependent status, marital status, etc.) so that analyses and planning of programs can be more needs-specific, and actual usage checked against assumptions.
- Work and family programs will continue to shift the focus on benefits from the cost (or actuarial value), to the value assigned to the benefit by the individual, based on how it meets his or her current life cycle needs.

Compensation Issue: Time Off and Pay Interchangeability: Competitive pressures, reengineering and other forces will continue to keep work demands at high levels. These forces, combined with increasing numbers of employees with dependent care responsibilities, cause time off to be valued as an attractive alternative to more compensation.

POSSIBLE STRATEGY IMPLICATIONS

- Vacation buy-backs will become a standard feature in flexible benefit and compensation programs. A significant number of individuals at all levels will avail themselves of the buy-back privilege.
- Part time and job sharing arrangements will become a common and accepted means to utilize and retain a diverse work force. The notion that benefits should be designed only for full time employees, who will stay with the company for a lengthy career, will be challenged.

Compensation Issue: "Democracy" in Compensation: Increasing diversity and willingness to speak out may create pressure for more "democratic" compensation structures and practices.

POSSIBLE STRATEGY IMPLICATIONS

- Pressure for smaller pay differentials between executives and the "troops in the trenches" will exacerbate, slowing the rate of growth in the pay gap.

- Status perks, (luxurious offices, company limo, and so on) will come under increasing pressure. The focus may change from the positive morale impact for the few who benefit from the practice, to the negative impact on the many who observe, but can never participate.

- Company support of executive participation in exclusionary clubs will be increasingly challenged as part of a diversity change process. Use of such facilities for company events involving diverse employees will entail unacceptable risks of negative reactions.

The list of issues cited above should be regarded not as conclusive, but only indicative of the future. As you think about the issues that face your particular organization, you can no doubt add to it.

DETERMINE IF DIVERSITY RESULTS SHOULD BE LINKED TO MANAGEMENT INCENTIVE PROGRAMS

One of the topics that is continually debated is the need or value of linking diversity progress to managerial performance appraisal and compensation. For many, the true test of senior management commitment to diversity results is the establishment of a pay-performance linkage. That debate leads directly to the second issue: if one were to attempt such linkages, what might be some workable approaches? In the remainder of the chapter I describe the rationale for and against specific diversity elements in the pay program, and provide a model incentive program to assess its practical value. First I need to lay out my assumptions about incentive compensation structures that you are likely to find.

Assumptions for the Analysis: To understand the conclusions it is necessary to understand some of my basic assumptions about the design of executive pay programs. If your company's profile differs from my assumptions, you could arrive at a different conclusion.

ASSUMPTION 1: I assume that it is difficult to provide a significant incentive for diversity performance through the administration of base salaries. With average *total* salary increases in the '90s running in the range of 3–5% there simply is not enough flexibility to set aside a meaningful portion just for diversity performance. As one manager said, *"The official guidelines say 3% to 6% but the budget controls limit the real flexibility between 3% to 4% max."* Let's assume that 25% of the total increase was based on diversity performance, which would be a heavy weighting for the typical line manager. That would mean that the difference between average and exceptional diversity performance would be .25% to 1.0% of salary, which does not seem like a big motivator.

ASSUMPTION 2: For most companies the largest portion of incentive compensation is driven by the financial results of the company, division or profit center where the individual centers his/her activities. The pressures for performance will dictate that such a weighting be continued in the future. As some managers have said to us, *"If the (profit) numbers aren't there, we won't need to worry about diversity. We will be out of jobs, or acquired by another company."*

ASSUMPTION 3: Despite the heavy reliance on financial performance, most bonus plans do provide for judgment of individual performance against predetermined objectives. In some instances the individual element may be quite high, but more frequently the individual component (as a practical matter) accounts for less than 35% of the variation in awards.

Using the three assumptions described above as background, let's look at the pros and cons of linking incentive pay to diversity performance.

The Case for Linking Diversity Results to Compensation: The arguments for rewarding progress on diversity objectives (or penalizing for lack of progress) are straightforward and appealing. The chief points made by proponents can be summarized as follows:

- An axiom in most organizations is that what gets rewarded gets done. The selection of performance measures for salary increases or bonuses tells a lot about the real priorities of the organization. Attaching compensation to diversity results may be viewed by key managers as the "acid test" of whether the CEO is serious about the company's professed commitment.
- There is a danger that diversity will be crowded from the agenda if it is not part of the comp structure. Diversity may be competing for attention with other strategic issues such as loss of market share, new challenges from competitors, "mega events" (e.g., mergers, restructuring) or toughened financial goals to meet shareholder and financial community expectations.
- Diversity progress will not come without effort, and perhaps some pain as well. Managers, for equity purposes, will want to be tangibly recognized for what many will perceive as the added burden of diversity management heaped on their already full plates.

The above rationale for directly linking compensation to diversity issues is compelling and holds a significant amount of surface logic, especially for those who retain reservations about the sincerity of the company's commitment to progress. Now let's examine the other side of the coin.

Arguments Against a Diversity Compensation Linkage: If the case for linking management incentives to diversity progress was overwhelming, there would be a lot more organizations already doing it. After all, management incentive programs are practically ubiquitous in companies of all sizes. However, the number of companies actually tying diversity measures to compensation is estimated at less than one fourth. Why the gap? Perhaps because there are several basic issues that organizations find difficult to resolve, including the following:

- Many areas of diversity progress are difficult to measure with any precision. As we discuss in more detail in Chapter 14, there are some specific and quantifiable goals that can be measured, especially those in such areas as hiring, promotions, EEO complaints, and so on. However, some of the measures are somewhat more qualitative, such as the perceived environment of respect, perceptions of discriminatory treatment (different from complaints actually filed), opportunities for advancement and the like. For these areas you may be limited to measuring changes in perceptions, or verifying that an activity has actually been accomplished, without measuring its impact on the company.

- There is a risk that you will not be able to allocate a sufficiently large portion of incentive pay to diversity to make it worthwhile, and to provide the correct message to the organization. Let's say that the individual's target bonus is 20% of base salary, with 60% of the bonus determined by finite financial measures of performance. That leaves only 40% of the bonus, or 8% of salary for all the remaining individual performance measures. Where the practice has been established, a typical line manager might have 25% of those individual measures determined by his/her diversity performance. (2) Thus the true range of diversity-based incentive is in the range of 0% to 2% of compensation. Most would judge this as insufficient to be a real incentive. In fact, one might argue that an incentive of that magnitude detracts from the importance of a diversity initiative, because the bonus plan would seem to devalue its relevance.

- Generally, incentive plans cover only a small portion of the workforce, so many would not have the incentive available. Depending on the philosophy of the company, its size and organization structure, a management bonus plan may cover only 3% to 10% of the salaried exempt employees. However, this may be the easiest argument to counter, because if the top of the organization is interested in diversity they have the power to hold their subordinates equally accountable for results.

- Inclusion of diversity could lead to micro-management of bonuses and administrative complexity. If diversity is to be included as a specific bonus element, why not include a dozen other activities that are inherent in a manager's job? Other examples that might be suggested are development of employees, quality performance, and so on. You could end up with a loss of focus on the **primary** performance issues.

- Some executives believe that managers should not be held accountable for what is essentially an organizational problem. For example, Xerox (one of the early leaders in tying affirmative action goals to compensation), discontinued the practice because recruitment and retention were considered to be heavily affected by organization issues (downsizing, restructuring) beyond the control of many managers.

The debate on *"should you?"* will continue. Let's shift to consideration of *"how would you?"* as a final test of the potential for a linkage between diversity performance and pay.

TEST YOUR PLAN DESIGN BEFORE IMPLEMENTING

Assume for the moment that you would like to further consider the formal integration of diversity measures into your management bonus plan. What follows is a description of one approach that illustrates how you might go about it. The Superior Gizmos Inc. Management Incentive Plan is outlined in Exhibit 11.3. This plan description incorporates many aspects of incentive plans that are found in organizations today. Note how some of the features might impact on the potential adaptability of the program to include diversity objectives:

Section III. Potential Award Levels: Total awards are large only for the officer and senior officer level (only so much $$ to work with.)

Section IV. Financial Performance: The primary bonus driver ties compensation to benefits that the shareholders are receiving. Generally broad gauge financial measures will not be significantly impacted on a short term basis by diversity progress.

Section V. Performance Measurement on Individual Goals: Significant variation is permitted here. However, as a practical matter, an award at only 60% of the maximum in many companies indicates very weak performance and is equivalent to being terminated. Also, there may be another six to ten key performance objectives that have to be considered for the personal performance piece.

Section VI. Diversity Performance Measures: We have provided a fairly long list of measures to choose from, including some with hard measures, and some that are more subjective or qualitative in nature. The 50% impact assigned to diversity progress probably would not be saleable in many organizations unless they are in some sort of "crisis mode" on diversity.

Section VII. Examples of Potential Bonus Awards: As you look at the bottom line, the difference between a high performer and a low performer for the various

EXHIBIT 11.3 Superior Gizmos Incorporated 1995 Management Incentive Plan: Guidelines and Measures

I. PLAN OBJECTIVES
   1. Motivate outstanding performance to achieve the strategic, financial and operational goals of the organization.
   2. Provide key managers an opportunity to directly share in the benefits of outstanding operating and financial performance.
   3. Provide focus on particular areas of corporate concern and reward performance in those areas. Focus area for the 1994–1995 fiscal years is managing diversity.

II. ELIGIBILITY FOR PARTICIPATION
   1. Recurrent participants: each year, managers in positions holding the title of Director, or other positions in salary grade 6 or higher.
   2. Periodic participants: each year individuals who are not recurrent participants may be nominated for a special one-time bonus award. Nominations to be made by the area Vice President, based on the following criteria:
      a. Performance is noticeably outstanding.
      b. The activity is above and beyond the normal requirements of the position.
      c. The activity is of strategic importance to the organization.

Note to Readers: The description under II.2. may be used to administer bonuses in companies that do not maintain formal ongoing management bonus programs.

III. POTENTIAL BONUS AWARD LEVELS

TARGET BONUS AS A % OF SALARY

Participant Position Level	Company Total Bonus %	Financial Performance	Individual Goals
1. President, Executive V.P.s, Senior V.P.s	55%	40%	15%
2. Vice Presidents	40%	25%	15%
3. Directors	28%	18%	10%
4. Others in grade 12 and above	18%	10%	8%
5. Those not included above, defined as "periodic participants"	Minimum award $1,000.00 Maximum award $7,500.00		

IV. FINANCIAL PERFORMANCE MEASUREMENT

Actual Return on Invested Capital versus Plan → YIELDS	Bonus Target Multiplier (see III. above)
110% and higher	1.30
108%	1.25
106	1.20
104	1.10
102	1.05
100	1.00
98	.95
96	.80
94	.70
92	.50
90% and below	Determined by Compensation Committee of the Board

(continued)

EXHIBIT 11.3 Continued

V. PERFORMANCE MEASUREMENT ON INDIVIDUAL GOALS

Performance Level*	Adjustment to Individual Target Bonus
1. Exceeds expectations	110% to 150%
2. Fully meets expectations	90% to 110%
3. Meets most expectations	75% to 90%
4. Missed key expectations	0% to 60%

*Performance levels defined in some detail in the performance appraisal manual.

VI. SPECIFIC DIVERSITY PERFORMANCE MEASURES FOR 1995–96

Diversity performance will be rated at 50% of the total for individual performance bonus determination. Principal indicators of performance are described below:

Goal Setting Category	Performance Indicators
EEO/AA Statistics	a. Performance versus industry average for % females & minorities employed in managerial, professional, and sales EEO - 1 categories b. Improvement in numbers of females and minorities employed in: • Grades 12 and above • Listed on back-up charts for grades 12 and above c. Number of EEO charges per 1,000 employees not to exceed industry average, show downward trend versus prior two years Gizmo data. d. Improve flow and hiring of minority recruitment candidates by 15% over prior year.
Training and Development	a. Completion of diversity awareness training for 60% of salaried employees with an overall rating of 4.0 or better (5 point scale) b. Complete diversity training pilot for hourly employees, execute program for 20% of employees on a prioritized location basis. c. Complete design of second wave of diversity training (diversity skills) for salaried employees. Run first 200 employees through pilot, and achieve quality ratings of 4.0 or higher. d. Develop strategy for incorporating diversity elements into ongoing management training programs: • Sales management • New manager training • Advanced leadership training
Diversity Initiatives	a. Complete semi-annual pay equity studies, resolve all issues identified within 90 days. b. Under guidance of division diversity steering committee, complete research to identify priority issues for resolution in 1994–95. c. Conduct focus groups on the effectiveness of current performance appraisal design and administration as perceived by employee groups. d. Develop description of position qualification standards for key career ladders: • Marketing: Marketing assistant to Vice President • Finance: Junior Accountant to division controllers, corporate department heads e. Incorporate position standards into succession planning reviews, train evaluators in the use of the factors. f. Expand job posting system to include positions at the director level.

EXHIBIT 11.3 Continued

VII. EXAMPLES OF POTENTIAL BONUS AWARDS

EXAMPLES OF BONUS AWARDS (% of salary)

BONUS STEPS	Exec. & Sen. V.P.	Vice Pres.	Directors	Other Eligible
1. Total target bonus by position. . . .	55%	40%	28%	18%
2. Financial performance target bonus. . . .	40%	25%	18%	10%
3. Multiplier assuming 104% of ROIC plan:	1.1	1.1	1.1	1.1
4. Adjusted bonus for financial performance [3. x 2. above] . . .	44%	27.5%	19.8%	11.0%
5. Bonus target for individual performance . . .	15%	15%	10%	8%
6. Bonus adjustment for individual performance:				
6. A. *High Rating Example*				
Diversity items	1.20			
Other items	1.10			
Avg. multiplier	1.15	1.15	1.15	1.15
6. A. Adjusted individual bonus [total multiplier x 5. above] . . .	17.25%	17.25%	11.50%	9.20%
6. B. *Low Rating Example*				
Diversity items	.65			
Other items	.75			
Total multiplier	.70	.70	.70	.70
6. B. Adjusted individual bonus	10.5%	10.5%	7.0%	5.6%
7. Total bonus:				
High Performer = 4 + 6.A.. . . .	61.25%	42.25%	31.3%	20.2%
Low Performer = 4 + 6.B.. . . .	54.50%	38.0%	26.8%	16.6%
Differential between high and low performer	6.75%	4.25%	4.5%	3.6%

positions is only 3.6% of salary for the lowest level participant to 6.75% for the senior officers. That differential has to capture all the elements that might be incorporated into the appraisal of the individual's performance for the year. Within the context of your own organization, you have to answer the question: "Is this a meaningful incentive?"

I have gone to some lengths to test the workability of connecting diversity performance with compensation. There are limits inherent in pay structures that make it difficult to make a heavy connection, and yet there are success stories. A Midwest supermarket chain tied 15% of its store managers' bonus to achievement of affirmative action goals for their own stores. The stores began demonstrating an immediate and significant improvement in their performance against those goals. At a lower incentive payout level, Levi Strauss bonus plan awards were based 2/3 on financial performance and the remaining 1/3 on individual performance measures. One-sixth of that remaining 1/3 (or 1/18 of the total bonus) is based on diversity performance. Levi Strauss describes that weighting for diversity as "heavy," and I am not prepared to argue otherwise. After all, from 1982 to

1992 Levi Strauss increased its percentage of minority managers from 18% to 36%, and the number of female managers from 32% to 53% (3) It seems to have worked for them, and that's the key!

IMPORTANT POINTS TO REMEMBER

1. Identify and correct any pay differentials that seem to follow group membership (gender, ethnicity, function).
2. Develop new compensation strategies that meet the interests and needs of the diverse work force.
   - Open systems to generate trust
   - Allow more flexibility to meet individual needs
   - Provide more compensation/time off interchange options
   - Prepare for criticism of executive pay practices
3. Determine if incentives for diversity progress make sense in your organization.
4. Test any incentive program before rolling it out.

12 How to Use Communications to Support a Diversity Change Process

The messages conveyed in a diversity change process cover a wide variety of subject matter. In fact, it is a bit artificial to set aside a chapter on communications, because virtually every step in a change process has a communication element. Some specific communication issues are discussed in relevant chapters.

The objective of this chapter is to help prepare you to develop and execute the *formal* aspects of a diversity communication strategy. To accomplish this, the following topics will be addressed:

- Identifying the constituencies that have a vested interest in a diversity process and describing the probable nature of that interest

- Describing specific strategies and activities for communicating to a diverse workforce during the change process

- Providing specific guidelines and examples for a half dozen diversity process "events" that will require communication support to reinforce the linkage of the individual activities to the process as a whole

DEVELOP YOUR STRATEGY TO MEET THE NEEDS AND INTERESTS OF THE DIVERSITY PROCESS STAKEHOLDERS

The list of individuals or groups who are potentially interested in your diversity initiatives can be quite extensive. Internally the interested parties may encompass responsibility levels from the janitor to senior management. Externally the audience may range from suppliers and civic organizations, to the shareholders of the company. An understanding of the communication targets and areas of self interest and concern is critical for planning your overall communication strategy, and in helping to develop the specific communication messages and vehicles you may wish to incorporate.

Protected Class Constituencies: One group of individuals having a great deal to gain or lose in a diversity change process are those who historically have been covered by affirmative action and anti-discrimination regulations. Individuals who are members of "protected classes" include at least the following:

- minorities (EEO-1 categories described in Chapter 9)
- physically challenged
- females
- foreign born
- persons over age 40
- Vietnam era veterans
- others protected in certain circumstances and jurisdictions (for example, gay and lesbian, severely obese)

Some of the concerns that protected class members will have about diversity programs include the following:

- Will the company lose focus on affirmative action as it shifts its attention to diversity, causing a backsliding from hard-won gains?
- Are the diversity and affirmative action activities related, and if so, in what way?
- Will the spotlight on diversity stir up white backlash, creating resentment regarding past and future progress of the members of their group? In other words, is it best to leave well enough alone?
- Does any continuing focus on females and minorities and others who are different further reinforce assumptions that "they can't make it on their own?"
- As diversity training progresses, will an open discussion of cultural differences create tensions and reinforce negative stereotypes, rather than the opposite goal for which the activity is intended?

The protected class constituencies in many organizations have heard a lot of promises over the years. They may be justified in having a healthy skepticism about the prospects for real and lasting change. In the words of an Asian female, *"I haven't seen any results on the employee survey or family issues survey. I am skeptical about this diversity push. You can only get your hopes up so many times."*

The tough questions can be answered, but anticipation of the concerns of these groups is important.

The White Male Constituency: White males are likely to perceive themselves as having the most to lose, and little to gain from a diversity initiative. Their concerns will revolve around the following questions.

- Syndicated columnist Mike Royko claims that the motto of politicians is *"Ubi est mea?"* (Where's mine?) Self-interest is a natural part of the human condition. With regard to diversity programs, self-interest may be expressed as one white male did: *"Affirmative action got them (females and minorities) here to begin with. Then diversity comes along and pushes them higher. Where is our program?"*

- Will quotas, set asides and other techniques be used to artificially (in their minds) increase the diversity at various organization levels? Will the progress of others come at the expense of white males?

- Will the communications or training implicitly lay the blame on them for the diversity issues the organization faces?

- Will their own point of view be fairly included in the development of the strategy and communication process?

- Will senior management accept responsibility for their role in creating the problems, and set a strong example for change? Or will they shift the blame to lower level managers?

When asked to generate a list of priorities, white males often will focus on the need for cost reduction, new strategies, more effective senior leadership, etc. They need periodic refreshers that diversity is a business issue, not just another "nice to have" or "flavor of the month" program. Furthermore, they would be reassured that managing diversity is not a guise for instituting racial and gender quotas.

Company Management Constituencies: Many participants will be viewing the diversity initiative from the point of view of the *short term* impact on the company. The types and levels involved include the following:

- *Senior management* who approve programs, set goals and hold managers accountable for results.

- *Middle managers* who implement programs.

- *Entry level managers* who may feel threatened, but are required to participate in the program.
- *The Board of Directors* who audits social responsibility performance.
- *Internal technical experts* (law, affirmative action, human resources) who examine communications from their technical viewpoints to protect company interests.

Some of the concerns of the management constituencies include the following:

- How much is this going to cost, and where will the budget come from?
- How much time will be required by me or my staff for the various activities?
  - Attending diversity training programs
  - Participating in diversity steering committees
  - Implementing whatever programs are generated from the process
- What are the potential positive and negative effects of an intervention process?
  - On day-to-day working relationships
  - Stirring up possible resentments that might better be left in a state of "benign neglect"
  - Improving or harming the company's public image
  - Improving individual and team effectiveness and productivity
  - Increasing market share through entry into new areas or protecting current customer bases
- Are the materials technically correct and do they avoid potentially damaging or misleading disclosures or commitments which may be difficult to fulfill?

Focusing on bottom line impacts is a good way to keep the attention of line managers at all levels. The short term costs must be positioned as a prerequisite for long term benefits.

External Constituencies: The impact of a diversity initiative often goes beyond the walls of the organization. Concern about the company fulfilling its obligations to be both socially and fiscally responsible may be shared by several groups.

- **Customers:** Organizations who buy the company's products or services who employ diverse decision makers, or who have established their own diversity programs will be alert to the existence of a similar level of commitment from their principal suppliers.
- **Consumers:** Those who use the company's products and services may won-

der how that company treats employees like themselves. The knowledge may or may not affect their buying decision.

- **Community organizations:** Organizations in your trading area are interested in the job opportunities and treatment of their members.

- **Shareholders/Investment community:** The concern is for positioning the company for competitive advantage and minimization of problems and distractions.

As an organization moves through a diversity change process, the needs of these and possibly other groups should be factored into the planning.

TAILOR COMMUNICATION STRATEGIES TO THE DYNAMICS OF A DIVERSITY CHANGE PROCESS

Diversity-related communications differ from some routine employee communication processes because of the potential sensitivity of the issues and the wide range of constituencies. To address the needs of the various target audiences previously described, Towers Perrin/Diversity Consultants communication specialists have found that a strategy for effective communications should contain the elements described briefly below.

Create a Diverse Planning Team: Diverse planning teams are often more effective than homogeneous teams in solving problems and coming up with more creative ideas. For example, in the work with a major restaurant chain, the project began with the formation of a diverse team to develop a game plan that will accommodate regional differences as well as differences in age, race, gender, store employees vs. corporate employees, etc. This collaboration process takes time, but better ideas result from this process. Most recently, for example, one such team came up with the idea of conducting an interactive telephone survey in both English and Spanish. The employee response to the change was extremely positive.

Research the Needs and Interests of Each Audience Segment: The needs of Spanish-speaking employees (or other language minorities), the lower paid employees, employees represented by unions—all need to be taken into account for various programs. A limited research probe involving two or three focus groups may be conducted to get a better appreciation of these varying needs and to determine what will be most effective in meeting those needs (see Chapter 7 for a discussion of focus group methodologies). You can then determine if distinct audiences will require any separate or special communication efforts.

Educate and Involve Senior Management: Senior management support of diversity initiatives is critical, and yet they may be far removed from the experiences and day-to-day issues that the programs are attempting to address. For example, a survey of CEOs of large companies was conducted by the *Wall Street Journal*. Of these, none had ever used any outside daycare or other child care services; 90% said their spouses had never worked full time for pay outside the home while the children were young.

Don't assume that senior managers have a sophisticated knowledge of the issues even within your own company! In large organizations there is a natural tendency to shield higher management from the problems festering in the trenches. Without "crying wolf" you need to raise their level of awareness and stay in front of them with tangible results and success stories to keep their commitment strong.

Train Diverse Teams as Front-Line Communicators: An often overlooked channel for information is the front-line communicators. Who do employees go to for interpretation when changes are made? In most organizations there is not enough HR staff to cover all the bases in a major communications intervention. You should consider training members of the diversity task force, members of advocacy groups as well as people in operations, secretarial and clerical positions to help conduct meetings as well as answer questions about diversity processes and programs.

One company with a significant population of Polish-speaking employees trained two Polish-speaking factory employees to serve as co-leaders and interpreters of a new human resources program. Employees who previously had not understood—but were hesitant to ask questions—now had a clear view of what the program meant to them.

Keep the Message Clear and Concise: Clarity and conciseness are absolutely critical—for the execs who don't bother to read, for those who don't like to read or don't read English well, and for those who are inherently resistant to the diversity message. The vision, concepts, and programs must be presented in a very abbreviated yet powerful way, with impact coming from clarity, repetition and expansion in other vehicles (e.g., diversity education).

To be effective you must start with a clear objective or what you want each target audience to *think*, to *feel*, and to *do*, as a result of the communications. Use concrete and compelling examples to create meaning for the listener or reader.

Provide Media Choices: Towers Perrin/DCI favors a combination of high tech with high touch. Use brochures, video, audiotapes, interactive phone, in combinations that are reinforcing and comfortably adaptable according to the listener's individual preference. Sometimes the most effective tools are the simple personalized communications. One company distributes a 20-minute staff meeting kit for managers. The five overheads and discussion outline give managers what they need to feel comfortable to include diversity on staff meeting agendas.

There is another level of choice required for diversity communications:

Should you use special communication vehicles for the diversity message, or should you incorporate those messages along with other internal communications? Some of the issues regarding this choice are as follows:

RATIONALE OF SEPARATE COMMUNICATION VEHICLES

- Helps to position diversity as an important business issue, not just something being fleetingly dabbled with on the periphery of the company.
- Raises diversity above the clutter of other ongoing communication activities of the organization.
- Permits development of a new communications style that sets itself apart from traditional company communications.

RATIONALE FOR USING EXISTING COMMUNICATION VEHICLES

- Inclusion with other communications positions diversity as a business issue, to be thought of as a natural part of managing for results.
- Inclusion in existing vehicles will probably be less expensive than separate communication vehicles and events.
- In a time of corporate downsizing, many will be critical of the introduction of separate new programs (i.e., diversity communications) that are perceived as having no short term impact.

Avoid the Trap of Traditionalism: In many diversity studies participants make reference to the "good old boys club," which determines (irrespective of formal systems) how things "really" get done around here. If the tone, the messages and the photos of your communications put you in mind of this anachronism, you will miss a large part of your audience. Your audience constantly will be asking themselves: "What is different?" "Is it real, or just show?". The communications look will provide them early clues as to the degree of change and commitment behind it. Consider using a diverse group of employees to complete a "diversity report card" on any communication piece before you go public with the piece.

These guidelines should be kept in mind as we discuss some of the event-related diversity communication opportunities in the remainder of this chapter.

SEIZE OPPORTUNITIES TO LEVERAGE EVENT-RELATED COMMUNICATIONS TO SUPPORT THE DIVERSITY PROCESS

Within an overall diversity communication strategy, some diversity communication needs will be event-driven. In too many cases the communications are handled almost as an afterthought in the process, rather than being viewed as a primary change tool. Communication events you should anticipate follow.

Introduce the Organization to Diversity: The objective of this early communication event is to signal the start of a change process by informing employees that diversity has been put on the corporate agenda. The typical vehicle is a letter from the Chairman or other senior officer which broadly positions the importance of diversity as a business issue and previews some likely activities.

Since this communication will raise diversity to a new level of awareness, the style and the content of the information are quite important. Some of the issues which must be managed include the following:

- Avoid creating an unrealistically optimistic set of expectations regarding the degree and pace of change. The process must be positioned as thorough, deliberate and balanced with other business priorities.

- A realistic timeline should be provided both to manage expectations and serve as a yardstick for measuring performance. Almost invariably the different stages of a diversity change process take longer than anticipated at the outset.

- Managing diversity (or whatever term is used) must be clearly defined and distinguished from affirmative action. The affirmative action concept still carries negative connotations for many which could lead to resistance.

- While defining how managing diversity differs from affirmative action, it is also important to verify the intended continuation of support for affirmative action.

- Behavioral expectations should begin to emerge in a non-threatening way. Use terms like "create a climate of mutual respect." Avoid the one situation where the CEO's first letter on diversity in essence said: *"We understand some people are prone to make derogatory comments about certain minority and ethnic groups. If we catch you doing this, you will be fired."* While the CEO was clear and concise, the message of threatened punishment overwhelmed everything else in his letter.

- Key elements in the change process should be spelled out if determined, or describe the organization body (for example, diversity task force) that will determine the makeup of the elements.

One of the toughest tasks in the early phases of the diversity change process may be to rein in the CEO's enthusiasm. The CEO's desire to demonstrate commitment may lead him to hint at the prospects for rapid progress even though he does not have a clear vision as to where the company is heading regarding diversity and what it takes to get there. Don't create another generation of skeptics by overpromising at the outset. It is better to under-promise and provide pleasant surprises as the process unfolds.

Example of a Positioning Communication: Exhibit 12.1 provides excerpts from an employee communication piece used by Sara Lee to position its diversity efforts. Note the care taken on the following:

EXHIBIT 12.1 Sample: Excerpts from A Positioning Communication

---

Sara Lee Corporation—Gary Grom, Senior Vice President, Human Resources

Q. What exactly does the term strategic diversity mean?

Sara Lee's definition of strategic diversity is, in the broadest sense, finding a way to develop all of our employees—employees who are different from one another in terms of ethnicity, personal background, genders, etc. Our goal is to impress upon every manager that there is tremendous value in hiring and retaining employees with unique backgrounds and perspectives.

All our diversity initiatives share a number of common objectives. These include creating an environment that is attractive to a culturally diverse work force, treating people as individuals by recognizing that each employee has value and varying needs and will need different kinds of support to succeed, and enabling every member of our work force to perform to his or her full potential.

Q. What distinguishes Sara Lee's strategic diversity initiatives from traditional affirmative action programs?

Affirmative action requires corporations in which women and minorities aren't adequately represented to hire more of them. When a corporation is faced with selecting one of two equally qualified candidates—one of whom happens to be a female or a minority—affirmative action says we should choose the female or minority.

Sara Lee strongly believes in affirmative action. We also know that it has allowed us to hire very capable women and minorities—and not by overlooking more qualified white males, as some would like to suggest.

But affirmative action is just one small part of strategic diversity, which focuses on the entire work force. While affirmative action and other legal compliance programs will continue to be necessary in those areas of our corporation where women and minorities are underutilized, we also will focus on much broader programs for all of our employees to help ensure their growth and development. These will include widespread mentoring programs, individualized development plans, more frequent reviews and feedback sessions and special assignment. One particularly important program we're initiating over the next few years is cultural awareness training.

Q. What does the corporation ultimately want to achieve through this intense commitment to strategic diversity?

Sara Lee wants to be recognized as the best among tough competition. And to be the best, we must be committed to identifying, attracting and retaining the creativity, talent, energy and power of our entire work force.

Reprinted with permission of the Sara Lee Corporation

- Diversity in the company context is defined (for example, "strategic diversity.")

- Affirmative action is adroitly distinguished from their broader diversity initiatives.

- Some of the anticipated activities and programs are mentioned very briefly, following a description of issues (which has been omitted for brevity).

Communicate About the Diversity Task Force to Convey Action: As discussed in Chapter 4, companies frequently will utilize a special committee or task force to guide diversity efforts. The first communication would be the letter to individuals who have been invited/appointed to join the diversity advisory organization. Some of the information items to be included in the participant invitation letter include the following:

- The mission of the organization
- Who the other members of the task force are, and the criteria for selection
- The scope of their responsibilities and authority (May be defined here or saved for the first meeting).
- How long it is anticipated that they will serve on the group
- The number and duration of meetings expected, along with target dates for the first several action steps
- Individual members are encouraged to fully and candidly express their points of view as the committee moves forward
- Advise that their supervisor is aware of this appointment and fully supports the individual's participation

To underscore the importance of the activity, CEOs or the local equivalent should express their interest in the work of the group. Reference to interaction with senior management (breakfast meeting, for example) further underscores the expectation that actions will result from their efforts.

Once the committee or task force has been formed, the general population should be advised of its existence, perhaps as part of an overall announcement of the diversity programming.

Announce a Diversity Research Process to Signal New Openness: Employees of many organizations have been conditioned through experience to pay little heed to the early letters from the chairman *on any subject*. However, the decision to seek diverse input signals a new level of commitment to the diversity issue. Employees who will participate in the research process are informed of the manner and objective of their participation. Those not directly providing input should still understand that the process is underway, and how the opinions of their group members will be gathered.

Include the following in the announcement of a diversity research project.

- Remind employees of what diversity is, and why the company is interested in it (in the off-chance they haven't saved the chairman's letter).
- Describe the techniques that will be used (questionnaires, focus groups, and so on) and why. Compare and contrast with approaches used for routine attitude surveys.
- Describe some of the general subject matter that will be covered in the data gathering.

- Indicate how the data will be used.

- Describe how they were selected for participation (for example, random sample).

- Encourage/mandate their participation in the process.

- Encourage candor and diverse input.

- Describe steps taken (for example, outside consultant) to maintain the confidentiality of the respondents.

- Provide a name/number for the reader to contact if he/she has any questions or input.

- Provide some time frame for when they might expect to see the results of survey.

Exhibit 12.2 provides a sample of what might be included in a letter to employees announcing a research project.

EXHIBIT 12.2 Excerpts from a Letter Announcing a Diversity
Research Process

After introductory comments referring to previous communications on diversity, and the formation of a Diversity Task Force:

One of the early conclusions of the Diversity Task Force is that it needs additional data to enable it to identify the issues that you feel are important and develop a list of diversity priorities. In representing the interests of all employees of Panoply Products Corporation, the task force wants to get your personal reactions to a short list of questions. These questions will provide the task force with an understanding of how you view the policies, practices and programs of the company as they apply to you.

Version for Recipients of Written Questionnaire

You were selected for participation on the basis of a random sampling of salaried employees. We will be sampling only about 25% of the workforce, so it is important that you complete and mail in the survey (prepaid envelope enclosed).

The tabulation and reporting of all the data will be handled by the XYZ Consulting Company whom we have engaged to conduct the study. They have performed similar studies for a number of companies.

You will note that, unlike some of our previous attitude surveys, the enclosed questionnaire calls for you to identify personal information such as race, gender, etc. This information is very important, because it is the only way that the consultants can identify whether the company's policies and programs are working for **all employees**.

You might feel that providing the data will enable someone to identify your questionnaire, especially if you are in one of the smaller divisions. The consultants will take all the necessary steps to make sure that your individual response will remain anonymous. For example, in providing detail on a division the Consultants will not provide us with breakouts for any group unless there are 10 or more in the group (e.g., Hispanic Exempt). However, your data would still be used in the process by combining it with that of similar employees for the company-wide profile. Your voice can be heard, so please complete and turn in the questionnaire.

(continued)

EXHIBIT 12.2 Continued

We appreciate your candid participation. Based on current estimates we believe that we can provide a summary of the results within two months, and a general action plan within two months after that.

If you have any questions regarding the survey, you can call Wilson Jones from XYZ Consultants (555–666–7777), or Mary Smith, Corporate Diversity Manager, or any members of the task force listed below.

Version for Focus Group Participants

We would like to obtain your viewpoints in this research effort through your participation in a focus group. A focus group, if you haven't participated in one before, is simply a small group of your fellow employees that meets to discuss a series of questions on your perceptions about various aspects of the company's programs, culture, policies, etc. as related to managing a diverse work force.

The focus group will be composed of individuals like yourself, that is, having the similar race and gender characteristics. The purpose is to provide a comfortable environment in which you can feel free to provide your candid comments.

The focus group will be led by a consultant from the XYZ Consulting Company. Any comments made during the focus group sessions will be treated on a confidential basis. The feedback from your group will be combined with other sessions being run by the consultants. The comments of any given individual will not be identifiable.

The meeting for your group is scheduled from 10:00 A.M. to noon on Thursday, September 14 in the first floor conference room. Your attendance at the meeting is very important. Julie Hansen of the Human Resources department will call to verify your attendance.

The information from the focus groups will be combined with the results of the written questionnaires which are going to a broader group of employees. We would hope to report back on overall results in about two months and have some action plans developed within two months after that.

Carefully Select the Appropriate Option for Communicating Research Results:
There will be great curiosity among employees about what was discovered as a result of the research and, more important, what might be done about the issues raised. There are three basic approaches to reporting on results, which are described below along with the advantages of each approach.

OPTION 1: BROAD DISCLOSURE OF DIVERSITY RESEARCH RESULTS

- *Description:* Option 1 entails extensive reporting on results, and actions planned. The communication piece may run ten or twenty pages and may cover all the basic issues and data that the diversity task force is using.

- *Advantages:* Broad disclosure can take some of the "mystery" out of the process, and signal an openness and willingness to share vital information. Everyone starts from the same information base, and so the possibility of surprises is reduced.

- *Disadvantages:* If information is reported which highlights the differential in perceptions of males versus females, minorities versus non-minorities, etc.

the reaction may be divisive. Information may also be taken out of context, for example, perceptions reported taken as fact, focus on the negatives while the positives are not mentioned equally.

OPTION 2: LIMITED DISCLOSURE OF RESEARCH RESULTS

- *Description*: Provide a summary overview, and specific results on just a few key questions, probably excluding any race/gender breakout of the data.
- *Advantages*: A limited summary probably meets the needs and interest level of many employees. It signals that action will be taken, without requiring an early and detailed commitment of action by the company.
- *Disadvantages*: If the issues are covered too broadly, skeptical employees may view it as a cover-up. Also, the lack of detail may prevent employees from understanding the reasons for specific action programs which follow.

OPTION 3: MODERATE DISCLOSURE OPTION

- *Description*: This option lies between the above two in length and detail. For example, comments would be made on general areas such as the overall climate for diversity, perceptions of fair treatment, the quality of working relationships, etc. If there are some pivotal issues, these would be highlighted.
- *Advantages:* It may provide unprecedented candor, yet not entail the risks described for the broad communication option (above).
- *Disadvantages*: It may not satisfy those who are intensely curious about the process and the results.

The length and variety of communications on research results makes it difficult to provide representative samples within the limits of this chapter.

Provide a Balanced Perspective: One of the highly sensitive issues in communicating research results is how to deal with the negative aspects of the feedback. As pointed out in Chapter 5, the feedback from a well structured research project can sometimes be disconcerting to senior management. In several instances, CEO's have reneged on their promise to make the data available to employees because the CEO viewed the results as too negative. This head-in-the-sand approach assumes that employees don't know what is going on in the organization until senior management tells them. All that this approach demonstrates actually, is that senior management may be the last to know what is going on in the organization.

Communicating to employees on the diversity issues the company hopes to address is a balancing act. Don't be afraid to claim credit for what seems to be working well, but remember that the Pollyanna approach won't be accepted by many employees. Therefore, you want to be candid and open with employees, yet not dwell only on negative perceptions. Employees are capable of understanding that despite a given issue, *it is still on balance a good place to work.* You want senior management of the company to take responsibility for the current status, but not picture them as being callous or disrespectful of individuals or the law. It is a difficult balancing act and employees recognize it as such. You are likely to find that they appreciate the candor and the sincerity of intent to the degree that they will not over-react to the information provided.

Communicate Action Plans to Make Commitments Public and to Shape Expectations: When preliminary decisions have been made regarding priorities and an action plan is developed along the lines described in Chapter 6, the highlights of the action plan should also be communicated broadly to employees who will be affected. Ideally, the information would be combined with research results which logically lead to the activities being announced. However, many organizations take some months to move from research information to an approved program, and you should not wait that long to communicate the research results.

Broadly speaking, a communication about the intended diversity activities of the organization should include the following elements:

Describe What Is Going to Be Done: Refer to a specific activity area, training, work and family, affirmative action, and so on, and specific activities within that area. Try to avoid broad references to "improved career planning processes" and the like that will be difficult for employees to truly understand how they may relate to them.

Explain Why the Action Is Being Taken: When describing the basis for a specific initiative or program adjustment, refer to specific research results if possible. Help employees make the connection between their input and the organization's response. For example, a perception of "closed" advancement systems could lead to a new or expanded posting system for job openings. Also relate the action being taken to the broad business benefits which might ensue.

Identify Who Will be Most Affected by the Actions Taken: Will the action benefit all employees (e.g., improved performance appraisal) or some specific portion of the employee population (for example, child care center established for employees' children from ages 1–5). The "Where's mine?" question is a natural employee response to change.

Specify Who Will be Responsible for Development and Implementation of the Changes: Will the steering committee\task force continue to guide the activity through implementation, or will it move into the province of the human resources group? Who can answer questions regarding the program?

Estimate When the Change Will be Implemented or Observable: Again we come to the issue of managing expectations. Be careful to be as specific as possible (for example, by June 30, by year end, by this time next year). If there are factors which might speed up or slow down the process, can they be identified without weakening the impact of the communication?

Communicating Specific Programs: In addition to the general diversity strategy issues covered here, there will be other specific program-related communication challenges. These may involve work and family programs, sexual harassment, changes in career mobility systems, affirmative action and so forth. These activities should be coordinated with the total diversity communication strategy and use the guidelines described earlier in this chapter.

IMPORTANT POINTS TO REMEMBER

1. Develop your communication strategy to meet the needs and interests of the various stakeholders, for example, members of protected class groups, white males, Board of Directors.

2. Tailor communication strategies to the dynamics of a diversity change process:

   - Create a diverse planning team
   - Educate and involve senior management
   - Keep the message clear and concise
   - Provide media choices

3. Use diversity process events as communication opportunities, such as:

   - Introduction to diversity
   - Diversity task force appointment
   - Results of a diversity research process
   - Action plans and timetables
   - Introduction of specific programs

13 Advance the Corporate Culture to Foster Diversity

The model for changing the behavior of an organization's employees shown in Chapter 1 identifies corporate culture as one of the important levers or influences in the change process. In fact, Dr. R. Roosevelt Thomas Jr. makes a convincing argument that sustainable progress is not possible unless the underlying cultural roots of the organization are compatible with the fundamental concepts of managing diversity. Yet we know that changing corporate cultures is a very difficult task, the nature of which is well captured by these words: "Change is intensely personal. For change to occur in any organization, each individual must think, feel, or do something different. . . . Think of this as 25,000 people having conversion experiences and ending up at a predetermined place at approximately the same time." (1) So let us begin the conversion experience.

In this chapter I will review some of the basic concepts of corporate culture as set forth by several of the leading business educators. Then we will examine some of the manifestations of culture that have been observed in various diversity strategy projects. Finally, we will describe several approaches for advancing the culture of your corporation in the direction of diversity success.

▬▬▬

BEGIN WITH AN UNDERSTANDING OF THE NATURE OF CORPORATE CULTURE

Like the term "diversity," culture has a broad range of meanings to different people. For our purposes I use the widely accepted definition, that culture is a basic pattern of assumptions that a given group has invented, discovered or developed in learning to cope with its problems of adapting to the external environment or integrating internal goals, strategies, conflicts, etc. The assumptions have worked well enough to be considered valid and tend to perpetuate themselves, often over long periods of time. Therefore, the assumptions are taught to new members of organizations as the correct way to perceive, think and feel in relation to problems the organization faces. Individuals are rewarded when they accept and conform to the norms, and may be ostracized when they do not. The importance of the phenomenon of culture in a business setting has been recognized for decades. (2)

To push the definition further, Kotter/Heskett (3) describe two levels of culture that differ in visibility and resistance to change.

LEVEL I: Group Behavior Norms, Visible and Relatively Easy to Change: Group behavior norms are common or pervasive ways of acting in a group that persist because group members teach the practices and underlying shared values to new members. Rewards are provided to those who conform, and sanctions are applied to those who do not. Some diversity-related examples of group behavior norms would include: the tendency to almost exclusively select individuals with a specific college degree for advancement opportunities, how new employees are welcomed into the organization, the patterns of informal association that develop within the work place, e.g., mono-cultural or inclusive. While these shared values are not easy to change, they are not as difficult as the Level II changes described later. An example of a Level I culture change is the following news item:

> *"BIG BLUE GOES PLAID—DRESS CODE RELAXED*
> *As part of the recent cultural house cleaning, IBM Canada President William Etherington is encouraging employees to dress in the garb that reflects the tastes of the company's clients." (4)*

IBM has long been known for its rather rigid employee dress code. In an apparent desire to mobilize the organization to address extremely serious business issues, the leadership was saying, "It's o.k. to show individuality in your choice of work clothing."

LEVEL II: Shared Values, Invisible and Relatively Difficult to Change: Shared values are the central concerns and goals shared by most of the people in the organization, that tend to shape group behavior, and persist over time even with changes in the group. Some diversity-related examples might include a "survival of the fittest" approach to employee development and advancement, and strong assumptions about the types or groups of individuals that are likely to be effective in key positions (e.g., women could not be delivery route drivers).

Again using the IBM example, the company broke with an important tenet of its culture when it reached outside its industry to bring in Louis Gerstner from RJR Nabisco to be its Chairman. It is widely assumed that this departure from its cultural norms could not have been made were it not for the billions of operating losses and share value that the company sustained. In fact it was the outside directors who forced the change. (5)

Three Aspects of Culture that Impact Diversity Success: In a diversity change process you are not trying to change all aspects of corporate culture, only those that most strongly impact the climate for diversity success. There are three principal aspects of the culture that can have an impact.

FACE VALIDITY: One of the most important aspects of corporate culture is a shared consensus on who is "in" and who is "out" and by what criteria one determines membership. The criteria may be determined by simple observation of tangible characteristics (race, gender, function) or by more subtle characteristics ("right school,") makes good presentations," etc.). The nature of these unwritten rules is critical to how "different" individuals feel welcomed and valued by the organization.

RELATIONSHIPS: The culture provides a consensus on criteria for intimacy, friendships and love, including rules for relationships between the sexes, and the manner in which openness and intimacy are handled. For example, are women in the organization viewed as equal business partners or are they expected to stay quietly in the background supporting those doing the "real work" of the organization?

REWARDS AND PUNISHMENTS: The criteria for determining heroic and sinful behavior are incorporated in the culture, along with criteria for rewarding or punishing behavior. If a manager perceives that there are few rewards for promoting diversity and no penalties for not doing so, the subject is unlikely to make his or her priority list.

New research is developing that specifically addresses the issues of diversity and corporate culture. For example, Cox suggests that a *High Prescription* culture is less suitable for diverse work groups than a *Low Prescription* culture.[1] Some of the typical characteristics of a High Prescription culture include: a narrow view of right or good behavior, quickness to evaluate and express criticism,

[1]Taylor Cox, Jr., *Cultural Diversity in Organizations*, pp. 169–170, Berret-Koehler Publishers, San Francisco, 1993.

risk aversion, intolerance of mistakes and detailed description by senior management of both strategies and methodologies.

In contrast, a Low Prescription culture accepts a wide range of work styles and behaviors so long as they are effective; risk taking is encouraged; judgments are made more deliberately and balanced with praise and criticism; and individuals are given greater latitude (within ethical and safety limits) to create their own approaches to the work.

The degree to which the culture is supportive of diversity will have a significant impact on the potential for successful initiatives. Next we review the steps to be taken to assess the culture and move it in the desired direction.

DEVELOP A BASELINE ASSESSMENT OF HOW YOUR EMPLOYEES VIEW THE CULTURE

If you want the answer, you have to be prepared to ask the question. In diversity research projects, information about the corporate culture can be garnered in a number of ways:

- Review the company's printed information describing the values and history of the company. This provides a perspective of what the company thinks it is, or is trying to be. Statements made by the chairman and other high profile people will give clues to their perception or goal for the culture. Printed information should be suspect, however, because many organizations have not "walked the talk." You should check the official position against the opinions of rank and file employees to test if the vision that has been articulated for the organization has been realized.

- Interviews with diverse employees at various levels can be used to provide their view of the culture. In this exercise you are looking for the first strong impression that comes to their minds. As you would expect, their perspectives are limitless and sometimes quite vivid. Some examples from several organizations are listed below:

"This company is like a meat grinder. You go in whole, but it is so tough on people—there isn't much left of you when you are done."

"Every morning when I come in here I feel like I am coming to the plantation. The 'mastah' sits up in the big house, and us niggers are going to be down here doing the dirty work the rest of our lives."

"Our culture is white male dominated, testosterone excessive, suburban Type A."

"A couple of years ago I could answer that. But ever since our company was acquired, we have become culture-less."

"This is the epitome of the 'old boy's club.' They lunch together, play golf together, live in the same neighborhood. It is a closed society."

"I know it sounds corny, but my job here is like working with my family. We all watch out for each other."

In a diversity research process it is important to measure some aspects of the perception of the culture. And yet there are so many things you are trying to measure, you can only afford to spend so much of your effort in this one area. Two dimensions that can be quickly checked are the overall environment for diversity, and the extent to which the organization utilizes its diverse skill base. Table 13.1 shows some questions and response patterns that demonstrate how employees in a small sampling of companies have viewed aspects of the corporate culture in which they were employed.

The data in Table 13.1 can tell you a lot about the environment of an organization. For example, if the data represented a single organization it seems that you could infer the following:

- Women and minorities do not feel their opinions are valued and as a result may be less inclined to attempt to contribute to their fullest potential.
- The majority of all of the groups feels that diverse input is not valued by management, and that it isn't safe to say what is on your mind. Thus the in-

TABLE 13.1 Seeking Out and Utilizing Diverse Input

	Percentage Agreeing With the Statement					
	Male Exempt		Female Exempt		Female Nonexempt	
Statement	White	Minority	White	Minority	White	Minority
Senior management values diverse opinions.	41%	33%	35%	43%	40%	29%
Business opinions of minorities are respected as well as non-minorities.	67	48	57	22	43	19
Business opinions of women respected as well as men.	73	58	45	30	34	20
It is safe to say what you think.	32%	24%	22%	9%	18%	5%

dividual (no matter what group) who has an opinion that is outside the mainstream, may be reluctant to express that point of view. Again, some potentially valuable input may be lost as the organization moves ahead on its course.

At the same time we see that data, there are some interesting anomalies. For example, it is typical that 70%–80% of all employee groups will say that they have the authority they need to get their jobs done. The point is that the environment will work as long as the old ways are working. However, if the old ways are not working, employees will be reluctant to speak up, and the organization may not adapt well to changes in the environment.

Another diversity element of the culture is the degree to which people feel they are treated with respect. Scores frequently run in a tight range, e.g., as a high of about 70% for exempt males, to 60% for nonexempt females. However, exceptions can be observed between organizations. For example:

- In one company only 30% of the nonexempt women felt they were treated with respect. In this particular case, there were clear perceptions of a two-class system, reinforced with different rules and policies for nonexempt employees that left the impression that they were neither highly valued nor trusted.

- In a second organization the female nonexempt employees provided the highest ratings of any group. Recent attempts to include them in team processes and departmental meetings provided a sense that their contributions were valued.

It is interesting to see that individuals seem to be able to view the organization climate as disembodied from the treatment they are accorded by their fellow employees. Even in organizations that have low scores such as those shown in the Table 13.1, it is not unusual for 60%–75% of the employees to say that they are treated with respect within their department or work group. So whatever they perceive to be going on elsewhere in the organization may not be affecting the day-to-day working relationships quite as seriously.

ASSESS THE PROSPECTS FOR SUCCESS

The task of identifying aspects of corporate culture that are not supportive of diversity is relatively straightforward. However, all the experts would lead us to believe that it is no easy task to change the beliefs, the cultural roots, or the values that underlie the behavior. A potentially useful step in the research process is to have participants provide their assessment of the likelihood of changing the environment sufficiently to establish diversity progress.

Hear What Your Employees Say About Prospects for Change: Your employees will have strong points of view on the odds for success. Here are some typical examples of responses from focus groups regarding their perceptions of the potential pace and breadth of change in the culture:

African American Male:
"I think the whole culture of the company has to change before anything will happen. There have to be more signals that risk-taking is worthwhile and will be rewarded. Without risk-taking, how can diversity really happen? Timid organizations do timid things. We'll just make some righteous noises and move on."

White Female:
"We get reports from the top, that such-and-such is a 'major concern.' After the hoopla is over, nothing has really happened except a few missed deadlines on what we were supposed to be doing. I guess this (diversity initiative) will just be another one of those."

Hispanic Male:
"The company doesn't want to hurt anyone. They want to manage like this was a home, not a company. The white male worker is their child. If they feel change might hurt their child, they will delay and delay until nobody even remembers what the fuss was all about in the first place."

White Male:
"TQM is the 'flavor of the year.' It's the newest craze, to be replaced by something else, maybe diversity. And then what?"

African American Male:
"Diversity won't happen! Senior management expresses the spirit, but the middle managers feel threatened. The middle managers are where they (senior management) were 15–20 years ago. They planted and grew these middle managers and know exactly what is going on. But if they don't plant some new style managers, you will never get at the root of the problem."

African American Female:
"There must be some federal audit or lawsuit coming up. I just can't see senior management getting all fired up about women and minorities unless there is some fear of a suit. So when the fear goes, the program goes. It's as simple as that."

Asian Female:
"The discrimination will just get more subtle and sophisticated. Nothing will change, except in form. For diversity to work, in this company senior management would have to be

visionary and courageous. Now look at this company. What chance do you really think there is of that happening?"

African American Male:
"Too many things begin here at Anonymous Corporation and then just fade away for lack of sustained interest. In fact you can get senior management interested in anything *for a while, but it never pans out. Maybe this will be an exception?" (laughter).*

Consider What the Experts Say About Prospects for Change: The pragmatic, experience-based skepticism of employees about the prospects for change is shared by some of the leading culture theoreticians. For example, some of the lead thinkers have this to say about the difficulty of changing corporate culture:

Peter Drucker suggests that culture is singularly persistent and that changing culture works best only if based on the existing culture. He suggests not changing the culture, but changing the practices, using the company's "best in class" to lead the way. (6)

Dr. R. Roosevelt Thomas suggests that "Fifteen or twenty years of consistent and conscientious efforts will be required before a culture change is naturally sustainable." (7)

Kotter/Heskett research of large corporations suggests that major culture change could take place within a period of four years or more. (3)

When managers hear sobering assessments of the degree of the challenge like those above, there is a tendency for eyes to glaze over. The time frames mean very different things to different people. For some of those in charge it could mean: *"That's a relief. I will be retired by then, so I don't have to worry about it."*

For others who have grown tired of waiting for opportunities and enduring subtle and blatant biases, the reaction may be: *"It sounds like just one more excuse. Be good little boys and girls, everything will be all right if you will just wait another ten or twenty years."*

Let's look at some action steps that realistically can be expected to have an impact on the organization.

ADVANCING THE ORGANIZATION IN A NEW DIRECTION

A company president who had been working hard on changing his organization used the analogy that changing his (large company) culture was analogous to changing the direction of a large ocean liner. His thought process was that you don't just slam on the brakes and head off in another direction. There is a sophisticated series of actions and maneuvers required, possibly with the help of some accompanying tugboats to advance (improve in position). An unexpected change of direction can be hard on the ship, the crew and the passengers.

For the corporate culture analogy, the same principle applies as did for the ocean liner. Let's focus on a gradual but inevitable change in direction of certain past behaviors of the organization's employees to better accommodate and utilize the diverse workforce that we absolutely know will be here. Even for a modest amount of progress, there are some specific steps that are important to progress. Listed below are eight culture characteristics that can have a significant impact on the odds for diversity success, plus a couple dozen options that can be used to advance the organization to a new position.

*1. **Utilizing Diverse Input:*** In the healthy organization management seeks input broadly for business decisions. Management listens carefully and utilizes a wide range of perspectives.

If this characteristic is not present, some of the implications include the following:

- The useful contributions of some groups (functional, level, gender, and so on) will not be captured. Though the cost of such lost input cannot be quantified, they are real nonetheless.

- Problems go unrecognized or unreported for extended periods of time because it may be risky to be the bearer of bad tidings.

- With no channel to communicate their concerns and frustrations, resentment can build up among employees. They may elect to go on to another employer in the hopes of leaving their anger behind.

ADVANCING OPTIONS

- Promote diverse managers into decision making groups, for example, Management Committee, succession planning committee.

- Rotate diverse employees through decision making groups for their development and input.

- Use diverse task teams to tackle important assignments or to provide input on specific key decisions.

- Use employee surveys and other input techniques which provide comfortable (i.e., confidential) channels for candid employee input that may run counter to senior management expectations.

- Use lunches, management by walking around, department meetings and other structured and unstructured opportunities to tap the input of employees who are not in the mainstream of company influence and decision making and to foster timely, candid two-way communications.

- Maintain ongoing contact with employee advocacy groups, affinity groups and networks.

2. People as Assets: In the diversity-supportive environment, people are valued as important resources to be developed and nurtured for the mutual benefit of themselves and the company. Because people are valued, the effective management of people is a prized and essential skill to be considered for advancement to senior levels.

If this culture characteristic is not present, human resources programs and practices are likely to be poorly developed, having a disproportionately negative impact on females and minorities. Future leaders of the organization are not developed for the perpetuation of the enterprise. Employees will view their position as a transitory experience rather than a career commitment.

Since people in general are not valued, diversity is likely to be seen as a negative to be neutralized or ignored, rather than being seen as a potential source of competitive advantage.

ADVANCING OPTIONS

- Develop and communicate a policy that commits to the development of all employees to their full potential.
- Identify good people managers, provide fast track promotions and publicize their success and the reasons for the success.
- Identify the costs and impact on operational effectiveness that can come from ineffective management of people generally:
  - Excessive turnover
  - Low productivity through poor communications and low employee commitment
- Incorporate basic people management skills into ongoing training programs. For example:
  - Influence skills: Achieving objectives without reliance on formal power and authority, creating atmosphere of openness and trust, selling ideas and resolving conflicts, positioning the organization for action.
  - Managing subordinates: Interviewing skills, performance management, providing feedback to the high and low performer, incorporating insights into cultural differences in feedback and coaching processes, mentoring for development, handling employee complaints.
  - Flexibility: Ability to use varied approaches based on the task at hand, the resources available, and the contribution that each team member can make. Support skills include listening skills, ability to accommodate to differing styles, awareness of personal style, and how it may impact on group and individual performance.

- Maintain a variety of high quality human resources programs and systems that work for all employees.

3. *Performance Expectations:* Employees know what is expected of them and are given reasonable degrees of autonomy, and may exercise flexibility in methods that may be used to arrive at the desired objective. If these characteristics are not present, individuals may be valued more on adherence to the standard operating procedures and fit with organization style rather than on results achieved and suggestions provided for continuous improvement.

ADVANCING OPTIONS

- Teach and practice empowerment management techniques at all levels of the organization.
- Develop highly focused teams to take on meaningful assignments.
- Train employees at all levels in results-based performance management techniques.
- Use multisource performance appraisals to provide candid and fair feedback, and to serve as a base for personal development.

4. *Preconceptions for Success:* It is assumed that a wide range of individuals can succeed in various jobs. There is no rigid mold used in evaluating job applicants or making promotion/advancement decisions. If these characteristics are not present, employees' performance and potential may be evaluated on the basis of diversity dimensions rather than on the basis of their ability or the objective value of their contributions.

An over-concentration of like individuals may develop at senior management levels based on their schools, functional discipline, and physical characteristics. The sameness of key managers could lead to group think, low creativity, and slow response to competitive challenges to existing products, methods and processes.

ADVANCING OPTIONS

- Critically review all the employee selection and job performance standards, eliminate requirements related to tradition, comfort, and convenience rather than to actual job requirements.
- Provide awareness training to help managers better understand and utilize differences.
- Engage teams of diverse employees in developing requirements for various positions.
- Conduct employee research to identify the perceptions of the current mold.
- Determine the potential "cost" of retaining the current mold; for example, turnover, lack of sufficient candidates to meet staffing needs internally.

5. *Absence of Assimilation Requirement:* In the diversity supportive culture there is no spoken or unspoken requirement for employees to assimilate into certain aspects of the dominant culture, that is, sacrifice a potentially important part of their individuality to gain acceptance.

If the assimilation requirement is in evidence, those who don't fit the mold are intensely aware of their points of difference, and undergo subtle and overt pressures to model themselves after the dominant group. As they attempt to de-emphasize their points of difference, the organization may lose some of the richness of diversity, while their discomfort remains.

ADVANCING OPTIONS

In addition to the options listed for the preceding culture characteristic (preconceptions for success), see that the following are done.

- Have the CEO provide a company policy/vision statement that is supportive of the differences that its employees bring to the workplace.
- Monitor career mobility systems to limit the impact of the Good Old Boy Network.
- Establish a mentoring program that helps employees distinguish between necessary and unnecessary adjustments of their differences to fit into the organization.
- Publicize actual examples of the benefits of diversity in the organization.

6. *Balancing Work and Life Demands:* Performance standards are demanding, but pressures for long hours and heavy travel are interspersed with periods allowing "decompression." If pressures are unrelentingly excessive, employees will be unable to balance their company and outside life responsibilities. This can lead to guilt feelings, excessive stress levels, dropping out of the workforce, moving to companies that provide a better balance.

ADVANCING OPTIONS

- Develop a corporate policy statement recognizing the validity of concerns about the balance of work and personal life.
- See that senior management leads by example and leaves by example (i.e., at a decent hour).
- Don't schedule routine meetings before 9:00 a.m. or after 4:00 p.m. so as not to interfere with flextime and dependent care arrangements.
- Award commendations more frequently for contributions made rather than for hours worked.
- When burdensome hours are a periodic business necessity, offset pressure with flexibility in where and during what part of the day the hours are worked.

- Train supervisors on the legitimacy and techniques of appropriate balancing of work/family demands.
- Sponsor parental support groups to share useful information and experiences and provide an outlet for concerns.

7. Environment of Mutual Respect: The diversity-supportive culture creates an expectation that all employees will be granted respect as individuals, the respect coming both from their fellow employees and the organization as an entity.

If the culture does not have this dimension, individuals not in the mainstream will struggle for acceptance as individuals, constantly trying to break out of the category to which they have been relegated. Comments, jokes and harassment based on diversity dimensions will be an accepted form of hazing behavior, entailing both legal risks and devastating morale impact.

ADVANCING OPTIONS

- Develop and communicate a company policy statement of respect for individuals, modeled and enforced by senior management.
- Provide awareness training in understanding and valuing differences.
- Make particular efforts to address the needs of groups who are often viewed as second class citizens, e.g., hourly and nonexempt salaried employees, those for whom English is a second language, those employed in low visibility support functions.
- Highlight the successes and contributions of members of the "out-groups."

8. Effective Teams Incorporate Diversity: In many organizations much of the work and problem solving of the organization is accomplished through high performance work teams, characterized by collaborative and empowered approaches to tasks. All employees are considered part of the team and their contributions are evaluated on their merit. Care is taken to foster productive working relationships within the teams that recognize cultural differences that may exist between men and women, minorities and non-minorities, older and younger employees, etc.

If this characteristic is not in place, tension will develop among team members that may remain unresolved and team productivity will suffer. Patterns of association develop on the basis of ethnicity and gender or other characteristics, rather than by work groups.

ADVANCING OPTIONS

- Provide team building training that incorporates relevant aspects of cultural conditioning of the participants.
- Use diverse task teams to tackle meaningful assignments.
- Celebrate the successes of diversity teams, and diagnose the sources of any failures.

HOW TO SECURE SENIOR MANAGEMENT COMMITMENT TO CULTURE CHANGE

Achieving culture change may be difficult at times, but it is virtually impossible without strong senior management commitment. In the research and practice of culture change the role of leadership looms very large. Executives are usually aware of the pivotal role they may play, and will ask "What can I do to help the diversity process take hold?" The response will vary according to the style of senior management and organization. For example, William D. Smithburg, CEO of the Quaker Oats Company communicated his commitment and the business context in a message to employees and shareholders in the Company's quarterly report (8). Key excerpts of the message are as follows (emphasis added by this book's author):

Q.: How has the company changed its expectations of employees?

WDS: *"We expect higher quality performance because we are constantly challenged to do more with less due to the ever-intensifying competitive environment . . . This situation provides an excellent opportunity to tap the talents of a more diverse work force–a work force that brings innovative ideas to challenge the old ways of doing things . . . while the composition of our work force has changed, the individual needs of our employees have also changed.*

We never stop trying to find the best way to realize the full potential of our employees. That in itself is a challenge-but the benefits are great for everyone involved.

Q: In the framework of all these changes, how do you perceive your job?

WDS: *As CEO, I am taking on an expanded role to act as the* **Company's chief human resource officer.** *One of my primary responsibilities is to assure the finest management team in our industry. I am actively involved in directing the resources we have, so that the talents and skills of our people produce the greatest benefit."*

Not every CEO will be prepared to take the strong public ownership position that Mr. Smithburg has. However, there are many things at many levels that can be done to establish the conditions for a successful diversity change. I have attempted to help senior managers envision their roles by developing a senior management diversity job description. The description in Exhibit 13.1 below outlines the principal roles where senior management influence is needed and can do the most good.

In Rosabeth Moss Kanter's *The Change Masters* (9), the importance of leadership ("prime mover" in her parlance) is covered in some depth. She notes that the leadership factor is especially important for changes that begin with pressures in the environment that were not sought by the corporation (for example, changes in response to regulatory pressures, a need to counter a competitor's strategy, and so on). In these circumstances it is important that the prime movers make it clear that they *believe* in the strategy, that it is oriented toward getting something

EXHIBIT 13.1 Senior Management Diversity Leadership Responsibilities

I. OVERALL ROLE

Provide senior leadership and direction in establishing an environment where the full potential of all employees can be utilized, in support of corporate objectives, without regard to irrelevant personal characteristics.

II. PRINCIPAL RESPONSIBILITIES AND ACTIVITIES

A. ESTABLISHING VISION AND STRATEGIES

1. Include diversity commentary as part of the organization's mission and strategy statements.
2. Be clear in articulating what needs to be changed; don't be a guardian of the status quo.
3. Develop a sound business rationale for allocating resources to diversity initiatives, identifying with clarity the potential adverse consequences of inaction.
4. Provide for linkage of diversity activities with other ongoing programs in the organization, such as total quality management, restructuring, etc.

B. ALLOCATING RESOURCES

1. Allocate sufficient budgets to sustain needed activities during both good and weak years of fiscal performance.
2. Provide for the appropriate staffing to move the diversity process forward to implemented programs.
3. Appoint senior executives to participate in task forces and other high visibility activities.

C. ESTABLISHING ACCOUNTABILITY

1. Work with senior managers to establish challenging but realistic goals for diversity interventions and measurable results.
2. Monitor the progress against objectives and include information on results in operational reports.
3. Provide appropriate financial or non-financial recognition of diversity progress, or withhold recognition and rewards when progress is disappointing.

D. MODELING LEADERSHIP BEHAVIOR

1. Participate in diversity education and training.
2. Complete a self-assessment of personal biases and preferences that might impede effectiveness in leading the diversity process.
3. Demonstrate a firm commitment in the face of backlash that might be stirred up by the diversity process.
4. Avoid becoming personally defensive about feedback identifying current problems, focusing energies instead on developing solutions.

E. PUTTING PRINCIPLES INTO PRACTICE

1. Create diverse work teams to address meaningful issues.
2. Question homogeneity in any company activity or at any level of the company.
3. Set policy against company-sponsored memberships for executives in discriminatory clubs.
4. Reinforce the diversity message in communications of all types, making it a normal part of doing business.
5. Incorporate diversity into succession planning processes.
6. Develop a personal understanding of the issues, through reading, training and contacts; use the knowledge to support changes in culture, systems and policies.

that the organization wants and needs. She cites affirmative action as one area where prime movers must find a way to see the changes as meeting *organizational* needs, and convey an unwavering commitment to improve the track record. The drive for change must become internalized, even if (like affirmative action) it originated externally. If the need for change cannot be internalized (that is, the business rationale for diversity) the prime movers cannot push with conviction, and the people around them can avoid wholehearted implementation, "faking it" for the time being.

CREATE A REALISTIC VISION OF THE NEXT PLATEAU

In looking at the vision for managing diversity, organizations may just become too overwhelmed with the degree of change necessary, and may be prone to give up before the task is started. You need to establish realistic interim goals that make sense for your organization, taking you from where you are to the new plateau.

Robert L. Lattimer, Managing Director of Diversity Consultants/Towers Perrin, finds it helpful for senior management to identify the values, beliefs and practices which made the company great in the past, and how those requirements might change in the future. This understanding is an important preparation for moving forward toward diversity success. Table 13.2 illustrates some of the "past" and "future" comparisons that might be included.

The type of organizational self analysis described in Table 13.2 does not fall

TABLE 13.2 Comparison of Past and Future Requirements for Success

Past Beliefs and Strategies Leading to Our Success	Current and Future Actions and Strategies Required
1. Family environment, hired people like ourselves.	1. Broader definition of "family" to create supportive environment, inclusive of those not previously in the mainstream.
2. Results achieved through autocratic and paternalistic leadership styles.	2. Results achieved through empowered and motivated work teams.
3. Centralized organization with policy directives flowing from the top.	3. Decentralized organization, with policies developed at the point where they have greatest relevance.
4. Top to bottom communications; employee input seldom sought.	4. Communications in every direction and a variety of formal and informal methods for seeking broad employee input on a variety of issues.

into the category of earthshaking breakthroughs in management science. Any strategically minded organization should be going through a process like this, whether or not they have a diversity initiative in place. If such a process does exist, it should be relatively easy to add the diversity dimensions to the analysis and forward planning.

A key executive activity in moving toward a new vision is to execute flawless "handoff" of diversity from the CEO or equivalent to other key managers in the organization. Diversity can't succeed based on CEO commitment alone. The vision has to be taken down to lower levels of the organization, to all the functions and locations. The vision has to be put into terms that makes sense to that group. For example, Jim Kochanski, Director of Human Resources at Northern Telecom, Inc. in Raleigh, developed a diversity continuum (Exhibit 13.2) for his human resources team, that was tailored to the mission of his group.

Jim Kochanski also developed an assessment instrument based on the factors in Exhibit 13.2 so that his team could periodically measure its progress against their diversity vision.

Balancing Priorities and Commitments: After exhorting the CEO to take a strong leadership position and hold people accountable for results, I need to add some balancing precautions.

EXHIBIT 13.2 The HR Diversity Team: Moving Constantly on a Continuum‡

Moving From		Moving To
"One Best Way," that is, fit the mold to succeed.	→	"Multiple Ways OK." Being different is valued, utilized.
We succeed as a function in spite of diversity.	→	We succeed as a function because of diversity.
Groups look and act segregated.	→	People move between homogeneous and heterogeneous groups. No group does harm to another.
Power is exclusive and limited. Highly dependent on level.	→	Influence is unlimited, shared by whoever is capable.
Minorities and women populate lower bands.	→	Any slice of the organization looks like a cross section of the community.
Skills and behaviors are prescribed—yet barriers to development exist.	→	People are valued "as they are," but get many opportunities to learn and develop.
Being different is uncomfortable, fearful.	→	Being yourself is OK; it is not a fearful place to work.

‡*Reprinted with permission of Northern Telecom, Inc.*

- Be careful how much you ask the organization to do at once. If you put too much on your managers' plates there will be confusion and overload in the organization. Much will be started; little will be finished.
- Use some of the prioritizing techniques described earlier in Chapter 6 to determine what you should be focusing on first.
- Keep a scorecard of your progress. With a great deal going on over a period of years, it will be easy to lose sight of the real progress that has been achieved. We will discuss measuring progress more fully in Chapter 14.

As in any change effort, senior management's role is a balancing act. There is a need to express impatience with what is, while recognizing that many managers are going to feel threatened by what may be. Senior managers are in a position to make those choices.

IMPORTANT POINTS TO REMEMBER

1. Begin with an understanding of the nature of corporate culture as it may affect diversity:
   - Group behavior norms are visible and relatively easy to change
   - Shared values are usually invisible and relatively difficult to change
2. Develop a baseline assessment of how your diverse employees view the culture as being effective in general, and supportive of diversity.
3. Assess the prospects for success to understand the pace and breadth of change that may be possible.
4. Advance the organization in new directions that support diversity:
   - Utilize diverse input
   - Value individuals as assets
   - Broaden the definition of employees that are likely to be successful
   - Soften the assimilation requirement
   - Provide for a balance of work/life demands
   - Create an environment fostering mutual respect
   - Capitalize on the value of diversity in the company's work teams
5. Senior management must play a strong and visible role for any significant changes to be effective.
6. Develop a realistic vision of diversity success for the organization to strive toward.

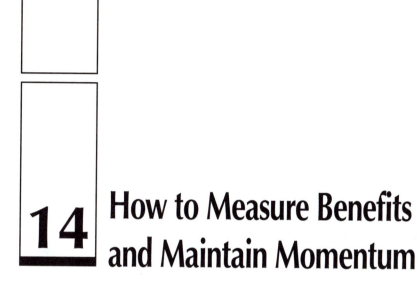

14 How to Measure Benefits and Maintain Momentum

As mentioned in several different chapters, the journey to diversity success in most organizations will be lengthy and full of challenges. Similar to any other type of intervention or activity, the sponsors (and doubters) will be seeking to measure the long-term value of the activity and to determine its appropriate place on the priority list.

This chapter explores the dimensions for measuring program benefits, and provides a number of examples of performance measures you may wish to consider. Furthermore, we describe seven specific strategies that you can use to keep the organization committed and energized to move toward the same diversity vision as the program progresses for a period of years.

DETERMINE HOW IMPORTANT MEASUREMENTS ARE FOR YOUR ORGANIZATION

A question frequently raised about diversity programs relates to the real impact they may have on the bottom line. Organizations may come to quite different conclusions regarding the need or desirability of specific measures, as illustrated by the two quotes below:

"We attempt to measure the impact of everything that we are doing. We must have metrics for our diversity programs."
CEO, large company

"Do Levi's (diversity programs) have any broader effect on the bottom line? That's anyone's guess. We've had six successive record years—because of diversity or in spite of it, I don't know."
Dan Chew
Manager Corporate Marketing, Levi Strauss (1)

These two quotes capture the essence of the polar opposites regarding employer concern over measuring results. Some have formed a special subcommittee to determine metrics for the diversity initiative. In other cases they are content that the diversity activity supports the overall vision and strategy, and are willing to settle for subjective assessments of the value of the programs, much as they would do for management development programs or communications activities.

It is natural that the question of measurement be raised, given the context of recent business trends in many organizations: severe pressures for improved profit performance; disillusionment with other broad-based interventions such as Total Quality Management; competition for management attention from globalization; new organization approaches; new marketing opportunities, and the like. Given the context in which organizations are operating, it is no surprise that tough questions are asked regarding the benefits of diversity initiatives. But before we talk about how to measure, keep in mind the potential metrics pitfalls that you can and should avoid.

Be Wary of the Dual Standard: While I don't question the sincerity of the interest in identifying the value of diversity interventions, I sometimes wonder if companies are not attempting to apply a tougher standard of evaluation for diversity processes than they do for other ongoing activities. For example, those who might be demanding some specific proofs for diversity programming, at the same time will be moving ahead on the following activities.

A meeting costing $500,000 is held for key managers and their significant others for "sharing of the strategic plan and chairman's vision," etc. The meeting is held at a posh resort during the work week, and much of the time is spent on the golf course, cocktail parties and tennis courts. The activity is felt to be essential to "morale, commitment, communications" and so on, but there is no attempt to measure the specific impact of the meeting.

Additions are made to the company jet fleet, and company limo service is expanded to enhance "executive productivity," without indicating how that productivity will specifically benefit shareholders, over and above the costs of the services.

I don't mean to be a nitpicking grouch. During my career in industry I have planned, implemented (and on occasion benefited from) the very kinds of activities described above. I am not suggesting those activities are without merit, but cite them as a possible incongruity. Should diversity activities (that potentially benefit so many employees as well as delivering business benefits to the organization) be held to a much tougher standard than other company programs? And will your employees infer that bias or a lack of commitment to diversity is the underlying cause of the dual standard?

Identifying Broad Impact in a Cluttered Landscape: Diversity activities are not conducted in a vacuum. In studies I have participated in or observed, it was not unusual to see various combinations of the following major events being conducted almost simultaneously within the organization.

- Termination of a number of employees as part of a permanent downsizing program.
- Major reorganization changing reporting relationships of divisions, departments and individuals.
- The organization may be going through a major strategic shift as represented by acquisitions, divestitures, entry into new markets, retreat from previous markets, plant closures.
- A total quality management effort is being rolled out, with numerous meetings for training and team building purposes.

Now for organizations going through one or more of the above activities simultaneously, how does one separate the specific effects of the diversity programs with any degree of accuracy? It should be understood from the outset that the attribution of specific causes and effects will not be easy.

Don't Expect to Identify Specific Program Elements Driving the Impact: As we suggested in earlier chapters, a broad-based diversity initiative will proceed along several tracks simultaneously. At various points in time there may be a dozen or more activities under the diversity program umbrella, leading to the following scenario. Situation: Management has noted that two years into its diversity program, the turnover of female managers has declined by 40%. This improvement has identifiable value to the organization in lower recruiting and training costs. But what caused the improvement among the following changes made during the time period?

- Introduction of extended parental leave option following maternity leave eases the transition back to work.
- Introduction of enhanced career planning activities, with special emphasis in the early stages in helping women and minorities develop realistic career options. The program included taking the job posting system up to the middle management job level.

- Flexible working hours were introduced to help employees balance their work requirements with other responsibilities.

- A women's support group was established providing an outlet to share experiences and strategy, and network about opportunities in the company.

- Due to the recession several major employers in the community terminated a substantial number of salaried employees, and announced hiring and salary freezes.

Now which among the above factors (if any) resulted in the 40% reduction in turnover? You may never know. On the other hand there are some measures that can and should be part of your diversity management process.

HOW TO SELECT MEASURES OF DIVERSITY EFFECTIVENESS

Despite the qualifications preceding, don't take away the impression that measurement of progress is a hopeless quest. In fact there are a number of specific measures that can be useful in gauging your progress. In Table 14.1 I have listed nine areas of activity, how the progress can be determined and some guesses as to how that progress could affect the bottom line of the organization.

Note that the potential dollar impact is usually on the side of expense reduction or cost avoidance, rather than revenue improvement. While there may be revenue implications of good or bad diversity performance, these are even harder to quantify than the expense reductions or cost avoidance.

The metrics of diversity are still in a developmental stage. However, even after further development the subjective evaluations may be as important as the quantitative justification. Like programs and activities in many areas of the company the impact on profits will be difficult to evaluate. Other activities that fall into the same category are public relations, corporate advertising, internal communications of any type and most management development programs. The benefits to the organization of these programs can be very real, even though you can't get your calipers around the issue, a phenomenon well understood by CEO's.

As time goes on, more and more information demonstrating benefits will become available. As an example of information now in the public domain, a number of company examples are summarized in Table 14.2.

In addition to benefits that can be measured in some way as reported in Table 14.2, there are a number of other totally unquantifiable benefits which diversity programs may deliver. Here are just a few examples that have been claimed by various organizations.

- Improved cooperation and communications within diverse work teams.
- Improved productivity through empowering management techniques.

TABLE 14.1 Quantitative Measures of Diversity Progress

Activity Focus	Measurement	Potential Profit Impact
Affirmative Action Hiring & Retention	1. Numbers of females and minorities hired versus • previous years actual • percentage in the applicant flow • percentages of area availability as determined by EEOC data	Good results cut risk of costly compliance sanctions
	2. Turnover of females and minorities versus • % for white males • previous year's trend line • external benchmark	Lower turnover can • reduce costs of recruiting replacements • reduce training costs • reduce expenses and lost revenues due to inexperience of new employees in jobs
	3. Percentage of mothers who return from maternity leave.	Same as above
Upward Mobility of target groups.	Numbers of females and minorities in key management positions and on backup slates.	Reduced expense for advertising, search and other employment costs to fill openings
Climate for Diversity	% of favorable responses to survey questions as compared with • previous survey • divisions within the company • external benchmarks	Early warning on developing issues can be used to avert high turnover, EEO charges, which in turn reduces costs (see above and below)
EEO Complaints	Number of AA/EEO related complaints per 1,000 employees as compared with • previous years • other parts of the company • community or industry benchmark	Reduced complaints lower cost of staff to investigate and defend the company, and provide financial settlements
EEO Legal Action	Costs of settlement of EEO charges (see above)	Reduced legal and court costs, reduced costs of settling cases.
Community Outreach	Amount of business done with minority/female-owned organizations.	May not have direct dollar benefit for purchaser
Program Flexibility	% of employees at various levels, age/race/gender utilizing options in flexible compensation and benefit programs	Satisfaction provided through more flexible use of current programs may forestall the need for costly enhancements, or make it possible to reduce other benefits with limited negative impact on employees

(continued)

TABLE 14.1 Continued

Activity Focus	Measurement	Potential Profit Impact
	Number of employees using flexible hours, job sharing, telecommute	Same as above plus reduced turnover costs and reduced costs associated with unplanned absenteeism
Compensation Equity Analysis	Wage and salary adjustments in excess of guideline increases	Correction of pay inequities adds to expense, but may reduce future costs of excessive turnover and defense of EEO charges and suits
Training & Development	Increased number of females, minorities using development programs.	Increased satisfaction reduces turnover and its associated costs and builds needed competencies within the organization
Productivity	Performance of homogeneous work groups versus diverse work teams. • Output quantity • Quality • Time to complete	Greater output reduces cost per unit, increasing profits. Greater creativity produces new products, ideas.
Diversity Related Training, e.g., sexual harassment	Numbers of complaints, dollar value of settlements	Reduced legal fees and settlement costs increase profits
Marketing to Diverse Consumers	Sales and market share before and after programs generated by diverse marketing team.	Sales dollars and profits from those sales

- Better relationships and acceptance among the diverse customer base.
- Development of more new approaches, processes and products through the contributions of diverse work teams.
- Improved company image resulting from a positive reputation and the presence of diverse employees in positions of importance.
- More effective upward communication to provide new perspectives to senior management for the operation of the business and the treatment of employees.

The intense profit pressures on just about any organization will create continuing scrutiny of the value added by diversity programs and interventions. If those programs do not deliver, they will fade away, but that has not been experi-

TABLE 14.2 Some Benefits of Company-Specific Diversity Interventions

Source/ Organization	Program Type	Benefit Claimed
Business Week, American Airlines	"Supertrack" for female managers to provide more rapid advancement.	Increased women in upper levels from 12% to 21% in a five-year period
Chicago Tribune Allstate Ins.	Work and family initiatives [broad]	The program saves money. It costs us $30–60,000 to train employees—work/family programs help keep turnover low
Unpublished survey/Aetna	On-site day care center	Post maternity turnover reduced from 23% to 12%
OAG	On-site day care center	Post maternity turnover reduced from 44% to 22%
Wall Street Journal Corning	Training in gender awareness ("Women as Colleagues")	Used to spend $4 million per year recruiting and training women. Since the diversity training started the dropout rate and expense has been cut in half
HRMagazine, Nynex	Mentoring circles for females and minorities	▪ Increase gender awareness by male mentors ▪ Defuse potential serious sexual harassment situations ▪ Provide visibility for upper level positions ▪ Build support system to improve productivity on the job
Wall Street Journal DuPont	Broad diversity program	Getting people to work together better on the job increases productivity
Wall Street Journal Xerox	Informal network of six female executives	▪ Change succession planning terms from masculine to sexually neutral ▪ Add a female to all succession planning discussions
Wall Street Journal Conference Board Survey	Flexible work programs- employer rationale e.g., Du Pont, Avon, Knight Ridder News, IBM	▪ Recruiting advantage ▪ Increase productivity ▪ Reduce turnover
Wall Street Journal	Understanding differences training	Improved understanding and reduced friction in working with non-U.S. employees

(continued)

TABLE 14.2 Continued

Source/Organization	Program Type	Benefit Claimed
Avon	Employee advocacy groups	Provide solidarity and career help for members, tackle subconscious
Harvard Business Review Digital	Training of thousands of employees in valuing or understanding differences	Help transform legal and social pressure into the competitive advantage of a more effective work force.
Human Resource Planning Two Federal agencies	Flextime results	Flextime users came to work earlier and gained increased family time in the evening
Wall Street Journal, Northern States Power Helene Curtis Household International	Mentoring & networking programs Extended maternity leave "Family Friendly" policies	Doubled the number of women officers/managers Turnover of new mothers reduced from 31% to 7% Cut new mother turnover from 40% to 25%

enced to date. In fact, a Towers Perrin survey of company diversity activities indicated that 80% of the companies had maintained or expanded their efforts in the midst of the recession of '91 to '93. (2) What that data suggests is that a number of line officers were making judgment calls on the potential value of a whole range of activities. They concluded that there were business benefits to diversity, and that the recession was not a valid reason to withdraw their support of diversity initiatives.

USE THESE EIGHT STRATEGIES TO MAINTAIN DIVERSITY MOMENTUM

In a sense, this section is premature because most organizations have not been working the diversity issues intensively for an extended period of years. Therefore, they may not have reached the point where boredom has set in, or other distractions have pulled them away from their diversity commitment. However, if your efforts have reached a wall of indifference or if you wish to anticipate that contingency, this section contains information that will be useful to you.

1. Dodge the Cost-Cutting Knife: As indicated in the earlier section, most companies have maintained or increased their diversity efforts during the recent recession. However, for the financially pressured company, no area of activity should be free from scrutiny, and in fact some companies have taken some embarrassing retrenchment steps (such as discontinuing diversity awareness training shortly after it had been announced, or eliminating the diversity staff).

If you are facing the threat of the cost-cutters' knives, it will be critical to be able to do the following:

- Have senior management reiterate the strategic business rationale for the company's diversity efforts.
- Identify the specific benefits that have been obtained to date, or which can be inferred from other organizations' experience as being realistic.
- Identify some of the potential adverse impacts (quantitative and qualitative) of discontinuing or de-emphasizing the activities and the organization's commitment.

Of course you must also realize that even a well-documented success story may be subject to some reduced spending limits. You can afford to sacrifice a few minor extremities, if you can preserve the heart of the program.

2. Celebrate Successes and Promptly Correct Failures: Who was it that said, "Success has a thousand fathers, but failure is an orphan"? Everyone wants to be associated with a winner, so don't be shy about publicizing the wins and the heroes that helped bring it about. Even those who have not been touched personally by the benefits of a particular intervention should be aware of success stories. The creation of enough success stories will broaden support and enthusiasm, making it very difficult for an organization to back away from diversity initiatives.

In a contrary vein, if something has not worked, quickly assess the situation, and fix or terminate the program. A diversity training program that is not meeting employee needs should not just be kept running interminably, simply because everyone has not been through it yet. Stop the program, fix it, or get rid of it.

3. Bring in Fresh Troops: Extended diversity interventions may involve the participation of support groups and task forces of a wide variety of individuals. Somewhere along the way, you will begin to see the effects of diminishing levels of interest. The reasons are probably varied, and quite expected, including:

- The need to focus more of their time on their full-time job.
- Frustration with the pace of change, or long-term nature of the process.
- Changes in their responsibilities since they started the effort (for example, added travel, promotion, transfer), which requires them to back off from their diversity involvement.

Don't try to pump up the troops who have served and are tired. Send them on their way with sincere thanks and recognition for their efforts (letter from the chairman). They can still be diversity advocates for you. You can then use the turnover opportunity to bring in fresh blood. Have the new recruits go through an education and awareness process to stimulate their enthusiasm and commitment. You then have a new core of diversity enthusiasts to help spread the principles through the organization.

4. *Make Diversity an Inseparable Part of HR Programs and Processes:* If you have really done the job well over time, your employees will stop thinking of diversity as a separate program in itself. Instead they will be thinking about the inherent diversity implications in such activities as compensation, performance appraisal, recruitment, career planning, communications, and team building. Managing diversity will be natural and part of the process of effective human resources management, not just an addendum to the program.

5. *Coordinate Diversity-Related Activities of All Departments:* Diversity related activities in larger organizations will run on a number of parallel tracks, often encompassing a number of different departments and individuals. The coordination of those activities will permit the greatest impact, especially when budgets are slim. For example, some potential areas of overlap include the following:

- Community relations: Creating linkages to ethnic, gender, disabled, gay and lesbian, and other special interest groups.
- Corporate contributions: Grants to predominantly minority educational institutions, research on family, women, minority issues.
- Investor communications: communicating benefits of diversity within the company to shareholders and the investment community.
- Government Relations: Maintaining positive working relationships with local, state and federal governmental units that have a legitimate interest in the representation and treatment of non-traditional individuals in the company's employment.
- Purchasing: Programs targeted toward minority, female business enterprises.
- Advertising/Marketing: Selection of target markets, positioning, use of ethnic media.
- Public relations: Positioning company with specific population groups.

The scope of possible diversity activities underscores the point that diversity is a normal and natural part of doing business.

6. *Provide Progress Reports:* As we discussed in the communication section, there are many interested constituencies for the diversity program. To maintain commitment and enthusiasm, keep them well informed of what has been done, why, and what has been achieved as a result. The message needs to be tailored to some degree to appeal to the enlightened self-interest of the different groups as described in Chapter 12. For example, here are just a few of the interests of stakeholders:

- The Board of Directors and shareholders want to know the impact on the bottom line and on the public relations and compliance profile of the company.
- Community advocacy groups will want to know how the programs have increased the employment and advancement opportunities for members of their group (African Americans, Hispanics, Asian, Jewish, Native American, working mothers, etc.). Internal advocacy/affinity groups will have a similar self-interest point of view.
- White males will want to know just what the diversity initiative has done for them. For example, an improved career planning and development program can benefit them as well as all other employees.

If you communicate well and often, enthusiasm for the program can be retained, and you can weather out the periods of retrenchment.

7. Provide for a Sponsor Succession Process: You will probably start a change process by securing the public commitment of the CEO or the local equivalent. However, folks in the trenches are used to hearing and reading high sounding pronouncements from the CEO. This is a CEO thing to do; this is what they are paid for. However, to keep a diversity change process moving long enough to realize results, you must provide cascading levels of highly visible sponsorship. The sponsorship should follow the natural power points of the organization. You should not assume that the torch will be picked up eagerly by successive levels of management. You need to win the hearts and minds at every level.

8. Integrate Diversity into Your Total Quality Management and Other Broad Programs: Frequently diversity interventions proceed along with total quality programs for management. The question is often raised whether the two should be integrated because there are some similarities:

Scope and Concept Similarities: (3)

- Both grounded in business rationale
  - Motivated by competitive realities
  - Often starts with CEO vision
- Both stress empowerment management
- Both represent "way of life" changes in the corporate culture to be sustainable
  - Comprehensive effort, dozens of changes
  - Sustained over a number of years

- Long term pioneering efforts are required, involving
    - False starts, ups and downs
    - Ambiguities that go with pioneering
    - Discomfort in "lead steer" role

Similarity of Implementation Strategies: (4)

- Requires visible, strong leadership
- Focus on customer results
    - Internal first, then external
    - Measure customer opinion
- Train all employees
    - Start with awareness, follow with skills
    - Subjects in common; empowerment, communications, team/group dynamics
- Participation and contributions are recognized
- Heavy communication of the program
- Specific process, tools and vocabulary developed

While there are significant similarities both in concepts and methodologies, I favor a linked but separate approach for diversity and total quality. The separation allows the following:

- Allows for communication of a strong commitment to diversity without dilution of the focus
- Minimizes complications of the chain of command—e.g., leaders reporting to two different officers
- Avoids diversity being totally overshadowed by the presence of the (often) more heavily funded total quality effort

However, there are also some disadvantages of totally separate approaches, including potential overlap of activity, confusion over priorities and system overload.

If both TQM (or total customer focus, etc.) are proceeding simultaneously, try to develop a linkage of the activities, programming and communications. For example, consider the following:

- Coordinate education and training activities so that one organization will not be hit with too many programs in the same year that require time away from the job.
- Look for linkages and overlapping objectives, e.g.

- Working with diverse teams/TQM team building activity
- Empowerment management techniques that focus on results achieved rather than on management style and adherence to standard operating procedures or the corporate culture
- Valuing and utilizing diverse input to develop more new ideas for improvement, processes and programs

While the coordinated approach can work for you, it is important not to let the diversity initiative become buried under the TQM program (which has probably been running longer with more resources). If diversity seems to be just a piece of TQM, employees will perceive a lack of commitment and very little may be accomplished.

As I stated at the outset of this chapter, there is much to be learned about measuring progress and maintaining the momentum or diversity programs. Within the next three to five years, there will be considerable progress made in these areas, further ingraining diversity into the culture and way of life of the organization.

IMPORTANT POINTS TO REMEMBER

1. Carefully decide how critical it is to measure the results of specific aspects of your diversity programs, and how soon you should begin trying to measure.

2. Select a mix of measures that incorporate both quantitative and qualitative assessments.

3. Utilize a mixture of strategies to maintain momentum for your diversity efforts:
   - Dodge the cost cutting knife by demonstrating program value
   - Celebrate successes and promptly correct failures
   - Bring in fresh troops to staff committees and serve as change agents
   - Make diversity an inseparable part of human resources processes and programs
   - Coordinate diversity related activities of all departments within the organization
   - Provide progress reports
   - Provide for sponsor succession
   - Coordinate with total quality initiatives

15 Panoply Products Corporation: Developing and Implementing Diversity Strategies

The various chapters of this book have each covered an important element of planning a diversity strategy and implementing programs intended to support that strategy and objectives. As a means to illustrate the connections between the various dimensions of a diversity initiative, and to test your understanding, the Panoply Products case is presented here for your analysis.

The PPC case is a very challenging exercise in that nearly all elements of the diversity process come into play in the case. With regard to the realism, the information and issues posed in the case study come from real life situations. However, it is not one company, but a variety of organizations from which the data is drawn. The picture portrayed by Panoply Products Corporation, in its totality, represents neither the very best nor the worst of what we have observed first hand or had described by others with whom we have come in contact.

The case can be read for its own enjoyment but we recommend that you try your hand at developing solutions for some of the tasks. The instructions at the end of the chapter are written on the assumption that small teams would undertake to develop short presentations on the various assignments. While there are no "perfect" answers, some of the key issues and possible solutions are included as an addendum to the case.

COMPANY HISTORY AND BUSINESS OPERATIONS

Panoply Products Corporation (PPC) was founded in the early 1920s by two brothers, Thaddeus and Leonard Zell. The Zell brothers had immigrated from eastern Europe in 1918. After failing at several small businesses they set up a small family business concocting and selling "garage brewed" cleaning and household products. Leonard was a chemist and handled the production side. Thaddeus handled the sales and finance, with various members of the immediate and extended family involved in various tasks.

A turning point for the business was when they landed a contract to produce private label products for Great Eastern, a large supermarket chain. As time went on they developed their own labeled products and sold directly to the retail trade or through wholesalers. They added production capacity cautiously as the business continued its steady but unspectacular growth.

By 1975 PPC grew to nearly one billion dollars in sales. Descendants of the family founders held a number of key positions during the company's early years. After the company was listed on the stock exchange in the late 1940's, the rapid growth necessitated that more and more key positions be filled with unrelated professional managers. Finally, in 1983 it became apparent that the third generation of Zells did not have the capacity or the desire to continue the tradition of family leadership of PPC. PPC was sold at that time to Global Corporation, a soft drink, publishing and transportation conglomerate based in New York City. Most of the family management left PPC (on good terms) in the two years after the sale to Global.

By 1994, PPC had grown to be a $2.5 billion sales subsidiary of Global. PPC's primary product lines were carried on from the original company: soaps, polishes, and other household cleaning products. In 1985–90 Global acquired several regional businesses in the personal products categories (shampoos, soaps, toothpaste, deodorants, etc.) and integrated them into PPC. The Personal Care division comprised about a fourth of PPC's overall sales. PPC products were typically marketed as "value" brands in supermarkets, discount stores, drug stores, etc. PPC did not have significant international sales (except Canada), but the parent company for several years had been urging PPC management to develop a strategic plan for entering markets in Europe or in the Pacific rim.

PPC had considerable autonomy to develop its own human resources, community and operational programs so long as financial performance met the tough standards of the parent holding company. Many consumers of PPC products were not even aware that it was part of the much larger Global corporation. Along with other subsidiaries of Global, PPC was subject to a periodic review of the public responsibility committee of the Global Corporation board of directors.

THE PPC CORPORATE CULTURE

The Zell family leadership, during its tenure, tried to instill a family atmosphere in the company. For example, they would attend the annual Company picnics at major locations, send birthday cards to employees, etc. Employee benefits and pay levels were quite competitive. Most of the plants were unionized, but relations with the unions were generally good. A recent Teamsters attempt to organize the headquarter's clerical work force had been defeated by a comfortable margin.

Many of the managers who remained from the Zell years still tried to maintain the "family" environment that they felt had worked well earlier in the company's history. However, employees who had come on board in the last ten years (and who had never seen a member of the Zell family) had little interest in, or patience with, the reminiscences of the "old geezers." This was especially true at PPC's Philadelphia headquarters office, where a substantial portion of the 1000 employees had less than ten years service.

Naturally the culture of the company changed as it grew in size and complexity. As more professional managers were brought into key positions by Global, the environment became more "professional" and formal. Internal competition for support of projects could be intense, and it was important to be seen as supportive of your own work team.

In mid-1993 PPC went through a restructuring and downsizing that eliminated about 5% of the salaried positions. Three older, inefficient factories were closed as well during this period. PPC increasingly became viewed by employees as hard charging and intensely demanding. Some linked the tougher environment with the advent of William Stevens, the current PPC president. Stevens was a linebacker on the Naval Academy football team in his college days and a naval carrier ship helicopter pilot. He was known to be very tough on managers who did not meet his expectations. He enjoyed describing his management style as "kicking ass and taking names." He felt Darwin had it right—only the most fit should survive. A current organization chart for the company is shown in Exhibit 15.1.

One of the legacies of the Zell years was an aversion to formal and detailed human resources systems and programs. Thus some departments developed their own approaches to performance appraisal. There was lip service provided on formal succession planning, mainly to meet requirements from Global Corporation for completed succession charts. There was a corporate training staff, but most of its work focused on training for first-line supervisors and the sales force.

A Total Quality Management program was introduced in 1992. The program was still in effect, but it had never been taken seriously outside the production and R & D groups.

EXHIBIT 15.1 Panoply Products Corporation Current Chart of Organization

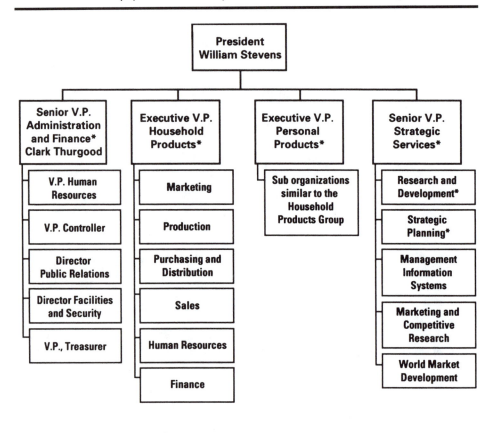

* *PPC Executive Operating Committee*

AFFIRMATIVE ACTION CONCERNS

During the early 1990s, PPC management became increasingly concerned about the turnover, discontent, and limited upward mobility of its minority and female employees. Among its salaried employees, symptoms of the underlying problems included the following:

- Voluntary turnover rates increased by 20% between 1990 and 1993. Minority turnover increased by 40% during this time.
- Complaints to PPC's Equal Employment Opportunity Department doubled

from 1990–1993. While most of these complaints were resolved without a formal charge being filed by the employee, the incidence rate was a concern nonetheless. While comparative data was sketchy, the incidence of complaints seemed to be high for its industry.

- The company was not able to achieve its ambitious affirmative action recruiting objectives. Blacks and Hispanics graduating from college and MBA programs did not have a positive perception of the company as a place to work. As a result, the better minority candidates were frequently lost to competitors.

- While numerous female graduates were hired into management training programs, very few stayed and worked their way into the middle management and officer ranks. Women who had been tagged for the "high potential" program had been lost for a variety of reasons. Very few minorities had managed to progress beyond middle manager levels, even though the PPC Chairman had expressed his interest in seeing more minority appointments at the director and officer level.

- In 1988 a Black Network group was formed by a small group of employees at the headquarters. Their stated purpose was to have a forum for discussion of common concerns and to support one another. Initially the human resource department tried to discourage the formation of the group. Soon after the HR group withdrew its opposition, similar groups were formed by Hispanic employees, and women managers. There were also rumors that a support group was being quietly organized by some gay and lesbian employees. There were jokes among certain white males that they were forming a group called W.H.A.D.—White Heterosexuals About to be Dumped on.

POTENTIAL IMPACT OF DIVERSITY ON THE BUSINESS

In the past several years there has been a growing awareness of the changing consumer demographics. John Pierce, the Vice President of Strategic Planning, was an outspoken critic of the company's limited understanding of how changing demographics could affect their business. At the annual long-range planning meeting held at the Founders Country Club, he made a presentation that included the following highlights:

1. Portion of purchases by minorities:
    - Personal goods   23%
    - Household products   29%

2. Percentage of professionals in marketing positions
   - who are minority managers: 4%
   - who are minority directors or officers: 2%

3. Purchasing decision maker
   - Personal Products   70% women
   - Household Cleaning Products   78% women

4. Percentage of directors and officers who are women: 8%

5. The fastest growing demographic group are those over age 60. However, the marketing managers (who have an average age of 31) have directed little or no attention to the special needs of this market segment. Competitors' niche market products are beginning to show up in test markets.

6. The company does not have a working relationship with any minority advertising agency or minority media.

7. The minority purchasing program is a paper shuffling activity that is handled on a part-time basis by a junior manager.

8. The corporate foundation allocates most of its gifts to local arts (symphony, ballet, art museum, and so on) and to Ivy League schools. Less than 10% of the funds go to the support of minority and women's groups and activities.

9. The company has floundered in its efforts to develop an international strategy that the parent company will support. No more than ten managers have lived outside of the U.S., it is estimated.

10. The human resources department has not developed any new programs to enable the company to attract, develop and retain women and people of color. The percentage of minorities in HR positions isn't much better than it is for the rest of the company.

11. Line managers' efforts to provide flexibility in work rules and benefit administration is routinely discouraged.

John Pierce summarized by saying, "It seems clear that we must understand better why we are doing well with our current loyal customers, so we can broaden our appeal to those we are not now reaching and reach into new markets. We must begin to build from the inside out. There is a need for a concerted and coordinated effort to focus meaningful company resources on this important issue."

The President, William Stevens, echoed his support of John Pierce's observations. Before adjourning to the golf course, Mr. Stevens suggested that Tod Walker, the recently hired V.P. of Human Resources, should be involved in the subject. Mr. Stevens promised to pass the word on to Tod and have him develop a recommended program for review.

RESPONDING TO THE PRESIDENT'S CHALLENGE

Even before hearing from the President on the subject, Tod Walker was feeling pressure to respond to the emerging issues of concern to senior management and employees. The word from the President just gave him the latitude to devote some time to the subject. However, Tod was at a loss on how to proceed with the diversity subject. Although Tod's previous employer had some sophisticated HR programs, they had not done much in the diversity area. He had heard of several companies in the city which had been working with employee support groups to identify issues. Like PPC, some companies had separate groups for female employees, African Americans and Hispanics and they attempted to involve these groups in their change efforts. Tod visited with several of his counterparts at other companies to find out how they approached the kinds of issues he was facing. He also checked out surveys regarding the kinds of diversity activities that seemed to be the most popular.

With the support of the President, Tod Walker elected to form a company-wide action group which was called the *Diversity Task Force* (DTF). DTF started with a dozen employees but soon expanded to 25 employees from all levels, and a variety of departments.

A few of the DTF members had been active in one of the special interest employee groups (e.g., Hispanics, women) that had developed. While some members of the existing groups were concerned about the role of DTF, Tod viewed DTF as a supplement rather than as a replacement for the special interest groups. DTF included females, minorities and white males. DTF conducted a series of meetings. Early sessions included an outside facilitator whose mission was to help participants understand issues in managing a diverse work force.

Even with the facilitator's help DTF had difficulty organizing itself, understanding what management wanted from them, and agreeing on priorities for action. Part of the issue seemed to be the size of the group itself (25 members). It was difficult to schedule meetings and attendance usually hovered around 50%. Moreover, the diversity of DTF's members also created wide variations in perceived needs. As one black male salesman said, "If management thinks that the needs of a white woman Vice President, who earns over $100,000 a year, have anything to do with my issues, they are hopelessly misinformed."

After three months of meetings, DTF participants concluded that they needed additional data and understanding of the issues before they could provide management with specific feedback on what steps should be taken. The chairpersons (a Black female and a Hispanic male) recommended to the Human Resources department that a survey of salaried employees be conducted to establish the nature and severity of the issues being faced. If the effort were a success for salaried employees, the model could be used at other PPC locations for hourly employees.

Unfortunately, Tod Walker's boss provided significant resistance to the diversity survey idea. "We spent $50,000 two years ago on employee surveys. Why can't we use the data already available?" He agreed to permit expenditure for the effort based on the President's interest, remarking "This better produce some brilliant stuff!"

THE DIVERSITY RESEARCH PHASE

A west coast consulting firm specializing in diversity issues (The Center for Creative Analysis, or CCA) and a small locally-based firm were invited to make proposals. Tod and his staff selected CCA for the project after listening to various firms' presentations. Because of the limited budget that Tod had to work with, CCA's work would be limited primarily to the gathering of the data with some overall observations. The development of detailed recommendations and action plans would be the responsibility of DTF.

Phase I of CCA's research study included sending surveys to about a third of the employee population. The researchers collected supplemental data by running focus groups that were broken out on the basis of race and gender. The researchers also examined a variety of written materials to understand PPC's vision, strategy, culture and equal opportunity efforts. The objective was to identify and analyze cultural and systemic factors that could hinder or facilitate effective management of employee diversity, and to identify and analyze the dynamics of upward mobility at PPC. While they were not charged with developing detailed program recommendations, it was assumed that their analysis would lead rather directly to the establishment of priorities upon which DTF and management could agree.

At the insistence of female members of DTF, a second survey was conducted to determine which issues were most important to employees who now had young children or who planned to become parents. Due to budget constraints, Tod decided to involve the company's internal market research department in designing and administering the study.

Participants in the dependent care survey were asked to allocate a hypothetical $1,000 spending allowance toward a variety of work and family-related benefits (for example, daycare, extended maternity leave, flexible policies). The objective of this targeted survey was to obtain clear feedback regarding possible improvements in company programs they would value most highly as working parents (or prospective parents).

Both surveys were introduced with a letter from the President in which he made it clear he personally felt that having a diverse work force was "the right thing to do" and he offered an optimistic assessment of future opportunities that would emerge from the study. Many white middle managers interpreted the letter as an expansion of affirmative action efforts which would limit their own opportunities for advancement. As one cynic scribbled on the President's letter, "*Diversity . . . clever name, same old game*—hiring and promoting according to quotas!"

MOVING FROM RESEARCH TO ACTION

Three months after the kickoff of the research phase of the PPC diversity initiatives, a special meeting of the DTF participants was called. The purpose of the meeting was to review the conclusions of the two surveys and develop a set of priorities for action. The external consultants presented the highlights of reports (see Attachment A on page 277). The PPC marketing research group provided a summary of the results of the work and family survey (Attachment B on page 278).

Unfortunately, about a third of the DTF members had scheduling conflicts and could not attend the all-day meeting to hear the reports on the results of the two studies. Among those who did attend the meeting, there was rapt attention to the presentations, followed by animated discussion. Unfortunately, the group could not come to a clear consensus on the top half dozen issues for which they would recommend priority efforts. Some wanted to focus on work and family issues, but other members felt they were ignoring some of the serious issues that seemed to indicate an environment not supportive of females, minorities or "anyone who doesn't look like they were a Naval Academy Midshipman," as one member put it. The DTF was also aware that a recent sales slump and earnings decline could result in any recommendation for a significant increase in costs being met with skepticism.

Furthermore, the group members were not well-versed on how some current human resources programs worked (for instance, succession planning decisions, maternity leave options, selection for training opportunities, tuition reimbursement, etc.). Thus they were not sure how their thoughts would mesh with existing efforts. In any case, the participants knew their primary job responsibilities would prevent them from allocating much of their time to the large chore of developing and implementing program modifications. Furthermore, they had some doubts that there was a true readiness on the part of senior management to change the basic cultural roots of the company. DTF adjourned at the end of the day with a number of the participants feeling frustrated and overwhelmed by the magnitude of the task.

The next morning, the DTF co-chairs gave their report to Tod Walker. While Tod was still enthusiastic about the process they had used and the information developed, he knew he had a difficult challenge to keep the DTF group committed to the process. Furthermore Tod's boss, Senior Vice President, Finance and Administration, was pressing him for some high profile (yet inexpensive) programs. Tod felt that his boss viewed the issues too narrowly, thinking that all that was needed was to gear up affirmative action efforts again.

Another pressure was developing in that the surveys conducted several months earlier had created some unrealistic expectations of major breakthroughs for minorities and females. Rumors of impending promotion opportunities were circulating. As one Hispanic employee said, "Maybe they finally realize that something more is needed beyond Mexican food day in the company cafeteria."

Furthermore, Tod was angered to learn that the Personal Products Division of PPC had announced a series of training seminars on valuing diversity led by a local university professor/consultant. The plan was to include all management employees over the next 18 months. Tod inquired of the division personnel director why they had elected to go their own way while the study results were still being analyzed. The personnel director said, "Look, my boss has been on me for six months to get something going. We just got tired of waiting for anything to come out of your department. I don't see how our program can harm your efforts." Tod was further concerned because he had received a half dozen phone mail messages complaining about the confrontational approach used by the outside trainer. Tod was concerned that the environment would be worsened if the first exposure to the subject of diversity resulted in a lot of employees being angered.

PREPARING FOR SENIOR MANAGEMENT BUY-IN

Tod was concerned about what to do next and what sort of recommendations to provide to his boss, and the President. The Executive Committee meeting at which he was to present was still a month away, but the pressure was on. He called in his direct reports to discuss the situation and seek their involvement. The key requests he made were for the following:

1. Success Factors: To identify the factors within PPC which will facilitate or hamper our efforts to bring about lasting improvement through diversity initiatives. How do we capitalize on our strengths and minimize the effects of our weaknesses? We need to confront the issues squarely, yet be realistic about what is achievable.

2. Work & Family Priorities: To determine which of the 3–4 issues in the family programs surveys should be dealt with first. The data and methods may not be your ideal, but we don't have a lot of time or money to reinvent the wheel. Given the needs, which one or two initiatives will best address the priorities?

3. Other Diversity Priorities: Based on the survey results provided by the Center for Creative Analysis, identify which issues are to be addressed first. Keep in mind that everyone may not recognize the long-term nature of this effort. What kind of decision criteria should we use? When applying the criteria you recommend, what priorities emerge as the focus? I can visualize a wide range of activities including our career planning programs, improved affirmative action recruiting and tracking, communications, and so forth. Are there some areas where we need more information before coming to a conclusion?

4. Selling Strategies: To develop a selling strategy to move toward approval and implementation. This would include:

- Developing a business rationale to justify the funding of the diversity commitments.
- Getting a senior management sponsor to help me push the changes through the system.
- Determining ways to get key line managers and divisional human resources heads behind the program.
- Anything else I haven't thought about.

5. Organization/Process/Strategy: What could I have done differently to better manage the process? We want to use our experience to help other divisions in the company when they begin their efforts. What steps should we take going forward to control the process, manage expectations and utilize all the talent available in moving toward our goals. For example, can we use the advocacy groups or some segment of the DTF as we sort out these issues? What involvement should we seek from the divisional HR directors?

"These are just a few things that come immediately to mind," Tod told his staff. "I'll need your help to develop a realistic, yet meaningful action plan to carry this project forward. If I have missed something, don't hesitate to express your point of view. I am open to criticism and we will only have one chance to get it right and nail down senior management support. Let's meet in three days to review your preliminary recommendations. An informal flip chart presentation is sufficient given the time constraints that we face."

ATTACHMENT A Panoply Products Corporation Work and Family Issues

---

SURVEY HIGHLIGHTS

METHODOLOGY

Respondents were asked to allocate a hypothetical $1,000 a year allowance from the company toward a variety of support programs. Their responses were to be based on the perceived value of the program to them, not its cost to the company. Thus, an optional 3-month unpaid maternity leave was ranked highly, even though the employee would, in effect, bear the full cost.

COMPANY DEMOGRAPHICS

Approximately 50% of headquarters employees are females. About 40% of all professional and management employees are women, spread through all departments. 80% of office and clerical are women.

The growth of the organization has resulted in a rather young salaried workforce. About 35% of all headquarters employees are women ages 18–40 (the primary childbearing years). Of the latter group, 70% have not had their first child.

DATA PRESENTATION

The overall data is summarized in Attachment A–1 below. The most popular programs, based on spending account allocation, are listed in order. The percentage of participants allocating some portion of their fund is shown in the right-hand column.

Author's Note: See Table 10.2–10.6 for a summary of competitive practices.

ATTACHMENT A–1 Employee Preferences for Family Support Initiatives

Type of Program/Policy Desired	Share of Funds*	% Respondents Allocating Dollars
1. Company-sponsored day care center (near headquarters, employee cost sharing)	19%	45%
2. Additional two weeks of paid maternity leave.	13%	50%
3. Up to three months optional unpaid maternity leave (immediately following paid leave)	12%	46%
4. Flexible hours	11%	40%
5. Part-time work	8%	35%
6. Flexible benefits	7%	25%
7. Job sharing	8%	24%
8. Pre-tax spending account for daycare	6%	20%

*all other items scored less than 5% each

ATTACHMENT B Summary of Diversity Research Results

PANOPLY PRODUCTS CORPORATION

I. BACKGROUND ON THE FOCUS GROUPS

Ten focus groups were held to supplement the data from the questionnaires, to surface other issues not covered by the survey and to develop solutions.

The focus groups were broken out by race, gender, and in some cases by organization level as well (exempt/nonexempt). Groups included:

- White male exempt (2 groups)
- Black Male exempt and nonexempt
- White female nonexempt
- Black female nonexempt
- White female exempt

- Black female exempt
- Hispanic male and female
- Asian male and female
- Gay and lesbian

Attendance for the groups varied from a low of seven to a high of twelve. Generally about 20% of the confirmed participants did not show. The attendance fall-off was attributed by some to the conflict with the current budgeting process which was in full swing at the time the focus groups were conducted. The focus groups were led by moderators of like race and gender. A summary of key comments from the various groups follows the data tables.

II. BACKGROUND ON THE QUESTIONNAIRES

During the month of March surveys were sent to about 1000 salaried employees at various company locations. White employees were selected through random sampling, and all minority employees received surveys so that confidence in the statistical validity of the data could be established.

The response rate on the survey was 43% for white male employees, and 59% for all other groups combined. The numbers of responses are sufficient for valid data reports on the following employee groups:

- White male exempt
- Minority male exempt
- White female nonexempt

- Minority female nonexempt
- White female exempt
- Minority female exempt

We did not have sufficient sample sizes to provide statistically reliable breakouts along divisional lines. Also, we did not have enough numbers to break out minority participants into black, Hispanic, and Asian groups as you had requested.

The data displayed in the tables at the end of this report represent responses to about half the questions in the survey. The entire survey with the detailed breakouts for each item will be available in two weeks. However, in our judgment, the key information necessary to develop action plans is contained in the data attached.

III. PRECAUTIONS ON THE DATA
Tonality

We understand the focus of your efforts is to identify needed areas of improvement. Therefore, we have reported our results as the percentages that *disagree* with the status quo, creating an impression more negative than is justified on balance.

Perception Versus Reality

Some of the responses seem to indicate a perception by some employees that certain practices do not meet various EEO/Affirmative Action federal or company standards. Keep in mind that we are reporting only perceptions. Gender- or race-based biases may result in over-reporting of problems, or misinterpretation of events. By the same token, the relatively more positive scores provided by white males may not be reflective of the environment either. We suggest focusing on the degree of difference in perceptions and the cause, rather than on the absolute score.

Analytical Commentary

Because of budgetary constraints and per our agreement we have restricted our role to developing the questionnaire and focus groups format, administering each activity and reporting the raw data. We have not evaluated the information nor have we developed recommendations or action plans which respond to the needs identified.

The members of the CCA project team thank you for the opportunity to serve you in this important research assignment.

Yours truly,

Center for Creative Analysis

Brief Summary of Key Focus Group Issues

Group	Activity Area	Concerns Expressed
White male	Diversity issues	1. Older employees not valued, not considered for promotions. 2. Have to look like a Navy quarterback to get on the fast track. 3. Favored groups (blacks, females) get all the attention. White male concerns ignored.
White male	Employment	1. Their children and neighbors have no chance to be hired because company is using a "quota" system to favor minorities and females.
White male	Communication	1. Open door policy operates in name only. 2. Plant manager goes around supervisors directly to union.
White male	Advancement & recognition	1. Too quick to go outside for hiring before fairly considering qualifications of internal people. 2. No assistance provided in determining future career paths and training needed to achieve goals.
Minority male & female	Diversity issues	1. Have to be "family" to be hired. 2. Promotions primarily determined by the "buddy system," not true merit.

Group	Activity Area	Concerns Expressed
		3. Use white female hiring and promotion to meet diversity numbers objectives.
		4. Sexual jokes and comments in sales and operations departments.
		5. Tardiness and absenteeism monitored more closely and dealt with more severely than for white employees. (nonexempt)
		6. Must look, act white to be promoted.
Minority male & female	Employment	1. Extra standards are applied to minority applicants.
		2. Asian applicants are favored/Black applicants are favored/White applicants are favored.
Minority male & female	Communication	1. No one to go to for discussion of problems.
		2. Any concerns raised generate overreaction from management and "trouble maker" label.
		3. Get most important information from their own grapevine. Official communication from management is infrequent and "meaningless."
		4. Not advised of the availability of training, how to be selected for attendance.
Minority male & female	Advancement & Recognition	1. No mentors to figure out development needs, determine the PPC "no-no's."
		2. Have to be "super black" to be promoted. Whites need only be mediocre to advance.
		3. Many of the good jobs are not run through the posting system/or, the candidates have already been pre-selected before the job posting goes on the board.
		4. Promotions heavily determined on the basis of sailing and golfing buddies.
		5. Performance reviews habitually late, just an empty ritual or used to "nail" you.
White Female	Diversity Issues	1. Sexual harassment and comments in several departments.
		2. Women excluded from some sales and supervisory jobs based on stereotypes.
		3. No flexibility around meeting parental responsibilities.
		4. Older males treated with respect, older women ignored or downgraded.
White Female	Communication	1. Taken for granted (especially at the nonexempt level).
		2. Legitimate complaints dismissed as "bitching" when made by females.
White Female	Advancement & Recognition	1. Promotions on the "good old boy" system.
		2. College degree required to advance even though not relevant to the work performed (nonexempt).
		3. No real training opportunities or guidance provided for career development.
		4. Senior management does not take women managers seriously (sophomoric jokes, etc).

Summary of PPC Survey Responses

	% of Respondents who Disagree with Statement					
Category/Statements	WHTE M Exempt	MNTY M Exempt	WHTE F Nonex.	MNTY F Nonex.	WHTE F Exempt	MNTY F Exempt
Climate for Diversity						
1. Changes necessary to provide environment in which diversity is valued.	28%	5%	9%	0%	17%	15%
2. Different views and opinions valued in decision-making.	22	24	37	46	35	38
3. It generally is safe to express your feelings here.	37	24	62	75	59	62
4. Business-related opinions of women are respected as well as men.	1	24	45	29	37	29
5. Business-related opinions of minorities are respected as well as non-minorities.	1	12	13	42	13	21
Category Mean Percentages	17.8%	17.8%	33.2%	38.4%	32.2%	33%
Advancement & Development						
1. Minorities have same advancement opportunities as other employees.	5%	55%	32%	66%	26%	38%
2. I have enough information to make informed decisions about career options.	20	25	18	40	21	21
3. The most qualified people are selected to fill openings.	22	30	42	67	35	15
4. I am satisfied with my opportunities for growth and development.	30	36	62	64	53	44
5. Female employees have same advancement opportunities as male employees.	7	30	43	51	41	32
Category Mean Percentages	16.8%	35.2%	39.4%	57.6%	35.2%	30.0%
Fair Treatment						
1. I am paid fairly compared with others in similar jobs.	28%	18%	32%	53%	32%	17%
2. I get fair and honest performance feedback.	16	24	45	36	25	21
3. I receive appropriate recognition for good performance.	19	25	50	57	39	27

% of Respondents who Disagree with Statement

Category/Statements	WHTE M Exempt	MNTY M Exempt	WHTE F Nonex.	MNTY F Nonex.	WHTE F Exempt	MNTY F Exempt
4. The procedures for considering employees for job openings are fair.	19	24	47	68	51	32
5. Pay is closely related to how well I perform my job.	30	30	65	72	48	24
Category Mean Percentages	22.4%	24.2%	47.8%	57.2%	39%	24.2%
Working Relationships						
1. I am treated with respect by my co-workers.	2%	24%	31%	23%	14%	9%
2. Minorities and non-minorities get along in my department.	2	24	15	27	14	34
3. Males and females work well together in my department.	0	5	12	16	19	22
Category Mean Percentages	1.3%	17.7%	19.3%	22.0%	15.7%	21.7%
Training						
1. Training for your current position meets your needs.	19%	36%	12%	29%	25%	9%
2. Your training helps you qualify for a better job.	29	36	52	62	42	21
3. A mentor has helped me in my development.	60	43	65	75	60	62
4. My immediate supervisor shows concern for my development.	45	55	58	48	60	68
Category Mean Percentages	38.3%	42.5%	46.8%	53.5%	46.8%	40.0%
Affirmative Action/Backlash						
1. Jokes and comments of a sexual nature aren't tolerated in my department.	27%	36%	18%	18%	35%	32%
2. Company should not give preferential treatment for females and minorities.	1	36	8	29	8	9
3. Racial and ethnic jokes are discouraged at my location.	22	30	22	33	26	38
4. Treatment of individual PPC employees is not affected by their race, gender, age or other irrelevant factors.	14	30	32	54	35	38
Category Mean Percentages	16.0%	33.0%	20.0%	33.5%	26.0%	29.3%

% of Respondents who Disagree with Statement

Category/Statements	WHTE M Exempt	MNTY M Exempt	WHTE F Nonex.	MNTY F Nonex.	WHTE F Exempt	MNTY F Exempt
Work & Family						
1. My immediate supervisor is responsive to my family needs.	7%	30%	22%	22%	21%	20%
2. PPC has policies designed to help employees balance their work and family responsibilities.	21	36	45	46	46	44
Category Mean Percentages	14.0%	33.0%	28.5%	39.0%	33.5%	32.0%
Productivity						
1. My job makes good use of my skills and abilities.	12%	11%	35%	29%	16%	15%
2. I understand what is expected of me in my job.	4	11	22	16	12	3
Category Mean Percentages	8.0%	11.0%	28.5%	22.5%	14.0%	9.0%
Overall Evaluation						
1. Within the next six months I plan to look for a job with another company.	65%	45%	42%	54%	42%	50%
2. I would recommend PPC as a good employer for females.	5	30	38	40	33	27
3. I would recommend PPC as a good employer for minorities.	5	49	18	44	26	56
Category Mean Percentages	25.0%	41.3%	32.7%	46.0%	33.7%	44.3%

INSTRUCTOR NOTES: PANOPLY PRODUCTS DIVERSITY CASE STUDY

The PPC case can be processed as a total group discussion, or by dividing participants into teams to focus on the areas that Tod Walker has outlined. If the team approach is used, each team would select at least two spokespersons to make a flip chart presentation of its findings. The group presenting would then defend its position and answer questions from the other participants.

There may be some overlap in the reports on the different areas. For example, the priority setting team might suggest that senior management education is a priority, and the selling team might also cover that as part of its strategy.

Using the subject areas assigned by Tod Walker as a frame of reference, lists of some of the potential issues and recommendations are summarized below each team heading:

THE SUCCESS FACTORS TEAM

Identify the factors at PPC that will facilitate or impede the establishment of a successful diversity process. Of the factors noted, choose one hindering factor and identify how its effects might be minimized. Select one facilitating factor and describe specifically how its presence might be built upon to further the program.

List of Facilitating Factors:

1. Strong business rationale—clear linkage to marketing opportunities, seemingly understood and supported by line management.

2. Highly decentralized organization—leaves room for PPC to determine what is right for them.

3. Heavy concentration of females of childbearing age provides rationale for work and family efforts.

4. Detailed survey information on which to build recommendations.

5. Groups of employees have been identifying issues and areas of common interest.

List of Hindering Factors:

1. Some guardians of the corporate culture savor the good old days—may represent some potential for backlash.

2. Senior management does not have a clear idea of diversity and does not seem to be much involved in the process as it has proceeded to date.

3. Diversity was created through acquisitions. Conflicting styles may require multiple approaches.

4. DTF role is poorly defined and they have not been prepared to provide leadership and support of initiatives.

5. Aversion to formal human resource systems may create resistance to improvements in performance appraisal, career planning, etc.

WORK AND FAMILY PRIORITIES TEAM

This team should determine which of the issues in the work and family survey should be dealt with first. It isn't necessary to develop the prescription in detail, but don't leave it too open-ended (for example, longer maternity leave). The key is not necessarily which specific interventions are chosen, but the criteria and rationale used to select the priorities.

1. The group needs to develop screening factors that are appropriate for the company in narrowing down the range of options to be pursued, for example:

   - Number of employees directly affected

   - Cost (inexpensive or produces savings?)

   - Degree of difficulty in implementing successfully

- Quick: grab some "low hanging plums" to show some upfront progress
- Business benefit of the intervention
- Systemic—lasting
- Multi-faceted to hit different needs, different employees

2. Are the interventions proposed consistent with the criteria the group developed?

3. Is the timetable for introduction realistic?

SELLING STRATEGIES TEAM

This team needs to develop a strategy to create awareness of the issues, build support and get buy-in to move the project forward. The strategy requires both work and family program issues.

Potential Selling Rationale for Diversity Initiatives

1. Develop a better understanding of, and more closely resemble the demographics of the marketplace.

2. Minimize turnover, especially for minorities and working mothers, which will yield cost savings and improve organizational effectiveness.

3. Provide a competitive advantage in recruiting.

4. Minimize legal costs and complaints.

5. Reduce the costs associated with excessive turnover.

6. Incorporate information on internal efforts in the external marketing and public relations (establish image as caring, committed employer)

Selling Activities

1. Interview key line managers and divisional HR staff to solicit data on perceived needs, clarify concepts and to build support for the program.

2. Provide educational/awareness building experience for key influencers.

3. Look for success stories to become role models.

4. Use consumer research to support the validity of the diversity initiative.

5. Identify project champions to lead the awareness and sales efforts.

6. Summit meeting chaired by CEO to approve the program elements and to underscore his personal commitment to a successful result.

ORGANIZATION/PROCESS TEAM

A review of the process utilized should yield a list of options that may have added to the effectiveness of Tod Walker's overall initiative.

1. Hold an educational session with senior management at the outset so that they would have true buy-in and understanding of the long-term nature of the process.

2. Create a closer linkage between the advocacy groups and the diversity task force by having the special interest employee groups choose their nominees for DTF participation.

3. Break DTF into separate subcommittees (for example, affirmative action, work & family) to make their task more manageable, and reduce the amount of program expertise they need to make sound decisions.

4. Provide DTF with more staff support and more clearly defined charter that they could manage.

5. Provide for closer linkage of divisional HR managers into the process for their contributions and support. Make them partners in the process to forestall preemptory actions on independent programming.

6. Structure research more carefully
   - broaden scope
   - demand recommendations from consultants
   - develop central themes for focus of efforts

7. Develop communication process control from start to finish; use process to condition employees on realistic expectations from the process.

8. Tod should educate his own boss in diversity, so he would become a champion and make sufficient budget available to do the work that is necessary.

9. Provide more process help to the DTF: someone who could work with them on the data, and develop action plans.

10. Get line support of the DTF, so that members would feel that their participation was valued, and that it would be recognized in some way.

GENERAL DIVERSITY ISSUES TEAM

Some system of setting priorities is necessary here as within the work and family team (Refer to Chapter 6 for examples of criteria selection.) Since the recommendations are being made to line management, the team should be in a position to sell the change on the basis of the need identified and the business benefits that might accrue, such as those described in Table 15.1:

TABLE 15.1 Some Possible Priority Areas and Action Steps

General Area	Possible Impact	Specific Activities
Climate for diversity	Not drawing full input from all employees, lose the benefits of diverse points of view.	Periodic climate surveys Train in listening skills Train in leading meetings and teams
	Frustration and turnover, lost input.	Train for awareness and valuing differences
Advancement & Development	Females and minorities may leave to seek a more favorable environment.	Provide individual counseling on career path options and steps needed to qualify. Train supervisors on coaching skills.
	Participation in the posting program declines, more outside hiring required.	Extend job posting to higher level jobs, communicate the program more extensively.
Fair treatment	Turnover due to non-competitive pay levels, or potential unfair practice charges.	Perform multiple regression analysis of individual pay levels, beginning in areas with highest female/minority concentration.
	Employees don't have access to candid performance feedback to aid in their self development.	Review steps in the performance appraisal system, provide training in cross-culture communications, use 360 degree appraisal process.
Affirmative Action	Turnover due to unfavorable climate.	Understanding differences awareness training. Company policy and communication on individual respect.

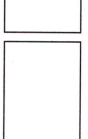

16 Background: Where We Have Been on Diversity and Where We Are Heading

It was my assumption in writing this book that the reader will have had some familiarity with underlying diversity issues and concepts. Thus, the introduction covered these only very briefly. This chapter is for those who would like to deepen their understanding of the driving forces responsible for the emerging interest in diversity, and to better understand Managing Diversity as a concept.

We will cover the 3"Ds," or driving forces, including the following:

1. The changing *Demographics* of the work force and the market place which is resulting in shifts in the talent pool and in markets for goods and services.
2. The *Disappointment* on the part of many organizations with the results of the traditional methods of utilizing the diversity of their workforce.
3. The *Demands* from employees for improved approaches to utilizing diversity, and the *Demands* for improved performance of the human assets of the organization, created by strategic and competitive challenges.

Further, we discuss the vision for change, and cite some balancing viewpoints regarding the appropriateness of that vision. We start with a brief review of key demographic trend information.

THE FIRST "D": DEMOGRAPHIC SHIFTS (U.S.)

In 1987 the Hudson Institute published the famous *Workforce 2000* report (1) which served as a wake-up call for corporate America. Focusing on workforce changes projected from 1985 to the year 2000, the report documented a shift in the labor force that many found difficult to believe. As shown in Table 16.1, the report projects dramatically varying rates of growth in the different ethnic and gender groupings that make up the workforce.

As the projections in the table indicate, white women were projected to represent the largest part of the increase, with the remaining growth driven by the increases in the numbers of native born minorities and immigrants. The column on the right shows the net effect of entrants and exits from the workforce. Since white males were the first into the workforce they now represent 42% of those leaving due to retirements and termination. Minority men and women represent only 12% of those leaving the workforce, and white women about one third. By combining the data on workforce entrants and exits, you come up with the often-misquoted statistic that 85% of the *net* growth in the workforce during 1985–2000 will be females, minorities and foreign born.

Under the surface of the major demographic changes there are many other subsets of change that could affect both the composition of the labor force and the consuming public. For example:

- in the 1960s 30% of the females with children under the age of six were in the work force. By 1990 that number had risen to 60%, with implications for labor supply and for programs to help employees balance work and family life.

TABLE 16.1 Projected Change in Workforce Composition 1985–2000

Population Group	1985 Labor Force	Net New Workers 1985–2000
Total	115.4 mill.	25.0 mill.
Native White Men	47%	15%
Native White Women	36%	42%
Native Non-White Men	5%	7%
Native Non-White Women	5%	13%
Immigrant Men	4%	13%
Immigrant Women	3%	9%

- The pattern of households was also changing, as the "traditional" family unit of the sixties (married with children) has become the exception, rather than the rule as evidenced by the statistics in Table 16.2.

Data such as that shown in these tables could be easily recognized for its potential impact on internal issues such as the availability of willing workers with the right skill set, benefit plan design, effective communications, development of teamwork among diverse employees, changed working patterns, and so on. External issues such as the emergence of new consumers or decline of the relative importance of traditional consumers also must come into the strategic planning mix. For example, in 1960, 9 of ten consumers were white. In the year 2000, 4 in ten consumers will be ethnic minorities. (2)

Changing Skill Base: Not only is the ethnic and gender makeup of the workforce changing profoundly, but the skill set of those workers is also changing, and not always for the better. Concerns about worker skills are driven by nagging evidence of the ineffectiveness of our educational system. Such concerns are frequently stimulated or reinforced by periodic reports on declining scores for standardized tests, and various studies of the quality of secondary school graduates. One study (3) conducted in Chicago city schools revealed the following key conclusions about the graduates of the local high schools:

TOP THIRD IN THE CLASS—"UNIVERSITY BOUND": Even the top third demonstrated deficiencies in math and science, particularly compared with the students of other countries with which the U.S. faces global competition.

MIDDLE THIRD IN THE CLASS—"COMMUNITY COLLEGE BOUND": In addition to the deficiencies of the top third, this group generally had inadequate computer skills, at a time when companies are becoming increasingly dependent upon computers for all phases of their operations. Students were increasingly opting

TABLE 16.2 Changes in Family Households (2)

Household Category	% of Households Represented		
	1960	2000	Change
"Traditional" Married:			
- With kids under age 18	44%	20%	− 24%
- No kids	31%	34%	+ 3%
Living Alone	13%	26%	+ 13%
Other	12%	20%	+ 8%

for "soft" subjects, avoiding math and science at the same time the labor market is moving in the other direction.

LOWER THIRD IN THE CLASS—"WORK BOUND": This group may be seriously deficient in math and reading skills. Employers have been known to screen applicants simply by observing whether an individual can fill out a job application competently. Some members of this group will not be fluent in English and may have difficulties in basic communications and interpersonal skills. According to the research they are more likely to have a negative self image, contributing to behavioral and other problems.

Counterpoint to the Demographic Arguments: A small segment of managers dispute the basic accuracy of the demographic projections. However, since the individuals represented by the aggregate statistics have already been born, are working their way through the school systems and into the workforce, those challenging the data can usually be answered. What is more common, however, is a discounting of the specific impact of the demographic changes on their own situation. What arguments do executives and managers raise to challenge the validity of the demographic impact on a given organization?

FEWER JOB OPENINGS/TOO MANY COLLEGE GRADUATES: The combination of economic malaise, technological advancements, repeated rounds of staff reductions and increased global competition will result in job formation being at the lowest level in the last fifty years. The number of jobs increased about 20% on average during the decades of the 50's through the '80s. However, during the 1990s, job growth is expected to be well under 10%. Nearly half of all major firms in the U.S. carried out layoffs in the July 1992 through July 1993 period. The percentage was about the same as the previous year, and about 40% of companies plan to carry out layoffs into 1994. (4)

Partially as a result of the above factors there is an excess of labor supply in a number of geographic areas and skill sets. For example, between 1990 and 2005 nearly one in three college graduates is expected to take a job that does not require a degree. That is up from 19% of college grads in 1980 who were either unemployed or in menial jobs. (5)

SHORT CORPORATE ATTENTION SPAN: To those looking toward the **long term competitiveness** and viability of their organizations, the demographics can be a potent motivator for concern and action. However, many organizations think in terms of the next *quarter*, not the next decade. Managers in the 1980s witnessed the wave of hostile takeovers and increasing shareholder activism and discontent. As beleaguered executives faced a second or third round of headcount reductions, the possibilities of skill shortages in five years may be of little interest. This Is Old News! For many organizations, Workforce 2000 hit them some years ago. The U.S. Census Bureau identifies 2000 counties, cities and towns in the U.S. where racial and ethnic minorities are in a majority. The present necessity of managing diversity can be illustrated by one Chicago area manufacturing facility which found in an employee census that there were fourteen different primary languages in existence in the plant! Another in Northern California listed 25 primary languages and distinguishable dialects among its workforce. Especially in the large urban centers, companies feel that Workforce 2000 has already arrived, and they are dealing with it. Why worry further, isn't it just a matter of degree?

THE DEMOGRAPHICS WON'T AFFECT US MUCH: There are some companies that don't feel they will be significantly affected by demographic shifts that have already occurred or are projected to happen. They will point out that a number of factors insulate them from the effects of the overall demographic shifts:

- There is little diversity in their primary labor market—such as rural Midwestern communities.
- The consumers of their product are not diverse—such as makers of luxury products.
- Individuals making buying decisions on their products and services are not diverse—such as certain financial services, management consulting services, defense and aerospace industries.
- While not everyone is thrilled with the climate for diversity in their organization, turnover is not a significant problem at this time.

The naysayers may indeed be correct in some circumstances, and at this point in time. This is why it is important for an organization to critically evaluate the potential strategic and competitive impact of demographics on their organization.

THE SECOND "D": DISAPPOINTMENT WITH TRADITIONAL METHODS FOR DEALING WITH DIVERSITY

The second of the forces driving interest in diversity is disappointment with the traditional methods for dealing with it in corporate America. Since equal employment opportunity became a legislated national objective in the early 1970's, organizations have relied upon the affirmative action model for dealing with diversity. Without getting bogged down in the technical aspects of affirmative action legislation, let's summarize its broader dimensions: (6)

- *Objective:* The objective at first was to open the doors to "protected classes"— initially, people of color and females. Later legislation included those with physical challenges, over age 40, and Vietnam era veterans.

- *Motivation:* Organizations engaged in affirmative action efforts so that they would be in compliance with legislation and executive orders. They also may have seen affirmative action as meeting what they saw as legitimate societal needs ("Do the right thing").

Change required:

Individuals coming into the organization were expected to bear the burden of adaptation to the existing norms, culture and practices of the organization. They were expected to go through the corporate "melting pot" in order to assimilate to the norms and standards of the organization.

Results of Affirmative Action:

An organization that was successful in affirmative action would have a diverse workforce, especially in the entry level jobs. The focus was on "getting the numbers" that assured a letter of compliance from the reviewing agency that examined the organization's record of efforts and progress.

Assumptions and Methods that Accompanied Affirmative Action: There were certain inherent assumptions for dealing with diversity that were made by organizations as they carried out their affirmative action mandates. The assumptions were made by those in the dominant group (usually white males) concerning those not in the dominant group. For these purposes we will call the outgroup **"others."** Others generally are females, minorities, foreign born, physically challenged, gay and lesbian. (7) Key assumptions about others include the following:

- If the others were different from the mainstream employees, it was assumed that they had some deficits, especially if they were labeled as "affirmative action" hires. Their differences may have been viewed as a potential threat to "the way things are done around here."

- Since white males were the success model in most organizations, it was assumed that the others had a strong desire to emulate the white males in behavior style (and hence) success.

- Since it was assumed that the others wanted to adapt, the burden of change fell entirely upon them. Little effort was made to adapt the culture and systems to make them more supportive of diversity. The others had to assimilate to whatever norms that they found in the organization.

- If the others politely expressed discomfort over the pressure to assimilate, they would be labeled as overly sensitive. If they were more bold in their criticism, they were labeled as troublemakers.

Dr. R. Roosevelt Thomas, Jr., in his lectures and writings, describes the assimilation/melting pot message companies give, as saying to your new employees something similar to the following:

"We find that this company has a special culture and that people who fit a given mold do better than those who do not. As you join us, we're going to hold up a mirror in front of you. In this mirror we have sketched the outline of the mold that works here. Compare yourself to the outline. If you fit, fine, come on in. If you don't fit, we invite you to step into our melting pot so that we can shape you to the appropriate mold. This is for our mutual benefit, as it will help to ensure that you have a productive relationship with the company."

Occasionally as an awareness raising exercise I will ask meeting participants to put themselves in the shoes of the senior management of the company. They are then asked to list the characteristics important to them (as senior executives of the company) in selecting and promoting executives. Invariably the responses include, white male, family man, age 35–50, rational and impersonal problem solving style, and so forth. In addition, there may be other more particular characteristics which are viewed as important by that organization, such as "MBA from _____ University," "golfer," "tall," and so forth.

If the employees are not able to fit the image in the mirror, the company may at least expect them to emulate the corporate model. There will often be a preferred management style in the company. The responses vary to some degree, but frequently the style preferred will call for characteristics such as "analytical," "hard charging," "tough minded," etc.

Often the style characteristics sought are those favored by Euro/white/ males, basically those that are in the positions of power in the organization. Individuals exhibiting other types of styles may encounter resistance even though they may be effective. For example, a manager who tries to work through issues by building consensus rather than win-lose confrontation as favored by the organization, may be seen as "weak." The employee showing emotion excessively (by company standards) may be labeled "volatile," "weepy," and so on. Such labels can get in the way of progress even if the characteristics do not prevent the individual from getting the job done.

Impact of Previous Assumptions and Methods on Others: In a company using the assimilation model, the "others" in the organization may encounter a number of obstacles to full utilization of all their talents.

Suppression of Differences: Individuals may become so intent on conforming to the mold that they are not fully productive. They can neither be themselves, nor meet the expectations of the mold makers (the woman trying to emulate the tough leader mold will be labeled a "bitch"). There is always the need for the others to meet the expectations for their own group, plus the standards in effect for white males. Feeling like they are always operating under a magnifying glass they hold back on expressing ideas for fear of being labeled in a way that will limit their opportunity to contribute, be recognized and advance on an equal footing. In the process their potentially unique contributions are not captured.

Assimilation Exercise: In diversity education and training seminars, we sometimes use a warmup exercise to illustrate the potential effects of assimilating, or suppressing differences. The exercise goes like this:

Exercise Instruction: Think back to a time in your life when you felt very different from those around you. In what way were you different? How did that difference make you feel? How did the difference cause you to behave? Typical feedback from this exercise is summarized in Table 16.3.

During exercises of the nature described in Table 16.3, several things become apparent:

- Differences usually result in some degree of discomfort, especially at the outset. The discomfort might be ameliorated by members of the dominant group.

- Frequently individuals would make some attempt to "fit in," using a number of adaptive devices such as clothing or speech. They may expend considerable mental energy moderating their behavior.

- Their sense of being different caused them to hold back, not providing their usual degree of contribution, perhaps reinforcing doubts about their competence that already exist.

- *Judged as a Group Member:* When white males fail, it is assumed to be an individual situation. The failure of a white male is not likely to result in a judgment that white males should not be considered for the positions. On the other hand, when an other fails, you frequently will hear, "I guess they (women, blacks, etc.) just can't do that kind of work. We will have to be careful before we throw another one into that position."

TABLE 16.3 Adaptation of Individual Differences to the Environment

Difference	Comfort Level	Adaptive Behavior
Living in a foreign country	Feel like an outsider	Avoid comparisons between native country and host country
Female was the tallest in her grade school class.	Embarrassed by taunts about her size	Physically slouched to appear more "normal"
Student from blue collar family attends prestigious graduate business school.	Conscious of differences in clothing, vocabulary and self-assuredness of classmates	Holds back on classroom participation for fear of saying something stupid or revealing his background
Was the first, or the only "one of a kind" in a given role or position level.	Feel like all eyes are on you. People testing for reinforcement of their views on members of your group.	Try to dress, talk or otherwise behave in a way that minimizes the obvious point of difference

- *Role Confusion:* Because of role preconceptions, the well-dressed black middle manager standing in the lobby may still be approached by someone assuming he is a security guard. The female manager at the meeting may be asked to serve coffee for the male managers in attendance. A classic case of role confusion is reported in Travis's *Racism American Style: A Corporate Gift (8):*

A black reporter was dispatched to cover a news conference at one of the major downtown Chicago hotels. As he was about to enter the room, he was challenged by a white public relations official at the door. The exchange reportedly went as follows:

PR Official: *"What do you want?"* the official asked abruptly.

Black Reporter: *" I am a reporter,"* he responded, surprised by the unfriendly reception.

PR Official: *"Porter? We didn't call for a porter!"*

Reporter: *"I didn't say I was a porter, I . . . (interrupted)"*

PR Official: *"Then what are you doing here?"*

Reporter: (loudly) *"I am a reporter, a newsman, a journalist. Do you understand?"*

PR Official: (finally learning the paper the reporter represented): *"I didn't know they had any colored reporters. I'm awfully sorry. Why didn't somebody tell me?"*

Unfortunately the story is not as exceptional as we might like to believe. There are numerous similar examples.

Isolation: Because the others don't feel comfortable with the constant pressure to conform to the mold, they will frequently seek the company of their ethnic/gender peers so that they can feel at ease for some part of the day. They may miss out on important informal communication channels as a result.

Members of the dominant group will refrain from invitations to those who are different because they do not feel comfortable with such individuals and visualize stronger differences of interests than may actually exist. Still they will object to the "clannishness" of the association of like individuals.

Stereotypes: A stereotyped bias exhibits itself when individuals are judged on the basis of characteristics assumed to be common in their ethnic/gender grouping. An example of members of the dominant group prejudging others using stereotypes would include the following:

- She's pregnant. We can't count on her any more!

- The (young) employee was late Monday morning. Must have partied too much on the weekend!

- The Asian applicant looks good. He said he wants marketing, but we will put him in financial analysis, since he is probably good at numbers, and his accent won't get in the way.

- Since Alice has a physical handicap she will probably have more sick days and have difficulty keeping up with the work pace.

Because of the discomfort of individuals who have had to assimilate, more and more employees are saying, "no thank you." Some excerpts from focus group discussions on the subject of assimilation are repeated later in this chapter to illustrate the point.

Disappointing Results of Previous Approaches: The affirmative action/assimilation model has been in place in most large companies for over 20 years. Although AA programs have opened the door for countless individuals, many companies are distressed with the way in which individuals are concentrated at the bottom of the corporate pyramid. In organization after organization—even those who have had strong affirmative action programs—women, people of color and others who are different tend to be stuck below the glass ceiling. The acknowledged existence of barriers to advancement, and a de facto limit to progress have yielded to a frustrating cycle entailing a variety of hidden costs.

- The costs of underutilizing your human resources
- The cost of excessive turnover
- The cost of complaints, people to handle the complaints
- The cost of people "checking out" without quitting

Even the others who have broken through the glass ceiling often pay a price for it. In many companies, 90% of male executives are married and have children. On the other hand, it would not be unusual to find that only one-third to two-thirds of the female executives are married with children. Minorities who reach key management levels talk about their continuing frustration, and sense of isolation—not accepted by their white peers, and distanced from the employee members of their own ethnic group.

The career pattern exemplified by the illustration often leads to a never-ending spiral of affirmative action efforts. This frustrating spiral (6) has been repeated in many organizations with distinguishable phases that include the following:

1. *Problem Discovery:* Management suddenly realizes that the numbers and distribution of females and minorities is not adequate. The problem has been created through excessive turnover, lack of upward mobility, unsupportive environment, etc.

2. *Target Recruiting Intervention:* When the diversity dearth is recognized, the initial response is typically affirmative action recruitment efforts directed at bringing in more members of protected class groups.

3. *Full Inventory:* The organization's talent inventory has now been filled with the "best" qualified females and minorities that could be attracted. Corporate management relaxes, as they assume that the newly hired individuals will "trickle up" through the organization, readily permeating the glass ceiling barrier.

4. *Disappointment:* Since there have been no changes in the culture and systems

of the company, the "others" in the pipeline find that the environment is not as supportive and accepting of their diversity as they had hoped. Management disappointment centers around the inability of the others to "fit in," become accepted team players, etc.

5. *Departure:* Issues fester, and people get tired of waiting for things to get better. If the job market is strong enough they vote with their feet. The high turnover leads to recognition of another crisis, and the cycle begins anew. If the job market is not strong, the individual's energy and commitment may dissipate, even though the individual remains on the payroll.

Companies have come to recognize that they must focus attention beyond the point of bringing diversity in the doors of the organization. Sustainable progress requires a change in the basic assumptions about those who are different from the mainstream.

THE THIRD "D": DEMANDS FOR BETTER METHODS OF DEALING WITH DIVERSITY

The Third D relates to demands for improved methods of dealing with diversity: demands from employees and demands of the market place.

Changing Employee Demands: For many years the assimilation model was accepted by minorities and females not in the white male mainstream as the necessary price of admission to "the club." However, members of these groups eventually recognized that their most valiant efforts were still likely to leave them outside the chosen inner circle. Interviews, surveys and focus groups covering thousands of employees suggest that employees are increasingly unwilling to check their ethnic and gender identity at the employer's door, even for the promise of a paycheck.

To illustrate the hypotheses, I have drawn comments from focus groups that were conducted separately on a race and gender basis. Some candid comments are often expressed on the assimilation pressures that employees experience in their organizations. Here are a few examples which illustrate the discomfort of nontraditional employees.

Asian American Male:
"To get ahead here you have to look white, act white, lose your accent and pat everyone on the back while kissing their asses. Sometimes it just isn't worth it."

African American Male:
"I think you can assimilate, but it only works up to a point. Most African American males choose not to because it requires too much compromising of your integrity. But if you try to maintain your identity, you are called a racist yourself for not wanting to fit in."

Asian American Female:
"You have to project yourself and sell yourself, be aggressive. You are told to talk loud because it shows confidence. But these are negative values in my culture, so I don't fit in here."

African American Male:
"You can't really be who you are. They didn't hire you for who you are. They hired you for how much like a white male you can be, while being the black male they had to hire."

Asian American Female:
"They say it is our job to adapt to them, and to some extent that is true. But they should think about getting the best that everyone has to offer, rather than just looking for clones of themselves."

African American Male:
"It is impossible to truly assimilate, and anyway it is undesirable. The Blank Company would be better off to value what my diversity contributes and use it whenever possible."

In some organizations the mold is so narrow and the pressures so severe, that even white males find it difficult and uncomfortable to fit in. Comments from two white males illustrate this point:

"This is a white "preppie" company. There is the look, the behavior pattern they seem to favor. I really don't feel comfortable playing a role just to meet their favor."

"In my work unit there is no divergence of opinion tolerated at all. Our management needs to have lock-step conformity at all times. Surely they are missing something through this approach."

Attitudes of the nature reported above are becoming more common and individuals are becoming more outspoken in their discontent with assimilation pressures. Assimilation can create difficulties for everyone, and may be unproductive for the organization as well.

Increased Competitive Demands: Anyone reading the U.S. business press in recent years is all too familiar with waves of hostile takeovers, "strategic divestitures," layoffs, downsizings, plant closings, bankruptcies, writeoffs and other sad stories. The competitive turmoil has taken its toll on employees as they tell about the longer working hours, increased job pressures and tougher demands of every type. My personal impression is that no existing survey truly captures the heightened expectations and requirements so commonplace in the business and not-for-profit worlds. Survival in the global markets seems to require that everyone contribute to his or her maximum potential. No one is allowed to coast.

To meet the increasing competitive pressures and the demands that senior management puts on its employees, companies are using a wide variety of approaches to tap the talents of the work force. Many of these approaches, such as total quality management, high performance work teams, etc. are dependent upon the effective functioning of small groups of employees, working as teams. In the work place, the team analogy that makes the most sense is not a sports team, but a surgical team in the operating room. In this analogy, all the chief surgeon sees of his team is their eyes and hands. At the critical points in their operation he couldn't care less what country they came from, their gender, or the color of their skin. What is important to that surgeon is the ability of each member to make a quality contribution to the total effort. Companies increasingly recognize that it is difficult for a team environment to be effective without the ability to manage diversity in a way that does not impede productivity. While that concern remains, there is a new trend to attempt to capitalize on the talents of a diverse work team, in order to capture the potential richness of the input of all group members.

A second element of the demand for better methods is the need for companies to adjust to the market place realities caused by the demographic shifts described earlier in this chapter. For example, in retail chains it is becoming more and more common for members of various groups to note that there are not too many people like themselves on the store staff where they do their shopping. The customer demand may create forces for change that the business organization had scarcely contemplated in its strategic planning.

DEFINING A DIVERSITY VISION FOR 2000 AND BEYOND

It takes less talent to catalogue the ills of the present than to identify a unifying and meaningful vision for the future. Therefore, I have relied heavily upon the research and concepts developed by my diversity mentor and a leading architect of the diversity movement, Dr. R. Roosevelt Thomas, Jr. (6) Dr. Thomas's research and work with organizations led him to conclude that the organizations that see diversity as an opportunity for competitive advantage can outrun their competition if they are willing to take on the challenge. What is required is a new way of thinking about diversity not as an "us versus them" confrontation to be contained, but as a resource to be leveraged for competitive advantage. Drawing liberally from Dr. Thomas's books, articles and lectures, we start with a definition and description of a new paradigm:

> *Managing diversity is a comprehensive managerial process for developing an environment that works naturally for all employees. Managing diversity seeks to tap the full potential of all employees, in pursuit of company objectives, where employees may progress without regard to (what should be) irrelevant considerations such as race, age, sex, etc.*

Defining managing diversity as a process highlights its evolutionary nature. It allows organizations to develop steps for generating a natural capability to tap the potential of **all employees.**

Diversity encompasses everyone including white males, who should not be excluded from diversity processes. Diversity is not defined solely by race or gender. Diversity also shows up with companies involved with acquisitions and mergers. In a number of companies, the toughest diversity issues are between functions and divisions, not race and gender. In other organizations the pressure point may be between the "old guard" and the "young warriors" who bring a different set of values to the work place. Although we should not overlook the broader aspects of managing diversity, most of our examples in this book deal with actions companies are taking to deal with the pain that they are feeling. Typically, the pain still centers on traditional race and gender issues.

MANAGING DIVERSITY COMPARED TO TRADITIONAL APPROACHES

In our nation we have traditionally thought of diversity in the context of legal or moral imperatives. Different perspectives within this context include:

- Civil Rights: seeks to end discrimination and racism and to comply with legal requirements.
- Women's rights: focuses on elimination of sexism in the workplace.
- Moral/Social Responsibility: Act in ways that benefit society because it is the "right thing to do."

The response to all these needs at the corporate level was typically affirmative action with an accompanying requirement to assimilate away their differences to better fit into the organization. However, since Affirmative Action has inherent limitations, something broader is needed.

Managing Diversity is a vehicle for escaping from the frustrating cycle of affirmative action. However, it should not be viewed as just an extension of affirmative action concepts. Some of the key perspectives of managing diversity are the following:

- Managing diversity means approaching diversity at three levels simultaneously: **Individual** (our own thoughts and feelings about those different from ourselves), **Interpersonal** (how we apply those feelings to others), and **Organizational** (how the culture, system and programs support diversity).
- Managing diversity approaches diversity from a *management* perspective. It deals with the way organizations are managed and how managers do their jobs. At its best, it means getting from employees not only everything you have a right to expect, but everything they have to offer.

- Managing diversity requires that line managers learn a new way. They are asked to spend less time "doing" the work and more time enabling employees to do the work.

- Managing diversity defines diversity broadly, addressing both the ways in which employees are different and the ways they are alike. It goes beyond race and gender as noted earlier. It is not about white males managing women and minorities; it is about all managers empowering whoever is in their workforce.

- Managing diversity assumes that adaptation is a two-way street, a mutual process between the individual and the company. The requirement that all employees assimilate to the corporate norms is relaxed, so that the burden of adapting does not rest solely on the individual who is different.

- Unlike more familiar approaches, managing diversity is not a program, not an orchestrated set of actions designed to "do" something. It calls for more than changing individual behaviors. It requires fundamental changes in the corporation's way of life, hence it often takes some years to fully implement.

- The driving force behind managing diversity is the business necessity of it. It is not done primarily out of a desire to be noble, moral, or have a positive public relations profile.

Just as managing diversity should not be confused with affirmative action programs, it should not be mistaken for "valuing differences" programs. Valuing differences programs are a derivative of affirmative action, and usually focus on one of several objectives:

- Fostering awareness of the nature of differences and acceptance of individual differences.

- Helping participants understand their own feelings and attitudes about people who are "different."

- Enhancing work relations between people who are different.

Valuing differences training assumes that undesirable behavior will be corrected as people enhance their awareness and understanding. But acceptance, tolerance and understanding of diversity are not by themselves enough to create an empowered work force. To empower a diverse group of employees to reach their full potential, you must both change the systems of the company as well as modify some elements of its core culture.

Some Challenges to the Managing Diversity Vision: In the interests of objectivity, it is only fair to point out that there are some critics of Dr. Thomas's *Managing Diversity* vision. As the field of knowledge about diversity issues is still evolving, the fact of the criticism should come as no surprise. Table 16.4 offers a brief sum-

TABLE 16.4 Some Viewpoints Countering the Managing Diversity Vision

Challenge	Response
Too Simplistic? It is too simple, too vague, too "pie in the sky."	To be a spur to action, a vision should be short, clear, uplifting and capable of being understood by the masses. The gritty details of how organizations implement a vision are left to others.
Too Unrealistic? MD Vision is unrealistic, optimistic beyond the realm of human experience in modern society.	While not fully achievable by 2000, satisfaction can be gained and benefits realized from **progress** from **whatever** the starting point of the organization.
Avoids the Heart of the Issues? Fancy new concepts aren't what's needed to address the issues. The problems are racism and discrimination, pure and simple.	Strong biases and racism, sexism, etc. are an important element in the inability of organizations to fully utilize all employees. However, some behaviors can be changed by raising awareness as to their cause and effects and placing them in a business context. Furthermore, the culture and systems must also be changed to support desired changes in behavior.
Undercuts Affirmative Action? The highlighting of the possible deficiencies of affirmative action further undermines a proven concept that is already under attack from various quarters.	The value of affirmative action in establishing diversity is well understood. However, a realistic assessment of the limitations of AA is a first step toward improving its total effectiveness. Managing Diversity involves effective implementation of a number of different activities simultaneously. Quite frequently a diversity study results in a refocused and more effective affirmative action effort.
Misleading Terminology? Managing equates to controlling people or minimizing damage. This implies diversity is a problem to be contained.	Think of management also as empowering employees, leveraging all the human assets of the organization. In this context the richness of diversity becomes an opportunity for competitive advantage. If the specific label doesn't feel right in your organization, adopt one that does while retaining the base concepts.

mary of some of the tough questions raised or contrary positions taken by others who are connected with the diversity area as educators, consultants, senior managers or human resources executives. In the interests of trying to continue a healthy debate, I provide my "responses" to the challenges as a point of view. Whether the response is conclusive with respect to the issue will be left to the reader to determine.

There may be other issues raised, even to the extent of dismissing the validity of any challenges to the assimilation/melting pot model used by U.S. organizations. For example, conservative icon Rush Limbaugh opines, *"If you want to prosper in America, if you want access to opportunity in America, you must be able to assimilate, to become part of the American culture. Just as in any other country in the world —if an American moved there, he would have to adapt to the culture to succeed. The so-called minorities in this country are not being done any favors when the multi-culturalist crowd forces their attitudinal segregation from mainstream society. The politics of cultural pride are actually the politics of alienation, in a different uniform."* (9) Since Rush says he is never wrong, I will just leave the comment as it stands.

POTENTIAL OBSTACLES IN A DIVERSITY CHANGE PROCESS

The managing diversity concepts described in this chapter have been widely accepted in corporate America and can be found in many company diversity vision statements. Nevertheless, few if any companies would claim to have attained or even approximated their vision objective. If managing diversity is such a great idea, why haven't more companies already succeeded at it?

Unfortunately in many organizations there exist some fundamental impediments to long-term progress in managing diversity:

- Individual and interpersonal dimensions
- Impact of organizational culture
- Impact of organization systems
- Focus on the quick fix

These impediments are described briefly below.

Individual and Interpersonal Dimensions: Our work places are not immune from the pressures and problems of our society in general. Your employees bring to the work place some strong opinions about those who are not like themselves, and those opinions are heavily influenced by the diversity dimensions of the opinion holders. And the pattern of biases is not as simple as one might imagine, as evidenced by a recent Louis Harris poll (10) on stereotypes held by different ethnic groups, summarized in Table 16.5.

TABLE 16.5 Stuck with Stereotypes

Stereotype Statement	Percentage of Respondents Who Agree			
	Non-Hispanic Blacks	Non-Black Hispanic	Asian American	Non-Hispanic Whites
Blacks want to live on welfare.		26%	31%	21%
Hispanics tend to have bigger families than they are able to support.	49%		68%	50%
Asian Americans are unscrupulously crafty and devious in business.	41%	46%		27%
Jews, when it comes to choosing between people and money, will choose money.	54%	43%	34%	27%

The data in Table 16.5 certainly demonstrate a number of issues that underlie the premise of the book, and the challenge of managing diversity:

- Negative stereotypes of groups other than our own abound, and are often widely held.
- No one is immune from prejudicial feelings. Even though the members of an ethnic group may have been victims of prejudice themselves, it does not stop them from forming their own negative biases of others.
- The attitudes we form from a range of associations carries over to the workplace, at least to a degree.

Corporate Culture as an Impediment: In addition to the preconceptions that employees bring to the workplace, their attitudes may be further shaped [for better or worse] or be reinforced by the culture of the organization. Dr. Thomas provides an analogy to help understand culture, likening corporate culture of an organization to a tree. In this organizational tree, the roots are the corporation's culture. The invisible roots give rise to the trunk, branches, and leaves—the visible parts of the tree. Nothing can grow in the branches and be sustained naturally unless it is congruent with the roots. You can graft peach limbs to an oak tree but they won't survive. You can graft incongruent diversity initiatives to an organization and they will not survive.

Often the culture is taken for granted and considered unremarkable by those who have grown up in it. The visitor in England would be more observant than the native to driving on the left hand side of the road, courteous and safety-minded cab drivers, etc. The others in the organization are similarly more attentive to the supportive or non-supportive aspects of the organization's culture.

As illustrated in Exhibit 16.1, some cultural roots are supportive of Manag-

EXHIBIT 16.1 The Tree of Corporate Culture

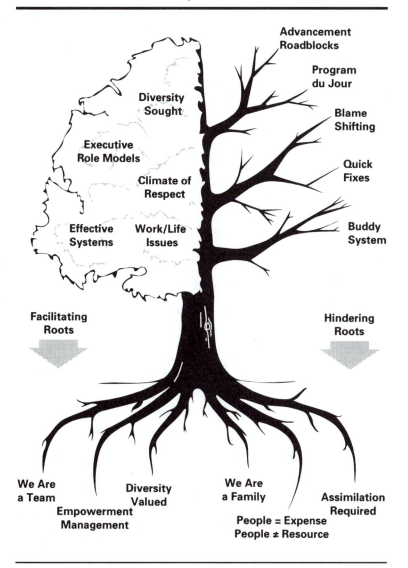

ing Diversity, such as those shown on the left side of the illustration. On the other hand, the roots shown on the right side of the tree will make it difficult for new concepts and practices to flourish on the branches.

Some practical illustrations of cultures that aid or inhibit diversity are summarized below:

Company A: In one organization, the success requirements were so narrowly defined that even some white males expressed discomfort with the degree of assimilation required.

Company B: The chairman of one organization reportedly stipulated a low percentage of minorities which could be hired into "visible" jobs.

Company C: In a company noted for its grueling working hours (and the impact on persons with dependent care obligations), a senior officer said that even he felt guilty leaving the office at the normal quitting time. Of course the pressure gets passed on down the line, with each organization layer waiting until its immediate supervisor leaves, before departing.

Changing corporate cultures is no easy task. Nevertheless, some progress can be made with broad and long-lasting efforts. (These methods and some specific aspects of corporate culture which sustain managing diversity or make it more difficult were described in Chapter 13.)

Impact of Company Systems: Even in an organization that has a supportive corporate culture, progress may be impeded by missing or ineffective human resources systems. In particular, the "career mobility systems" may aid or impede the progress of Others in the organization. In some cases the career mobility systems are quite formal and well documented with forms, timetables, training in the application of the system and multiple levels of involvement. Still, the concentration of females and minorities at the lower end of the corporate tower suggests that career mobility systems have not worked well for all employees. Chapter 7 identified the deficiencies that are often observed in those systems and some possible remedies.

There are a number of other impediments to managing diversity that may come up, such as the tendency for companies to go for the "quick fix" solutions.

MOVING TOWARD THE MANAGING DIVERSITY VISION

In moving along the way toward the end vision, it is useful to think of it as a progressive journey. While many organizations have adopted the "managing diversity" vision that was described in this chapter, many are still at the affirmative action stage. Their initiatives will help move them through transition stages from affirmative action to the next phase of development. Each organization must move at its own pace toward its vision of "diversity success." The guidelines presented in this book will aid your journey immeasurably.

NOTES TO CHAPTERS

CHAPTER 1

1. John P. Kotter, James L. Heskett, *Corporate Culture and Performance*, pp. 5–8, The Free Press, New York, N.Y., 1992.

CHAPTER 2

1. Marilyn Loden, Judy B. Rosener, *Workforce America—Managing Employee Diversity As A Vital Resource*, Business One Irwin, Homewood, IL, 1991.

2. Lee Seligman and Susan Welch, *Black Americans' Views of Racial Inequality—The Dream Deferred*, Cambridge University Press, Cambridge, Mass., 1991.

3. Gordon W. Allport, *The Nature of Prejudice*—25th Anniversary Edition, Addison-Wesley Press, Reading, Mass. 1979. Much of the material in pages 17–20 is adapted from this book with permission of the publisher. A similar intensity scale for prejudice is provided in *Racial and Cultural Minorities*, George Simpson and Milton Yinger, Harper and Row, 1965.

4. American Society for Training and Development, *Basics of Intercultural Communication*, ASTD, Alexandria, Virginia, 1991.

CHAPTER 3

1. Fred R. Bleakly, "The Best Laid Plans: Many Companies Try Management Fads, Only to See Them Flop," *Wall Street Journal*, New York, N.Y., p. 1, Jul. 27, 1993.

2. 1993 Society for Human Resource Management/Commerce Clearing House Study

3. Jayne O'Donnell, "Cadillac Focuses on Black Buyers," *USA Today*, Feb. 28, 1993, p. B2.

4. John Huey, "The New Post-Heroic Leadership," Fortune, p. 50, Feb. 21, 1994.

5. Vine Deloria, Jr., *Custer Died for Your Sins, An Indian Manifesto*, pp. 7–8, University of Oklahoma Press, Oklahoma City, OK, 1988.

6. Mary Louise Kelly, *New Dekalb Clinic in Diversity Dilemma*, The Atlanta Journal and Constitution, C1, Feb. 9, 1994.

CHAPTER 4

1. Lee Gardenswartz, Anita Rowe, *Managing Diversity* pp. 149–150, reprinted with permission of Business One Irwin, Homewood, Il., 1993.

CHAPTER 5

1. Larry Baytos, "Launching Successful Diversity Initiatives," *HR Magazine*, Jan. 1992.

2. Earl Shorris, *Latinos: A Biography of the People*, W.W. Norton & Co., New York, N.Y., 1992.

CHAPTER 7

1. A.M. Morrison, R.P. White and A. Van Velsor, *Breaking the Glass Ceiling*, pp. 54–56, reprinted with permission, Addison-Wesley Publishing, Reading, Mass., 1987.

2. R. W. Cameron, *The Minority Executives' Handbook: Your Essential Map and Guide to Success Up the Corporate Ladder*, New York, Warner Books, Inc., 1989.

3. "The Labor Letter: Mentoring Programs Face Hard Times in the 90's," *The Wall Street Journal*, March 24, 1992, p. 1.

4. Dr. Jeffalyn Johnson, *A Blueprint for Success*, pp. 9–24, Executive Leadership Council Study, Washington, D.C., 1991.

5. A.M. Morrison, R.P. White, A. Van Velsor, *Breaking the Glass Ceiling*, pp. 83–98, reprinted with permission, Addison-Wesley Publishing, Reading Mass., 1987.

6. P.R. Sacket, C.L.Z. DuBois, A.W. Noe, "Tokenism in Performance Evaluation: The Effects of Work Group Representation On Male-Female and White-Black Differences in Performance Ratings," *Journal of Applied Psychology*, Vol. 76, April 1991, pp. 262–67.

7. Mark R. Edwards, *Sustaining Culture Change with Multiple Rater Systems for Career Development and Performance Appraisal Systems*, 1993, cited by permission of the author.

8. Mark R. Edwards, "In-situ Team Evaluation: A New Paradigm for Measuring and Developing Leadership at Work," from *Impact of Leadership*, Center for Creative Leadership, 1992, pp. 443–58.

9. Lee Gardenswartz and Anita Rowe, *Managing Diversity*, reprinted with permission, Business One Irwin, Homewood, IL, 1993, p. 198.

CHAPTER 8

1. Dr. Ben Rosen, Dr. Sara Rynes, *1993 SHRM/CCH Survey*, Commerce Clearing House, Chicago, IL, 1993.

2. Conference Board Survey of 131 companies, 1991.

3. Anne Delatte, Ph.D., Larry Baytos, "Guidelines for Successful Diversity Training," January 1993, Lakewood Publications.

4. Michele Galen and Ann Therese Palmer, "White, Male & Worried," *Business Week*, January 31, 1994, pp. 50–56.

CHAPTER 9

1. "Many Voices: Changes in Black America," *The Wall Street Journal*, May 6, 1992, A8.

2. Robert Staples, *Lure and Loathing: Essays on Race, Identity, and the Ambivalence of Assimilation*, The Penguin Press, Middlesex, England, 1993, pp. 227–45.

3. "Equal Opportunity Pays," *The Wall Street Journal*, May 4, 1993, A.1.

4. "Blacks Face Discrimination," *The Wall Street Journal*, Nov. 3, 1993.

5. Shelby Steele, *The Content of Our Character*, Harper Collins Publishers, New York, 1992.

6. David Gates, "White Male Paranoia," *Newsweek*, March 29, 1993, p. 52.

7. "Labor in Review," *The Wall Street Journal*, Dec. 1993, p. 1.

8. Dr. R. Roosevelt Thomas, Jr., *Beyond Race and Gender*, adapted with permission, AMACOM Publishing, New York, N.Y., 1991, p. 28.

CHAPTER 10

1. Michele Galen and Ann Therese Palmer, "White, Male and Worried," Jan. 31, 1993. *Business Week*, McGraw-Hill, New York, NY, pp. 50–55.

2. Dr. R. Roosevelt Thomas, Jr., *Beyond Race and Gender*, reprinted with permission, AMACOM, New York, N.Y., 1991.

3. Julie Amparano Lopez, "Making Work-Family Programs Sound More Inclusive," *The Wall Street Journal*, May, 1993.

4. Michelle Neely Martinez, "Family Support Makes Business Sense," *HR Magazine*, Jan. 1993, pp. 38–50.

5. Sue Shellenbarger, "The Aging Of America Is Making 'Elder Care' A Big Workplace Issue," *The Wall Street Journal*, Feb. 16, 1994. p.1.

CHAPTER 11

1. Bureau of Labor Statistics, Analysis/News and Background Information, Vol. 141, LRR 251.

2. Barbara Ettore, "Breaking the Glass Ceiling, Or Just Window Dressing?" *Management Review*, American Management Association, March 1992, p. 19.

3. Jenny Crowe-Innes, Director of Diversity & Employment, Levi Strauss & Co., in a presentation to the Human Resources Management Association of Chicago, December, 1993.

CHAPTER 13

1. Jeanie Daniel Duck, "Managing Change: the Art of Balancing," *Harvard Business Review*, Nov.–Dec. 1993, p. 109.

2. Edgar H. Schein, "Coming To A New Awareness of Organization Culture," *Sloan Management Review*, 1984.

3. James L. Heskett, John P. Kotter, *Corporate Culture and Performance*, The Free Press, New York, N.Y., 1992.

4. Carolyn Leitch, *Big Blue Goes Plaid*, Toronto Globe and Mail, March 25, 1993, B1.

5. Judith H. Dobrzynski, "Rethinking IBM," *Business Week*, October 4, 1993, pp. 87–97.

6. Peter Drucker, *Managing for the Future*, pp. 192–93, Truman Talley Books/Dutton, New York, N.Y., 1992.

7. Dr. R. Roosevelt Thomas, Jr., *Beyond Race and Gender*, AMACOM, New York, N.Y.

8. Quaker Oats Company quarterly report to shareholders, July 1993.

9. Rosabeth Moss Kanter, *The Change Masters*, Simon and Schuster, Inc., New York, N.Y., 1983, p. 297.

CHAPTER 14

1. Alice Cuneo, "Diverse By Design," *Business Week, Reinventing America 1992*, p. 72.

2. Towers Perrin, *Workforce 2000 Today: A Bottom Line Concern*, Towers Perrin, New York, N.Y., 1992.

3. Dr. R. Roosevelt Thomas, Jr., *Total Quality, Managing Diversity: Keys to Competitive Advantage in the 1990's*, paper published by the Executive Leadership Council, 1992.

4. David Luther, V.P. Total Quality, Corning Corporation, presentation on *Corning Total Quality Strategies*, 1990.

CHAPTER 16

1. The Hudson Institute, *Workforce 2000: An Executive Summary*, New York, N.Y. 1987.

2. Martha Farnsworth Riche, *The Shape of the American Marketplace*, American Demographics, Ithaca, New York, 1990.

3. The Institute for Urban Economic Development, *Identifying Employment Opportunities for Chicago Area Residents*, Chicago, IL, 1991.

4. Joanne S. Lublin, "Survivors of Layoffs Battle Angst, Anger, Hurting Productivity," *The Wall Street Journal*, August 3, 1993. p. 1

5. Christina Duff, "Poor Prospects, Young Graduates Anxiety," *Wall Street Journal*, July 28, 1993.

6. Dr. R. Roosevelt Thomas Jr., *Beyond Race and Gender*, AMACOM, New York, N.Y. 1991. Material adapted with permission.

7. Marilyn Loden, Judy B. Rosener, *Workforce America*, Business One Irwin, Homewood, IL, 1991. Material adapted with permission.

8. Dempsey J. Travis, *Racism: American Style, A Corporate Gift*, Urban Research Press, Chicago, IL, 1992, p. 82–83.

9. Rush Limbaugh, *The Way Things Ought To Be*, Pocket Books, New York, N.Y., 1993

11. Raymond R. Coffey, "Racial Stereotypes Pervade All Cultures," *Chicago Sun Times*, March 3, 1994, p.4.

Bibliography

Allport, Gordon W., *The Nature Of Prejudice*. Reading, MA.: Addison-Wesley Publishing Company.

Augenbraum, Harold and Han Stavans, *Growing Up Latino*. New York: Houghton Mifflin, 1993.

Boyett, Joseph H. and Henry P. Conn, *Workplace 2000*. New York: Dutton-Penguin, 1991.

Cameron, R.W., *The Minority Executives' Handbook*. New York: Warner Books, 1989.

Carson, Clayborne, ed. et al., *Eyes on the Prize Civil Rights Reader*. New York: Penguin Books, 1991.

Carter, Steven, *Reflections of an Affirmative Action Baby*. New York: Basic Books Division of Harper Collins, 1991.

Cose, Ellis, *The Rage Of A Privileged Class*. New York: Harper Collins, 1993.

Cox, Taylor Jr., *Cultural Diversity In Organizations*. San Francisco: Berrett-Koehler Publishers, Inc., 1993.

Deloria, Vine, Jr., *Custer Died for Your Sins, An Indian Manifesto,* Oklahoma City, OK: University of Oklahoma Press, 1988.

Dewart, Janet, ed., *The State of Black America 1991*. New York: National Urban League, 1991.

Drucker, Peter, *Managing for the Future*. New York: Truman/Talley Books, Dutton, 1992.

Galinsky, Ellen, James T. Bond and Dana Friedman, *The Changing Workforce*. New York: Families and Work Institute, 1993.

Gardenswartz, Lee and Anita Rowe, *Managing Diversity*. Homewood, IL: Business One Irwin, 1993.

Heskett, James L. and John P. Kotter, *Corporate Culture and Performance*. New York: Macmillan Free Press, 1992.

Jamieson, David and Julie O'Mara, *Managing Workforce 2000*. San Francisco: Jossey-Bass Publishers, 1991.

Jaynes, Gerald David and Robin M. Williams, Jr., ed., *A Common Destiny*. Washington: National Academy Press, 1989.

Johnson, Dr. Jeffalyn, *A Blueprint For Success*. Washington, DC: Executive Leadership Council, 1991.

Kanter, Rosabeth Moss, *The Change Masters*. University of Chicago Press, 1983.

Lattimer, Robert L., *Managing Diversity For Strategic and Competitive Advantage*. New York: Bantam Doubleday, 1994.

Loden, Marilyn and Judy B. Rosener, *Workforce America*. Homewood, IL: Business One Irwin, 1991.

Malcolm X, *The Autobiography of Malcolm X*, as told to Alex Haley.

Lemann, Nicholas, *The Promised Land*. New York: Alfred A. Knopf, 1991.

McCann, Nancy Dodd and Thomas A. Mcginn, *Harassed*. Homewood, IL: Business One Irwin, 1992.

Morrison, Ann M., *The New Leaders*. San Francisco: Jossey-Bass Publishers, 1992.

Morrison, Ann M., R.P. White, and A. Van Velsor, *Breaking The Glass Ceiling*. Reading, MA: Addison-Wesley Publishing, 1987.

Seligman, Lee and Susan Welch, *Black Americans' Views of Racial Inequality—The Dream Deferred*. Cambridge MA: Cambridge University Press, 1991.

Schwartz, Felice N., *Breaking With Tradition*. New York: Warner Books Inc., 1992.

Shorris, Earl, *Latinos: A Biography Of The People*. New York: W.W. Norton & Co., 1992.

Staples, Robert, *Love and Loathing: Essays on Race, Identity, and the Ambivalence of Assimilation*, Middlesex, England: The Penguin Press, 1993.

Steele, Shelby, *The Content of Our Character*, New York: Harper Collins Publishers, 1992.

Tannen, Deborah, Ph.D., *You Just Don't Understand*. New York: Ballantine Books, 1990.

Thomas Jr., Dr. R. Roosevelt, *Beyond Race And Gender*. New York: AMACOM, 1991.

Thomas Jr., Dr. R. Roosevelt, *Differences Do Make A Difference*. Atlanta: The American Institute for Managing Diversity, 1992.

Travis, Dempsey, J., *Racism: American Style, a Corporate Gift*, Chicago, IL: Urban Research Press, 1992.

Tripp, C.A. , Ph.D., *The Homosexual Matrix*. New York: Penguin Books, 1987.

INDEX